Air Fryer Cookb

CW01502212

500 Recipes

for

Beginners and Advanced Users

By

Amelia Clark

Table of contents

Introduction

While food choices like fresh salad or sandwich can be easy to consume for some people, others find them difficult to eat. A person's inability to have a taste of his/her favorite meals can be disappointing most especially for people have been fed with deep fried food from a very young age. However, as for those who have lived their life eating deep fried food, but have long aspired to eat healthier food, the opportunity is now available as a result of the recent creation called Air Fryer.

The air fryer is one of the most recent kitchen gadget which enables users to fry food without the use of oil. Many will wonder how that could be possible? Well, it is possible as the hot air fryer is designed to cook fried foods without oil. Many will argue that such food is most likely to taste bad since deep-frying with a substantial level of oil has always been the customary way of frying food which is not only crunchy on the outside but soft on the inside.

Without a doubt, many people love eating fried foods; however, what has been a major source of concern for most people is the side-effect of consuming one. Such side-effect could be digestion difficulties, weight gain, and the presence oils filling the skin pores. Almost everyone will wish to eat fried foods such as chickens, fries among others without having any side-effects. Actually, such wish has become a reality with the invention of Air fryer.

This cookbook contains 500 recipes which are strongly healthy to consume. Also, you will get to know about some useful tips concerning air fryer, details on how to purchase air fryer, and a checklist on how to make use of air fryer. Lastly, you will find beneficial information on how to reduce fat and salt, and yet, enhance the food's flavor.

Technology of the Air Fryer

Air Fryer is still a recent innovation among other popular kitchen gadgets. Although some people have already get used to the air fryer as one of their favorite kitchen appliances; however, several hundreds of people are still uninformed about this modern invention.

The Basic Mechanism of Operation

If you are still one of the uninformed people concerning air fryer, then I will be revealing some basic but useful information about the mechanism of an Air Fryer.

Why is Air Fryer outstanding?

The cooking mechanism of an air fryer can be considered as the most special aspect of the gadget. For instance, most of the kitchen appliances were designed to use the conduction technique to prepare foods; whereas, air fryer is created to use Convection – or airflow – for its cooking procedure.

With the use of Rapid Air Technology and Air, an air fryer can quickly and easily get your meals done with a small amount of oil.

The Rapid Air Technology

Don't be surprised to know that Rapid Air Technology is not a Tech-material; instead, it is a Tech-procedure. Let me describe the procedure as simple as possible.

The air fryer is designed to suck in air from the atmosphere, and once the gadget sucks up enough air, the appliance becomes superheated to about 390☐ Fahrenheit. Then, the hot air will move into a compartmentalized heating chamber which supports the cooking process.

The described procedure, which is simply known as Rapid Air Technology, prevent the use of a large amount of oil while grilling, frying, roasting or baking. Also, the process ensures that the cooking process ends within a relatively short period.

Structure of the Air Fryer

As for those who will be using the air fryer for the first time, it can be quite confusing to understand the several parts of the appliance. However, there is no need to worry as I have listed and explained each of the components in here for you to understand within a few minutes.

An air fryer is made of:

1. Cooking chamber

This chamber is where the whole process takes place including getting the meal ready. While the principle of operation remains the same, the functionality of a cooking chamber may differ based on whether your model is made with a single tray or multiple layers of a tray.

2. Heating Element

This part determines the amount of heat which is required to mix up with the flowing air. One of the most beloved qualities of the heating element of an Air Fryer is that it switches off automatically once the required temperature necessary for cooking has been ascertained – this quality saves power and curbs excessive overheating.

3. Fan and Grill

This pair works jointly to make sure that the superheated air is supplied to the meal evenly. The way in which the grill is designed enables it to change the direction of airflow which is a significant aspect of the overall cooking activity.

4. Exhaust System

This system is structured to assist in maintaining an internal balance pressure and block the accumulation of toxic air. You can get some models with a filter, which remove the dust and any remaining particles to clear the exhausted air. By doing this, there won't be any emission of unpleasant odor.

5. Movable Food Tray

Primarily, the trays are designed to transfer food which is to be cooked. Some models come with few boundary walls on the tray which enables the cooking of different meals at the same time. Also, you can get some brand's model with a universal handle which can be used to remove the tray from the heating chamber quickly.

Some outstanding advantages of Air Fryer

- With air fryer, you can prepare healthy fried foods which are better than those cooked with the conventional frying technique.
- It is easy to use.
- It requires low maintenance and is convenient to clean.
- Air fryer cooks food in a relatively short period.
- It is better to use in terms of safety.
- And most importantly, it requires little oil to prepare a meal without jeopardizing the taste of the meal – and consequently, it assists in alleviating additional calories effortlessly.

Wings in a Peach-Bourbon Sauce

Prep + Cook Time: 50 minutes | Servings: 2-4

Ingredients:

- ½ cup peach preserves
- 1 tbsp brown sugar
- ¼ tsp kosher salt
- 1 garlic cloves, minced
- 2 tbsp white vinegar (or white wine)
- 2 tbsp bourbon
- 1 tsp cornstarch
- 1 tsp water
- Olive oil cooking spray
- 2 lbs chicken wings, without wing tips

Directions:

1. Clean your blender or food processor. Put the peach preserves, sugar, salt, and garlic in it and blend until the mixture is smooth.
2. Get a clean saucepan and transfer the blended peach mixture into it.
3. On medium-high heat, boil the mixture of vinegar and bourbon. When boiling, reduce the heat and simmer of about four to six minutes, until there is a little thickness.
4. Make a mixture of cornstarch and water in a clean bowl, and stir until you have a smooth mixture.
5. Add the cornstarch mixture to the peach mixture. Boil and allow to cook for one to two minutes with frequent stirring. Keep ¼ of this sauce separately.
6. Ensure that your Air Fryer is preheated to 400 F, after which you spray the interior with a cooking spray.
7. Brush each wing with the sauce. Each brushed wing should be arranged in a single layer in the basket.
8. Allow to cook for seven minutes before flipping and brushing the other side of the wing with the sauce. Then allow cooking for additional 8 minutes.
9. For best results, you may have to divide the wings into two groups and treat each group separately.
10. Serve the cooked wings with the ¼ sauce reserved.

Buffalo Style Skinny Chicken Wings

Prep + Cook Time: 25 minutes | Servings: 2-4

Ingredients:

- ½ cup frank's hot sauce
- 1 lb chicken wings, fresh
- Blue cheese, crumbled, optional

Directions:

1. Apply the hot sauce on all sides of the chicken wings.
2. Ensure that your air fryer is preheated to 400 F.
3. Transfer the chicken wings in the air fryer, maintain a single layer of arrangement.
4. Allow to cook for 18 minutes, and shake twice or thrice while cooking.
5. Add blue cheese and celery as toppings on the cooked chicken wings.
6. Serve.

Garlic Parmesan Breaded Fried Chicken Wings

Prep + Cook Time: 40 minutes | Servings: 4-6

Ingredients:

- 16 chicken wing drumettes
- Chicken seasoning to taste
- Ground black pepper to taste
- 2 tbsp soy sauce
- ½ cup flour
- 1 tsp garlic powder
- ¼ cup parmesan, grated
- ¼ cup buttermilk, low-fat
- Cooking spray
- 1 tsp parmesan, grated

Directions:

1. With the aid of a paper towel, clean and pat dry the chicken wing drumettes.
2. Add chicken seasoning as well as black pepper, preferably in sprinkles.
3. Put in a Ziploc bag after a quick brush with a soy sauce, and refrigerate the bag for 60 to 120 minutes.
4. Mix flour, garlic powder, and ¼ cup of parmesan in another bowl.
5. Pour the buttermilk in a new bowl.
6. Now, take each of the refrigerated chicken drumettes and dip in the buttermilk, before coating them with the mixture in (4) above.
7. Ensure that the Air Fryer is preheated to 400 F.
8. Before placing the chicken in the air fryer pan, spray the inside with the cooking spray.
9. Now, sprinkle the cooking spray over the drummettes.
10. Proceed to cook for about 20 minutes. Shake the pot twice or thrice while cooking.
11. After 20 minutes of cooking, let the wings cool down a little before serving with one tablespoon of parmesan.

Barbeque Chicken Wings

Prep + Cook Time: 25 minutes | Servings: 2-4

Ingredients:

- 2 tbsp honey
- Salt and ground black pepper to taste
- BBQ chicken seasoning
- 1 tbsp olive oil
- 1 lb chicken wings

Directions:

1. Get a clean bowl and in it, mix the honey, salt, pepper, BBQ chicken seasoning, and the olive oil.
2. Using the BBQ mixture, brush the chicken wings generously.
3. Ensure that your air fryer is preheated to 400 F.
4. Transfer the chicken wings into the air fryer, while maintaining a single layer.
5. Allow frying for 18 minutes, while turning the wings after 9 minutes.
6. Withdraw when both sides are fried.
7. Serve.

Chicken Wings in Nandos Marinade

Prep + Cook Time: 25 minutes | Servings: 2-4

Ingredients:

- 1½ lbs chicken wings
- Salt and ground black pepper to taste
- 10 oz homemade Nandos marinade

Directions:

1. Season the chicken wings by rubbing thoroughly with pepper and salt.
2. Transfer the seasoned chickens in a Ziplock bag or foil. Cover the wings with about 3 oz Nandos marinade and lock the Ziplock bag.
3. Place in the fridge and leave for 10-12 hours.
4. The following day, ensure that your air fryer is preheated to 360 F.
5. Withdraw the chicken from the fridge and place them in the air fryer.
6. Set the timer to 20 minutes and allow cooking.
7. The unused Nandos marinade should be served alongside the cooked wings as the dipping sauce.

Chicken Wings in Orange Sauce

Prep + Cook Time: 1 hour 5 minutes | Servings: 2

Ingredients:

- 6 chicken wings
- Orange juice from 1 orange
- 1 tsp orange zest
- 1½ tbsp Worcestershire sauce
- Country herbs (basil, oregano, mint, parsley, thyme, rosemary and sage)
- 1 tbsp sugar
- Salt and ground black pepper to taste

Directions:

1. Ensure that the chicken wings are washed well and pat dry.
2. Mix juice and orange zest in a big clean bowl.
3. Place the chicken wings inside the bowl and stir well until the wings are fully coated.
4. Make a mixture of Worcestershire sauce, country herbs, sugar, salt, and black pepper in another bowl.
5. Rub all sides of the wing with this mixture.
6. Ensure that the Air Fryer is preheated to 360 F.
7. Wrap the rubbed/coated chicken wings, alongside the sauce, with an aluminum foil.
8. Transfer the wrapped wings into the air fryer and let it cook for 20 minutes.
9. Remove the cooked chicken wings with the sauce and place them in a bowl.
10. Using the sauce, brush the wings before returning them into the air fryer. Do not dispose of the remains of the orange sauce.
11. Let the wings cook for another 15 minutes in the air fryer. Remove and brush again with the remains of the orange source.
12. Cook for an additional ten minutes.
13. Remove from the fryer and serve.

Spicy and Crispy Chicken Wing Drumettes

Prep + Cook Time: 40 minutes | Servings: 2

Ingredients:

- 10 large chicken wing drumettes
- Cooking spray
- 1 tbsp soy sauce
- 3/8 tsp red pepper, crushed
- 2 tbsp chicken stock, unsalted
- 1 clove garlic, chopped
- ¼ cup rice vinegar
- 1 tbsp toasted sesame oil
- 3 tbsp honey
- 2 tbsp roasted peanuts, unsalted and chopped
- 1 tbsp fresh chives, chopped

Directions:

1. Ensure that the Air Fryer is preheated to 400 F.
2. For better space management, arrange the drumettes to the sides of the chicken in the air fryer basket.
3. While in the basket, spray them with the cooking spray.
4. Allow the sprayed chicken to cook for 15 minutes before flipping on the other side and allowing to cook for 15 minutes again.
5. Make a mixture of soy sauce, red pepper, chicken stock, garlic, rice vinegar, sesame oil, and honey in a clean skillet.
6. Using a medium-height heat, stir and bring the honey sauce till it simmers. Then cook for 6 minutes – the sauce will appear slightly thickened.
7. Put the cooked chicken wings into a clean bowl and add the honey sauce, then stir mildly.
8. Once the wings are well coated, sprinkle with peanuts and chopped chives. Serve.

Air-Fried Chicken Drumettes

Prep + Cook Time: 30 minutes | Servings: 2-4

Ingredients:

- 1½ lbs chicken wing drumettes
- Olive oil cooking spray
- 1 tbsp lower-sodium soy sauce
- ½ tsp cornstarch
- 1 tsp finely chopped garlic
- ½ tsp finely chopped fresh ginger
- 1 tsp sambal oelek (ground fresh chili paste)
- 1/8 tsp kosher salt
- 1 tsp fresh lime juice
- 2 tsp honey
- 2 tbsp chopped scallions

Directions:

1. Pat the rinsed chicken drumettes dry using the paper towels and then spray with olive oil.
2. Ensure that your air fryer is preheated to 400 F.
3. Transfer the chicken drumettes in the air fryer, maintaining a single layer.
4. Allow cooking in the air fryer for 22 minutes, while shaking twice or thrice.
5. Withdraw the drumettes when crispy.
6. With the drumettes in the air fryer, get a clean saucepan, and combine the soy sauce and cornstarch.
7. Toss in the garlic, ginger, sambal, salt, lime juice, and honey.
8. Stir the mixture thoroughly and transfer to medium-high heat.
9. Cook until the mixture becomes thickened and starts to form bubbles.
10. Remove the chicken drumettes and place them in a big bowl.
11. Pour the sauce mixture over the drumettes and stir mildly.
12. Add chopped scallions and toppings before serving.

Spicy Drumsticks with Barbecue Marinade

Prep + Cook Time: 45 minutes | Servings: 4

Ingredients:

- 1 tsp chili powder
- 2 tsp brown sugar
- 1 clove garlic, crushed
- ½ tbsp mustard
- A pinch of salt
- Freshly ground black pepper
- 1 tbsp olive oil
- 4 drumsticks

Directions:

1. Ensure that the Air Fryer is preheated to 390 F.
2. Create a mixture of the chili powder, brown sugar, garlic, mustard, and add a pinch of salt and freshly ground pepper to taste.
3. Add oil to this mixture, stir.
4. Do a thorough rubbing of the drumsticks, using the marinade and allow the rubbed sticks to marinate for 20 minutes.
5. Now, place the drumsticks in the basket, and put the basket into the Air Fryer, allowing to roast for 10 minutes, or until they are brown.
6. Drop the air fryer temperature to 300 F and allow them to roast for additional 10 minutes.
7. Remove the roasted drumsticks and serve with French bread and corn salad.

Southern Chicken Drumsticks

Prep + Cook Time: 55 minutes | Servings: 4

Ingredients:

- 2 large slices bread
- Salt and ground black pepper to taste
- 1 tbsp dried garlic and onion
- 1 tsp basil
- ½ tsp cayenne pepper
- 1 tbsp plain flour
- 2 tbsp paprika
- 5 oz buttermilk
- 4 chicken drumsticks
- 1 tbsp oregano
- 1 tbsp rosemary
- 1 tbsp thyme
- 1 tsp olive oil

Directions:

1. Ensure that the Air Fryer is preheated to about 365 F – it takes about two minutes.
2. In addition to the bread, add the salt, pepper, dried garlic, onion, basil, and a pinch of cayenne. Blend the mixture in the blender until the blend looks like breadcrumbs. Put the blend into a separate bowl and set aside.
3. In a new bowl, add flour and mix with ½ the paprika, while adding pepper and salt to taste. Set aside this bowl also.
4. Get a third bowl and make a mixture of the buttermilk, the chicken drumsticks, and the rest of the seasonings. Stir the mixture well, while the drumsticks are submerged.
5. Take out each chicken drumstick from the bowl and place it in the flour, and after that in the breadcrumbs.
6. Once you are done with the dipping for each, place them into the basket in your air fryer.
7. After coating all the chicken drumsticks, sprinkle a bit of olive oil to ensure that they do not dry while improving their taste.
8. Place all coated and oiled drumsticks in the air fryer and cook for about 30 minutes at 365 F. Reduce the heat to 345 F and cook for an extra two minutes.
9. Remove from the air fryer and serve.

Nando's Chicken Drumsticks

Prep + Cook Time: 35 minutes | Servings: 4

Ingredients:

- 2 corn on the cobs
- 1 small fresh red chilli
- ½ bunch of fresh parsley, chopped
- 1 tsp paprika
- 5 garlic cloves, peeled
- 3 bay leaves

- 3 tbsp olive oil
- 8 chicken drumsticks
- Salt and ground black pepper to taste
- ½ tsp Piri Piri seasoning
- 1 tsp butter

Directions:

1. Pick each corn on the cob and chop it into three equal pieces, thus giving you six equal small pieces of chopped corn. Put these pieces into the steamer basket of your Instant Pot, which already has 1 cup of water under it. Seal the lid and allow to cook for 15 minutes on the Steamer button.
2. Open the blender and add the red chili, parsley, paprika, garlic, bay leaves, and olive oil. Blend until you have a grainy or almost-smooth blend.
3. On a clean chopping board, arrange the chicken drumsticks and drizzle on them salt and pepper. With the aid of your pastry brush, brush each drumstick with the blended marinade.
4. Proceed by placing the brushed drumsticks into the grill pan of the air fryer. Set the temperature to 355 F and cook for 12 minutes.
5. Once you get a beep tone from the Instant Pot, remove the corn on the cob by using the Quick pressure release. Transfer it to the chopping board, and season with Piri Piri seasoning, alongside salt and pepper to taste.
6. Set the temperature to 390 F and allow this to cook for an extra three minutes on the other side, plus the corn on the cob. This will give them that barbecue well done look..
7. You can add a little butter to the corn on the cob, before serving with the Peri Peri chicken drumettes.

Coconut and Turmeric Chicken

Prep + Cook Time: 4 hours 40 minutes | Servings: 2-3

Ingredients:

- 3 pcs whole chicken leg (de-skin or with skin is totally up to you)
- 4-5 tsp ground turmeric
- ½ tbsp salt

- 2 oz galangal
- 2 oz pure coconut paste (or coconut milk)
- 2 oz old ginger

Direction:

1. Do not pound or blend the chicken meat; all other ingredients should be pounded or blended.
2. With a focus on the thick parts, cut a few slits on the leg of the chicken. The cuttings will increase the absorption of the flavor during marinating.
3. Add the blended ingredients to the chicken and allow to marinate for not less than four hours, or if possible, overnight. During the marinating process, the seasoned chicken should be wrapped with a cling film and stored inside the refrigerator.
4. Set the Air Fryer to 375 F and allow to preheat at this temperature, then air-fry the chicken for about 20-25 minutes, frying each side for half of the total time.
5. Once you have a golden brown chicken, you can proceed to serve.

Spicy Air-Fried Chicken Thighs

Prep + Cook Time: 6 hours 30 minutes | Servings: 4

Ingredients:

- ½ tsp cayenne pepper
- 1 tsp paprika
- 2 cups low-fat buttermilk
- 4 (6- to 7-oz.) boneless, skinless chicken thighs
- 1 cup (about 4¼ oz.) all-purpose flour
- 2 large eggs

- 2 tbsp water
- 2 cups whole-wheat panko (Japanese-style breadcrumbs)
- ½ tsp kosher salt
- Cooking spray
- 2 tsp hot sauce (such as Franks RedHot)

Directions:

1. Get a large, clean bowl and make a mixture of cayenne pepper, paprika, and buttermilk inside it.
2. Add the chicken thighs, allowing both sides to coat. Then cover and marinate the coated chicken thighs in the refrigerator overnight or for not less than 6 hours.
3. In a shallow dish, add some flour.
4. In another shallow dish, add eggs and water and whisk the mixture mildly.
5. Get a third shallow dish and place the panko in it.
6. Remove the chicken from the marinade and dispose of the remnants.
7. Sprinkle the chicken with salt and then dredge in flour. Shake the chicken to get rid of the excess flour.
8. Dip into the egg mixture, and allowing excess egg to drip off.
9. Dredge the chicken in the panko, while adding a bit of force for adherence, before coating the chicken on either side, using the cooking spray.
10. Spray the air fryer basket mildly with the cooking spray. The chicken is best placed in the basket in a single layer, and start cooking in batches, at 400 F for each batch. Continue this until a thermometer placed in the chicken reads 165 F, with the coating turning golden brown and crispy. Leave for 16 minutes. Ensure that you turn the chicken over midway through cooking.
11. It is best served immediately, with each chicken thigh on a plate, drizzled with ½ teaspoon hot sauce.

Simply Fried Chicken Thighs

Prep + Cook Time: 30 minutes | Servings: 4

Ingredients:

- 1 tsp kosher salt
- ½ cup all purpose flour
- 1 egg beaten

- 4 small chicken thighs
- 1½ tbsp Old Bay cajun seasoning

Directions:

1. Ensure that your Air Fryer is preheated to 390 F.
2. Combine the salt, flour, and the Old Bay, and mix the mixture.
3. Submerge the chicken in the flour mixture, and into the egg, before taking it back into the flour mixture again. Remove all excess flour by shaking them off.
4. Transfer the four chicken thighs into the cooking compartment of your Air Fryer – preferably at the bottom. Allow to cook for 25 minutes in this position, or until the chicken reaches the temperature of 180 F.
5. Once either of this happens, it means the chicken is ready.
6. Remove and serve.

Buttermilk Chicken Thighs

Prep + Cook Time: 6 hours 45 minutes | Servings: 3-4

Ingredients:

2 lbs chicken thighs (skin on, bone in)

Marinade:
2 tsp black pepper
2 tsp kosher salt
1 tsp paprika powder
2 cups buttermilk

Seasoned Flour:
1 tbsp garlic powder
1 tsp kosher salt
1 tbsp paprika powder
1 tbsp baking powder
2 cups all-purpose flour

Directions:

1. Get rid of any visible residue or fat from the chicken thighs by rinsing, then pat dry using paper towels.
2. Get a large, clean bowl, put the chicken pieces in it and add black pepper, salt, and paprika.
3. Pour your buttermilk over the chicken until the entire chicken is coated. Place inside the refrigerator overnight or for not less than 6 hours.
4. Ensure your Air Fryer is preheated at 355 F
5. Get another bowl, and mix garlic powder, salt, paprika, baking powder, and flour.
6. Now, take each piece of the chicken from the buttermilk, dredging them in the flour mixture. To get rid of any excess flour, shake the dredged chicken before transferring to a plate.
7. Place the chicken pieces in one layer of the basket in your fryer, such that the skin side is facing upwards.
8. Now, slide the basket containing the chicken into the air fryer. Let it air fry for 8 minutes – you can set the air fryer's timer. After 8 minutes, remove the tray and change the sides of the chicken such that the skin side is facing downwards. Air fry for another 10 minutes.
9. Withdraw the air-fried chickens on paper towels (to drain) before serving.

Healthy Chicken Tenders

Prep + Cook Time: 20 minutes | Servings: 1-2

Ingredients:

- 12 oz of chicken breasts
- Salt and ground black pepper to taste
- 1/8 cup flour
- 1 egg white
- 1¼ oz panko bread crumbs

Directions:

1. Before you cut the chicken breast into tenders, remove any excess fat by trimming. Use the combination of salt and pepper to season each side.
2. Get your flour, egg, and panko breadcrumbs into different clean bowls.
3. Then dip the chicken tenders into flour, eggs, and panko breadcrumbs respectively.
4. Arrange the coated chicken into the basket of your air fryer, and spray with olive spray.
5. Set your air fryer to 350 F and cook.
6. Let the chicken cook through – for about 10 minutes.

Air Fryer Chicken Breast

Prep + Cook Time: 15 minutes | Servings: 2

Ingredients:

- 2 chicken breasts
- 2 tsp olive oil
- Salt and ground black pepper to taste

Directions:

1. Switch the air fryer basket in your air fryer with a grill pan.
2. Arrange the chicken breasts in the grill pan.
3. On each breast, apply a combination of a teaspoon of olive oil, salt, and pepper (as seasoning).
4. Set your Air Fryer to 350 F and let the chicken breasts cook for 12 minutes.
5. Slice the cooked chicken to your taste with your knife.
6. Serve.

Spicy Air Fryer Chicken Breasts

Prep + Cook Time: 1 hour 45 minutes | Servings: 8

Ingredients:

- 2 tbsp Dijon mustard
- 2 cups buttermilk
- ½ tsp garlic powder
- 2 tsp salt
- 2 tsp hot pepper sauce
- 8 bone-in chicken breast halves, skin removed (8 oz each)
- 2 cups soft bread crumbs
- ½ tsp cayenne pepper
- ¼ tsp dried parsley flakes
- ½ tsp poultry seasoning
- ½ tsp paprika
- ½ tsp ground mustard
- ¼ tsp dried oregano
- 1 cup cornmeal
- 2 tbsp canola oil

Directions:

1. Ensure that your Air Fryer is preheated at 375 F.
2. Get a large bowl and make a mixture of the first five ingredients on the list above.
3. Coat the chicken with this mixture. Keep the coated chicken in the refrigerator, covered, for an hour or overnight.
4. Drain the chicken of excess coatings and dispose of the marinade.
5. In another shallow dish, add all the unused ingredients together and stir to mix.
6. Coat each piece of the chicken with this spice mixture, and transfer them into the basket of the air fryer in a single layer. Ensure that the air fryer basket has already been sprayed.
7. Air fry the chicken until you have a reading of 170 F on the thermometer. This will take about 20 minutes, and you need to turn the chicken halfway. Do the same for the remaining chicken.
8. After all the chicken is cooked, transfer all of them to the basket again. Air fry for about two or three minutes to heat through.

Chicken Breasts in a Bag

Prep + Cook Time: 1 hour 10 minutes | Servings: 1-2

Ingredients:

- 1 carrot (thinly sliced)
- Butter
- Salt and ground black pepper to taste
- 2 chicken breast halves
- 1 lemon (halves)
- Bunch of sage

Directions:

1. Ensure that your air fryer is preheated at 375 F.
2. Cut your parchment papers (2 pcs) into a square shape. Divide the sliced carrots equally on each paper. To each portion, add a sufficient lump of butter plus pepper and salt (or other seasonings).
3. Place the chicken breast on the carrot slices.
4. Then add a squeeze of lemon juice, a couple of sage leaves, and finally, a knob of butter again.
5. Fold all the four corners of each parchment paper to make it air tight.
6. Place the first bag on the baking tray, and allow to bake for about 20-25 minutes. You can remove once the carrot feels soft.
7. Do the same for the other bag.
8. Open the bag and serve the baked chicken.

Balsamic Glazed Chicken Breasts

Prep + Cook Time: 3 hours 20 minutes | Servings: 2

Ingredients:

- 1 large mango
- 15 tsp olive oil
- 4 garlic cloves
- 5 tbsp balsamic vinegar
- 1 tbsp parsley
- 1 tbsp oregano
- Salt and ground black pepper to taste
- Pinch mustard powder
- 2 chicken breasts
- 1 medium avocado
- 1 red pepper
- Fresh parsley to garnish

Directions:

1. After peeling and getting rid of the stone in your mango, set aside about ¾ of it into a separate bowl, and dice the remaining.
2. Place the diced mango, olive oil, garlic, the balsamic vinegar, and all the seasonings into your blender. Blend until you have a smooth mixture.
3. Transfer the blended mixture into a clean bowl, and submerge the whole chicken breasts in it. Refrigerate for about 3 hours to allow it to soak.
4. Separate the chicken and the marinade.
5. Switch your air fryer basket with the grill pan.
6. Coat the top of the chicken with the marinade using a pastry brush.
7. Set your Air Fryer to 355 F and allow the coated chicken breast to cook for 12 minutes. When the coking is halfway, withdraw the pan and turn the chicken to the other side, giving it another balsamic coating. This ensures that the two sides have the coating.
8. Slice the mango, pepper, and avocado thinly.
9. Add some drizzles of some balsamic vinegar.
10. Serve with fresh parsley.

Buffalo Chicken Breasts

Prep + Cook Time: 40 minutes | Servings: 3-4

Ingredients:

- 1 tsp hot sauce (such as Frank's)
- 1 tbsp hot sauce (such as Frank's)
- ¼ cup egg substitute
- ½ cup plain fat-free Greek yogurt
- 1 tbsp cayenne pepper
- 1 tbsp garlic pepper seasoning
- 1 tbsp sweet paprika
- 1 cup panko breadcrumbs
- 1 lb skinless, boneless chicken breasts, cut into 1-inch strips

Directions:

1. Get a clean bowl and add one teaspoon and one tablespoon hot sauce, egg substitute, and Greek yogurt. Whisk the mixture.
2. In another clean bowl, make a mix of cayenne pepper, garlic pepper, paprika, and breadcrumbs.
3. Set your Air Fryer to 355 F.
4. Dip each chicken strip into the yogurt mixture.
5. Coat the dipped chicken strips with the panko breadcrumb mixture.
6. Place the coated chicken strips in your air fryer, such that they all are in a single layer.
7. Cook in the air fryer for about 8 minutes, turn the chicken to the other side and cook for another eight minutes. It is cooked when the chicken is evenly browned.
8. Serve.

Philadelphia Herby Chicken Breasts

Prep + Cook Time: 20 minutes | Servings: 2

Ingredients:

- 2 chicken breasts
- Mixed herbs chicken seasoning
- Salt and ground black pepper to taste
- 2 tbsp soft cheese

Directions:

1. Ensure that your Air Fryer is preheated to 355 F.
2. Slice midway into the breasts to create ample space to accommodate the seasoning.
3. Add salt and pepper into the spaces created.
4. Cover the entire chicken with soft cheese; use your hands to ensure a nice creamy layer.
5. Have the seasoned chicken breasts rolled in the mixed herbs.
6. Place them on a reusable baking mat and transfer into the air fryer.
7. Cook until the chicken breasts are cooked in the middle (for about 15 minutes).
8. Serve.

Mexican-Style Stuffed Chicken Breasts

Prep + Cook Time: 30 minutes | Servings: 2

Ingredients:

- 4 extra-long toothpicks
- 4 tsp ground cumin, divided
- 4 tsp chili powder, divided
- 1 skinless, boneless chicken breast
- 2 tsp chipotle flakes
- Salt and ground black pepper to taste

- 2 tsp Mexican oregano
- ½ red bell pepper, sliced into thin strips
- 1 fresh jalapeno pepper, sliced into thin strips
- ½ onion, sliced into thin strips
- 2 tsp olive oil
- ½ lime, juiced

Directions:

1. Soak your toothpicks into a small bowl of water. This ensures that they do not burn while cooking.
2. Get a shallow dish and make a mixture of 2 teaspoons cumin and two teaspoons of chili powder.
3. Ensure that your air fryer is preheated at 400 F.
4. While placing on a flat work surface, slice the chicken horizontally through the middle. With the aid of a rolling pin or kitchen mallet, pound each half of the chicken until you have a thickness of about ¼ inch.
5. Mix the remaining chili powder, cumin, chipotle, pepper, salt, and oregano. Sprinkle the mixture on each breast half, equally. Place ½ of the bell pepper, jalapeno, and onion in the center of one breast half. With the aid of two toothpicks, keep the chicken in the position where the tapered end faces upward.
6. Repeat the process for the other breast – add spices, vegetables, and secure with the unused toothpicks.
7. Roll each breast half in the chili-cumin mixture. Then, drizzle olive oil on them until it covers all the surface evenly.
8. Transfer the roll-ups into the air-fryer basket such that the toothpick side faces up. Set your air fryer timer to six minutes.
9. After six minutes, turn the roll-ups over on the other side. Cook again in the air fryer, and continue until the juices run clear and a reading of 165 F is seen on an instant-read thermometer. Cook at this temperature for an additional five minutes.
10. Withdraw the roll-ups from the air fryer, and drizzle lime juice on each evenly. Serve.

Chicken Kiev Supper Breasts

Prep + Cook Time: 40 minutes | Servings: 2

Ingredients:

- ¼ tsp garlic puree
- 4 oz soft cheese
- 1 tsp parsley
- 2 chicken breasts

- 4 oz breadcrumbs
- Salt and ground black pepper to taste
- 1 medium egg, beaten

Directions:

1. Make a blend of the garlic, soft cheese, and the parsley (half).
2. Using a rolling pin, flatten out the chicken breast. Chop the flattened breast into half – you then get a chicken breast with the distinct upper and lower part, which makes stuffing easy.
3. Put the mixture in the middle and then press the two chicken breasts together.
4. Create another blend in a mixing bowl by adding the breadcrumbs, the remaining half of the parsley, pepper, and salt.
5. Immerse the chicken in the beaten egg before rolling it in the breadcrumbs mixture.
6. Set your Air Fryer to 355 F and cook until the chicken is cooked (for about 25 minutes). Serve.

Syn Free Slimming World Chicken Tikka

Prep + Cook Time: 20 minutes | Servings: 4

Ingredients:

- 2 large chicken breasts

Chicken tikka marinade:

- 10 oz greek yoghurt
- ½ small diced onion
- 2 tsp garlic puree
- 2 tsp paprika
- 2 tsp cumin

- 2 tsp garam masala
- 2 tsp turmeric
- 1 tsp grated ginger
- Pinch of chilli
- Juice and rind of 1 lemon

Directions:

1. Make a smooth mixture of all the chicken tikka marinade ingredients in a clean mixing bowl.
2. Place the chicken breasts into the bowl and leave overnight to marinade.
3. The next day, separate the chicken breasts from the marinade.
4. Transfer the chicken breasts to a chopping board, and chop the chicken into tikka bite shapes.
5. Switch your air fryer basket with a grill pan. Cook the chopped chicken in the pan at a temperature of 360 F for about 10 minutes.
6. Serve the cooked chicken while warm.

Simply Air Fried Chicken Schnitzel

Prep + Cook Time: 25 minutes | Servings: 3-4

Ingredients:

- 2 chicken breasts
- Salt and ground black pepper to taste
- 2 medium eggs

- 12 tbsp gluten free oats
- 2 tbsp mustard powder
- Fresh parsley, chopped

Directions:

1. Flatten out your chicken breasts on a clean chopping board, such that there are four flat pieces of them.
2. Season the flat pieces with pepper and salt on either side – to ensure thorough seasoning.
3. Get a separate mixing bowl, and beat two eggs in it using a fork.
4. Place the gluten free oats, mustard, the fresh parsley, and another round of salt and pepper in your blender. Blend until you have the appearance of coarse breadcrumbs.
5. Transfer the blend into another separate dish.
6. First roll the chicken in the oats, before transferring it into the egg. Return it to the oats again.
7. Place the rolled chicken in your air fryer's grill pan, and set the temperature to 350 F. Allow cooking for 12 minutes.
8. With the aid of tongs, turn the chicken halfway through.
9. Serve the cooked chicken warm alongside warm potatoes.

Thai Mango Chicken

Prep + Cook Time: 20 minutes | Servings: 2

Ingredients:

- Mixed herbs chicken seasoning
- ½ mango peeled and diced
- Salt and ground black pepper to taste
- Spicy chicken seasoning
- 1 tsp red Thai curry paste
- 2 tbsp olive oil
- 1 lime rind and juice
- 2 chicken breasts

Directions:

1. Ensure that your Air Fryer is preheated to 355 F.
2. Make a mixture of your mixed herbs seasoning, mango, salt, pepper, spicy chicken seasoning, Red Thai Curry Paste, olive oil, and lime into a clean mixing bowl. Ensure that you mix thoroughly so that the seasoning is evenly distributed in the mixture.
3. With the aid of your vegetable knife, cut slightly into your chicken without the cut reaching the bottom of the breasts.
4. Sprinkle the seasoning mixture in the mixing bowl and ensured that sufficient seasoning gets into the cuts.
5. Transfer the sprinkled chicken into your air fryer, on the baking mat. Set the timer for 15 minutes and allow to cook. Always check well to ensure that the chicken is well-cooked in the center.
6. Garnish some fresh tomatoes and extra lime, and serve with the cooked chicken.

Lemon Pepper Chicken Breasts

Prep + Cook Time: 20 minutes | Servings: 1-2

Ingredients:

- 2 lemons rind and juice
- 1 tbsp chicken seasoning
- Handful black peppercorns
- 1 tsp garlic puree
- 1 chicken breast
- Salt and ground black pepper to taste

Directions:

1. Ensure that your air fryer is preheated to 360 F.
2. Prepare your workstation by first placing a large silver foil sheet on the worktop and then adding it to the lemon rind and all the seasonings.
3. With your chicken breasts spread on a chopping board, trim off any fatty parts or little bones present.
4. Using pepper and salt, season each side generously until you have a slightly different color.
5. Transfer the seasoned chicken onto the silver foil sheet and rub again to ensure that the seasoning is evenly distributed.
6. Then seal the foil up tightly such that air cannot enter. This is to ensure that the flavor penetrates the chicken well.
7. Slap the sealed chicken with a rolling pin. This flattens it out while ensuring that it releases more flavor.
8. Place the chicken in the air fryer and cook for 15 minutes. Ensure that it is cooked in the middle before taking it off the fryer. Serve.

Crispy Coconut Chicken

Prep + Cook Time: 40 minutes | Servings: 4

Ingredients:

- Vegetable oil for frying
- 1 tsp cayenne pepper, optional
- ¼ tsp salt
- 1/8 tsp ground black pepper
- ½ cup cornstarch
- 3 large eggs, lightly beaten
- 3 - 4 cups of sweetened coconut flakes (Baker's Coconut)
- 3 - 4 medium boneless, skinless, chicken breasts, cut into strips or nuggets

Directions:

1. Get a medium-sized pot and pour about 2 to 3 inches of oil. Heat on a medium burner of about 365 F.
2. Get a bowl, make a mixture of cayenne pepper, salt, black pepper and cornstarch, and set aside.
3. Get another bowl and beat three eggs lightly.
4. Get a third bowl and add coconut flakes in it.
5. Douse each of the chicken in the cornstarch mixture, then in the eggs, ensuring that it is evenly covered. Finally, dip it in the coconut flakes and set them aside.
6. After dipping all the chicken, check if the oil is ready by placing the end of a wooden spoon in it. Once there is the formation of bubbles around the spoon, you can proceed to cook. If not, allow the oil to heat further.
7. To cook, add each chicken piece gently into the oil while ensuring that the chicken does not touch and stick together after entering into the oil.
8. Allow the chicken pieces to cook for about 4 minutes before turning the other side and cooking for an extra four minutes.
9. Once the chicken appears golden, withdraw and transfer them onto a paper towel lined plate. You may cook in batches if the pan isn't large enough to take all at once.
10. Served the cooked chicken alongside your preferred sauce, alongside honey, orange, or sweet and sour sauce.

Chicken Cutlets

Prep + Cook Time: 15 minutes | Servings: 6

Ingredients:

- 3 medium chicken breasts
- 7 oz gluten free oats
- 2 medium eggs beaten
- Salt and ground black pepper
- 1 tbsp mustard powder
- 1 tbsp basil, dried
- 1 oz parmesan cheese, grated
- 2 tbsp garlic, dried

Directions:

1. The first step is to butterfly your chicken. In the end, you will have six pieces of butterfly chicken if you used three chicken breasts.
2. Divide your gluten-free oats into two; blend one half until they give the appearance of fine oats.
3. Get three clean bowls – add your egg; blended oats; and unblended oats in each bowl.
4. Combine the blended oats and ¼ of the unblended oats, and add pepper, salt, and mustard powered to taste.
5. Combine unblended oats and ¼ of the blended oats, and add pepper, salt, basil, parmesan cheese, and dried garlic.
6. Place the chicken cutlets in the fake flour first, then the egg, and the fake breadcrumbs.
7. Set your Air Fryer to 350 F and cook at 11 minutes. For best results, cook two cutlets at a go. Serve.

Shredded Chicken

Prep + Cook Time: 20 minutes | Servings: 2

Ingredients:

- 1 tsp honey
- 1 tsp mustard
- 1 tsp garlic puree

- 2 large chicken breasts
- Salt and ground black pepper to taste

Directions:

1. Combine the whole marinade ingredients into the baking pan of the air fryer and stir very well.
2. Immerse the chicken breasts into the marinade, while seasoning the top of the chicken breasts with pepper and salt.
3. Allow the seasoned chicken to cook for 15 minutes in the air fryer, at 360 F.
4. After the first five minutes of cooking, slice the chicken breasts into thirds and pour some marinade into the openings. This is to ensure that the breasts cook fast and are well-flavored.
5. Transfer the well-cooked chicken into a chopping board and leave for about two minutes.
6. Chop the cooked chicken into small pieces using a knife and fork. Serve.

Greek Chicken Kebabs

Prep + Cook Time: 25 minutes | Servings: 2

Ingredients:

- 1 chicken breast
- 3 garlic cloves
- 1 tbsp oregano, dried
- 1 tsp coconut oil

- Salt and ground black pepper to taste
- Pinch thyme
- 1 small lemon juice and rind
- 1 tsp greek yoghurt

Directions:

1. Ensure that your chicken has been chopped into pieces of medium sizes.
2. After peeling your garlic, dice it into thin pieces, then add seasoning and lemon to make a mixture. Transfer the mixture and the chicken into a mixing bowl and mix well with your hands.
3. Keep the mixed chicken in the storage container and leave it in the fridge overnight.
4. Bring out the chicken from the fridge the next day and immerse it in Greek yogurt and coconut oil.
5. Transfer the immersed chicken onto the skewers and then into the grill pan of the air fryer.
6. Set the air fryer to 350 F and cook for about 9 minutes.
7. At about 4 ½ minutes, turn the chicken with thongs to ensure the presence of a crispy grill-like coating on both sides.
8. Serve alongside fresh oregano.

Chicken Wrapped In Bacon

Prep + Cook Time: 20 minutes | Servings: 3

Ingredients:

- 1 chicken breast
- 6 back bacon
- 1 tbsp garlic soft cheese

Directions:

1. Ensure that your chicken breast has been cut into six bite-sized pieces.
2. After laying out your bacon rashers, spread them using a small layer of soft cheese.
3. Roll your chicken on the cheese, and have them secured with a cocktail stick.
4. Transfer them into the air fryer, set it to 355 F and allow to cook for 15 minutes.

Perfect Healthy Chicken Dippers

Prep + Cook Time: 1 hour 45 minutes | Servings: 4

Ingredients:

- 2 chicken breasts
- 2 slices wholemeal bread made into breadcrumbs
- 1 tsp oregano, dried
- 1 tsp mustard powder
- 2 tsp parsley, dried
- Salt and ground black pepper to taste
- 1 large egg

Directions:

1. Ensure that your air fryer is preheated to 360 F.
2. Cut your chicken breasts into different pieces with sizes similar to chicken dippers. Keep the chopped chicken pieces somewhere.
3. Get a clean baking tray and make a mixture of breadcrumbs and seasoning in it.
4. Get a clean bowl and beat the egg in it.
5. Ensure that every chicken piece is covered in the egg, and then in the breadcrumbs.
6. Transfer the covered eggs into a plate and fridge it for an hour.
7. Remove from the fridge and place on a sheet of baking paper in the air fryer. Set the temperature at 360 F and allow to cook until you have crispy breadcrumbs and a well-cooked chicken, especially at the center. This takes about 25 minutes.
8. Serve alongside Wasabi Mayonnaise.

Chicken Nuggets

Prep + Cook Time: 35 minutes | Servings: 4

Ingredients:

- Salt and ground black pepper to taste
- 1 tsp paprika
- 1 tbsp olive oil
- 10 oz chicken breast, chopped into pieces
- 1 tsp garlic puree
- 1 tsp parsley
- 1 tsp tomato ketchup
- 2 medium eggs, beaten
- 2 slices wholemeal bread, made into breadcrumbs

Directions:

1. Make a mixture of pepper, salt, and paprika into a clean bowl.
2. To the mixture, add the olive oil to make a nice batter.
3. In a food processor, puree the chicken while adding garlic, parsley, ketchup, and one beaten egg.
4. Beat the second egg in a clean bowl (to be used for batter coating).
5. Transform the chicken mixture into chicken nugget shapes, before covering it in the egg and the breadcrumbs respectively.
6. Allow cooking for 10 minutes at 390 F. Serve.

Flourless Truly Crispy Chicken Nuggets

Prep + Cook Time: 25 minutes | Servings: 2-3

Ingredients:

- 1 chicken breast
- 1 large egg beaten
- 1 cup gluten free oats
- 1 tbsp thyme
- 1 tbsp parsley
- Salt and ground black pepper to taste

Directions:

1. Ensure that your air fryer is preheated to 355 F.
2. Process your chicken breast in a food processor or blender until it appears like chicken mince.
3. Transfer the processed chicken into a clean mixing bowl.
4. Put the egg in a separate bowl.
5. Using a food processor or blender, blend your oats until it appears like breadcrumbs.
6. Into the mixing bowl containing the chicken, add thyme, parsley, pepper, and salt. Then mix well.
7. Take a piece of the chicken mixture (already chopped into chicken nugget sizes), and mold it into the desired shape with your hands.
8. Dip it into the blended oats and egg respectively. Then, dip into the oats again.
9. Do the same for all the chicken nuggets, one after the other, and transfer them onto a baking sheet in the air fryer.
10. Allow the chicken pieces to cook for 10 minutes at 180°C.
11. Serve alongside mustard and tomato ketchup.

Panko Breaded Chicken Parmesan with Marinara Sauce

Prep + Cook Time: 35 minutes | Servings: 4

Ingredients:

- Cooking spray
- 16 oz skinless chicken breasts sliced in half to make 4 breasts
- ½ cup parmesan cheese, grated
- 1 cup panko bread crumbs
- 2 tsp Italian Seasoning
- Salt and ground black pepper to taste
- 1/8 cup egg whites
- ¾ cup marinara sauce
- ½ cup mozarella cheese, shredded

Directions:

1. Ensure that the air fryer is preheated at 400 F, with the basket well sprayed with the cooking spray.
2. Create four thinner chicken breasts by cutting the chicken breasts horizontally into half. Pound the chicken breasts on a hard surface to flatten them completely.
3. Grate your parmesan cheese and set it aside.
4. Get a large, clean bowl and mix the grated cheese, panko breadcrumbs, and seasonings. Stir to have a uniform mixture.
5. Get another bowl of similar size and place the egg whites in it.
6. Immerse the chicken into the bowl containing the egg whites, and then the one containing the breadcrumbs mixture.
7. Transfer the immersed chicken into the air fryer, with the top sprayed with the cooking spray.
8. Allow the chicken to cook for 7 minutes in the air fryer. After this, use the marinara sauce and the shredded mozzarella to top the breasts.
9. The topped chicken should be cooked until the cheese melts completely (for about 3 minutes).
10. Serve.

Chicken Parmesan and Fries

Prep + Cook Time: 35 minutes | Servings: 4

Ingredients:

- 2 large potatoes
- 2 medium eggs
- 1 tbsp basil, dried
- 1 tbsp oregano, dried
- Salt and ground black pepper to taste
- 1 tbsp garlic puree
- Parmesan crisps
- 2 medium chicken breasts
- 1 tbsp olive oil
- 1 oz mozzarella cheese, shredded
- 1 oz parmesan cheese, grated

Directions:

1. Without removing the skin, chop the potatoes into French Fries.
2. Create your production line. Get a bowl and beat the eggs in it, adding the basil, oregano, salt, pepper, and some garlic puree. Blend the crisps until you have a fine texture and transfer it into a separate bowl, adding black pepper and a handful of unused breadcrumbs, then mix everything thoroughly.
3. Butterfly the chicken before transferring them onto a clean chopping board.
4. With the French Fries in the air fryer, set it to 360 F, and add a tablespoon of olive oil before cooking for 12 minutes.
5. After withdrawing the basket from the air fryer, insert the grill pan.
6. Dip the butterflied chicken completely in the parmesan coating, then in the egg, and the parmesan coating again.
7. Transfer the dipped chicken to the grill pan. Set the air fryer to 360°F before cooking the chicken for 10 minutes.
8. When the air fryer beeps, place the chicken over the French Fries and decorate the upper part with the cheese.
9. Place in the air fryer again and cook at the same temperature for an additional four minutes.

Crumbed Chicken Tenderloins

Prep + Cook Time: 30 minutes | Servings: 4

Ingredients:

- 1 egg
- ½ cup dry breadcrumbs
- 2 tbsp vegetable oil
- 8 chicken tenderloins

Directions:

1. Ensure that your Air Fryer is preheated to 350°F.
2. Get two clean bowls; in the first bowl, whisk an egg, in the other bowl, make a loose and crumbly mixture of oil and breadcrumbs.
3. Place each chicken tenderloin into the bowl containing whisked egg. Remove any extra egg by shaking.
4. Then immerse in the crumb mixture until the mixture covers the chicken thoroughly and evenly.
5. Place the chicken tenderloins carefully into the air fryer basket.
6. Cook the chicken for about 12 minutes, or until you can no longer see the pink in the middle.
7. Once cooked, measure the temperature with an instant-read thermometer inserted into the center of the chicken. It should read not less than 165 F.
8. Serve.

Chicken Tenders

Prep + Cook Time: 15 minutes | Servings: 6

Ingredients:

- 2 large eggs
- 2 small lemons, juice only
- ½ tsp garlic puree
- 8 oz gluten free oats
- Salt and ground black pepper to taste
- 1 tbsp parsley, dried
- 1 tbsp mustard powder
- 2 tbsp basil
- 3 medium chicken breasts
- 1 tbsp mayonnaise, optional

Directions:

1. In a clean bowl, make a mixture of egg and half of the lemon juice, alongside the garlic puree. Keep the mix somewhere safe.
2. Blend a combination of ½ of the gluten-free oats until it appears like fine oats.
3. The blended oats should be transferred into a bowl and the non-blended oats into another bowl.
4. Mix both the blended oats and the non-blended oats by adding ¼ of the blended oats into the non-blended, and another ¼ non-blended oat into the blended oats.
5. After the mixing, you should have two bowls – one containing more of blended oats, and the other containing more of unblended oats.
6. Use the unblended oats mixture as your fake breadcrumbs and the blended oats mixture as your fake flour.
7. Add salt, pepper, parsley, and mustard to the fake flour.
8. Add salt, pepper, and basil to the fake breadcrumbs.
9. Cut the chicken breast such that you have tender shapes of medium sizes.
10. Place the chicken tenders into the flour bowl, before soaking it in the egg mixture.
11. Coat the soaked chicken tenders with the breadcrumbs mixture.
12. Transfer the coated tenders into the air fryer basket.
13. Set your Air Fryer to 350 F and cook for about 10 minutes.
14. While the chickens are cooking, prepare your mayonnaise mixture by adding pepper, salt, lemon, and a bit of mustard powder and mixing well. Serve.

Spatchcock Chicken

Prep + Cook Time: 55 minutes | Servings: 4

Ingredients:

- 1 tsp mixed herbs
- 1 tbsp garlic puree
- 2 tsp olive oil
- Salt and ground black pepper to taste
- 2 lbs spatchcock chicken

Directions:

1. Create a really thick paste by combining all the seasonings, including the garlic puree and the olive oil.
2. While placing the spatchcock chicken on the grill pan of the air fryer, apply the garlic paste on every visible part of the skin to ensure that you have an even and total coating.
3. Set your air fryer to 360°F and cook each side of the chicken for 25 minutes.
4. Serve warm with salad and rice.

Notes:

The usual practice is to cook the whole chickens in the main basket of the air fryer. However, the chicken was longer than normal this time around. Thus, only the grill pan can accommodate it conveniently. You may reduce the cooking time by five minutes if you are working with a thawed chicken.

Air fryers work differently, thus, be sure to check that the chicken is cooked before serving. You can avoid getting burnt while turning the spatchcock chicken over by using kitchen tongs.

Southern-Style Chicken

Prep + Cook Time: 40 minutes | Servings: 6

Ingredients:

- 1 tbsp minced fresh parsley
- 1 tsp paprika
- 1 tsp garlic salt
- 2 cups crushed Ritz crackers (about 50)
- ½ tsp pepper
- ¼ tsp rubbed sage
- ¼ tsp ground cumin
- 1 large egg, beaten
- 1 chicken (3 to 4 lbs), cut up

Directions:

1. Ensure that your Air Fryer is preheated to 375 F, and spritz the basket using a cooking spray.
2. Get a clean shallow bowl. In the bowl, make a mixture of the first seven ingredients.
3. Get another clean shallow bowl and place the egg in it. After dipping the chicken in the egg, dip again in the cracker mixture, while patting, to ensure that the coating doesn't remove. Arrange the chickens in a single layer in the air fryer basket and spritz with cooking spray.
4. Allow the chicken to cook for 10 minutes before turning and spraying with additional cooking spray. Cook again (for about 10-20 minutes) until you have a golden brown color and juices running clear.
5. Do the same for the remaining chicken.

General Tso's Chicken

Prep + Cook Time: 40 minutes | Servings: 4

Ingredients:

- 1 lb boneless, skinless chicken thighs, patted dry and cut into1 to 1¼ -inch chunks
- 1 large egg
- 1/3 cup plus 2 tsp cornstarch, divided
- ¼ tsp ground white pepper
- ¼ tsp kosher salt
- 2 tbsp ketchup
- 2 tbsp soy sauce
- 2 tsp sugar
- 7 tbsp chicken broth
- 2 tsp unseasoned rice vinegar
- 1½ tbsp canola oil
- 3 to 4 chiles de árbol, chopped and deseeded
- 1 tbsp finely chopped garlic
- 1 tbsp finely chopped fresh ginger
- 1 tsp toasted sesame oil
- 2 tbsp thinly sliced green onion
- ½ tsp toasted sesame seeds

Directions:

1. In a large bowl, coat your chicken well in the beaten egg.
2. In another bowl, make a mixture of 1/3 cup cornstarch, pepper, and salt. Using a fork, transfer the chicken into the cornstarch mixture. Ensure that every area is well coated by using a spatula.
3. Divide the chickens into batches, and transfer them into the air-fryer basket. If you are using the air-fryer oven racks instead, you can cook the entire chicken by moving them into the oven racks but leaving little space between the pieces. Set your Air Fryer to 400 F and allow it to preheat for 3 minutes.
4. Place the battered chicken and allow to cook for 12 to 16 minutes, while shaking midway. Allow the cooked chicken to dry for three to five minutes, if a side of the chicken is still damp, cook again for about 1 or 2 minutes.
5. Whisk the remaining two teaspoons of cornstarch alongside ketchup, soy sauce, sugar, broth, and rice vinegar.
6. Get a large, clean skillet and heat canola oil and chiles in it over medium heat. Once the mixture starts to sizzle, add the garlic and ginger, and cook for about 30 seconds until you have a fragrance.
7. Whisk the cornstarch mixture again, and stir into a mixture in the skillet. Set the heat to medium-high, and once you have the sauce bubbling, add the chicken. Stir the chicken to ensure even coating, and continue cooking until you have a thickened sauce that clutches to the chicken tightly. This takes about one and a half minutes. Turn off the heat and stir the chicken in 1 tablespoon sesame oil and 1 tablespoon green onion.
8. Transfer into a serving plate, and add the remaining one tablespoon green onion as well as the sesame seeds.

Rotisserie Chicken

Prep + Cook Time: 45 minutes | Servings: 4-5

Ingredients:

1 whole chicken (3 lbs)

Brine:

2 tsp thyme

1 tbsp paprika

Salt and ground black pepper to taste

1 chicken oxo cube

Chicken Rub:

1 tsp celery salt

1 tbsp paprika

1 tbsp olive oil

Salt and ground black pepper to taste

Directions:

1. Collect all your brine ingredients into a freezing bag. Place the whole chicken inside, and then fill it up with cold water until the chicken is immersed. Zip the freezing bag, and place it in the fridge overnight.
2. When you are ready to cook the next day, withdraw the chicken from the freezing bag and remove the giblets. Separate the brine stock also and dry the entire chicken by patting it dry with a kitchen towel.
3. Get a clean bowl and prepare your chicken rub in it.
4. With the breast facing down, put the entire chicken in the air fryer basket/pan. Rub every visible part of the chicken skin with ½ of the chicken rub and ½ of the olive oil.
5. Set your Air Fryer to 370 F and allow the chicken to cook at this temperature for 20 minutes.
6. Using the kitchen tongs, turn over the chicken to the other side and add the remaining oil and chicken rub, then cook again for another 20 minutes without changing the temperature.
7. Serve warm.

Thai Peanut Chicken Egg Rolls

Prep + Cook Time: 20 minutes | Servings: 3-4

Ingredients:

- 2 cups rotisserie chicken, shredded
- ¼ cup Thai peanut sauce
- 4 egg roll wrappers
- 1 medium carrot, very thinly sliced or ribboned
- ¼ red bell pepper, julienned
- 3 green onions, chopped
- Non-stick cooking spray or sesame oil

Directions:

1. Ensure that your air fryer is preheated to 390 F.
2. Get a small bowl and place the chicken in it alongside the Thai peanut sauce.
3. With the egg roll wrappers laid out on a clean, dry surface, arrange ¼ carrot, bell pepper, and onions to accommodate the bottom third of the egg roll wrapper.
4. Spread ½ cup of the chicken mixture over the vegetables.
5. Using water, moisten the outer edges of the wrapper. Roll the wrapper tightly by folding the sides of the wrapper towards the center.
6. Do the same for the other wrappers (pending this time, cover them with a damp paper towel).
7. Using a non-stick cooking spray, spread both sides of the assembled egg rolls well.
8. Transfer the sprayed egg rolls into your air fryer. Bake for 6-8 minutes at 390 F or until you have a crispy and golden brown appearance.
9. Slice the baked chicken into half and serve with extra Thai Peanut Sauce for dipping.

Friendly Airfryer Whole Chicken

Prep + Cook Time: 45 minutes | Servings: 4

Ingredients:

- Medium whole chicken (about 3 lbs)
- Salt and ground black pepper to taste
- 1 tbsp mixed herbs
- 1 tbsp olive oil
- 1 large onion

Directions:

1. Ensure that your air fryer is preheated to 340 F.
2. To the skin of your nice and dry chicken, sprinkle salt, pepper, and mixed herbs, before rubbing olive oil.
3. Take away the giblets present in the chicken. Without removing the skin of the onion, chop it into half and place in the chicken's cavity.
4. Transfer the chicken into the air fryer upside down and with the bottom stuck in the air. Allow cooking for 20 minutes before turning it over. This time around, the breast faces up. Cook for another 20 minutes.
5. Remove and serve warm.

KFC Chicken in the Air Fryer

Prep + Cook Time: 30 minutes | Servings: 4

Ingredients:

- 1 whole chicken
- 1 oz KFC spice blend
- 10 oz bread crumbs
- 4 oz plain flour
- 3 small eggs beaten

Directions:

1. After chopping your chicken into pieces of desired sizes, set them aside.
2. You may separate the wings, things, drumsticks, and breast, or have the wings and the breast together.
3. Get a clean bowl, and make a mixture of the KFC spice and breadcrumbs.
4. Get another clean bowl and place your flour.
5. In a third clean bowl, place your beaten eggs.
6. After rolling the chicken pieces in the flour, roll it in the egg, and finally in the spicy breadcrumbs.
7. Set your air fryer to 360 F and cook the rolled chicken for 18 minutes. Do not withdraw until it is well cooked in the middle.
8. Serve.

KFC Easy Chicken Strips in the Air Fryer

Prep + Cook Time: 25 minutes | Servings: 2

Ingredients:

- 1 chicken breast, chopped into strips
- Salt and ground black pepper to taste
- 3 oz bread crumbs
- ½ oz plain oats
- ½ oz desiccated coconut
- ¼ oz KFC spice blend get our recipe here
- 2 oz plain flour
- 1 small egg, beaten

Directions:

1. Make strips out of your chicken breast.
2. Get a clean bowl, and make a mixture of salt, pepper, breadcrumbs, oats, coconut, and the KFC spice blend.
3. Get another clean bowl and place your egg.
4. In the third clean bowl, add your plain flour.
5. Dip the strips in the plain flour first, before the egg, and finally the spicy layer.
6. Set your Air Fryer to 360 F and cook the dipped chicken for eight minutes.
7. Reduce the temperature to 320 F and cook for an extra four minutes to ensure that the chicken cooks well in the middle.
8. Serve.

KFC Popcorn Chicken in the Air Fryer

Prep + Cook Time: 25 minutes | Servings: 2

Ingredients:

- 1 chicken breast
- 2 oz plain flour
- 1 small egg, beaten
- Salt and ground black pepper to taste
- 2 oz bread crumbs
- ¼ oz KFC spice blend get the recipe here

Directions:

1. Blend your chicken in your food processor until you have something like a minced chicken.
2. Create your factory line – first bowl containing your flour; the second containing your beaten egg; and the third containing a mixture of salt, pepper, bread crumbs, and finally the KFC spice blend.
3. Like another factory line, transform the minced chicken into balls.
4. Roll the balls in the flour first, then in the egg, and finally in the spiced breadcrumbs.
5. Transfer the rolled chicken balls into the air fryer. Set it to 360 F and cook for about 10 to 12 minutes, or until you are sure the chicken is well cooked in the middle.

Everything Bagel Chicken Strips

Prep + Cook Time: 25 minutes | Servings: 4

Ingredients:

- 1 day-old everything bagel, torn
- ½ cup panko bread crumbs
- ½ cup grated parmesan cheese
- ¼ tsp red pepper flakes, crushed
- 1 lb chicken tenderloins
- ½ tsp salt
- ¼ cup butter, cubed

Directions:

1. Ensure that your Air Fryer is preheated to 400 F.
2. Pulse the torn bagel in a food processor and withdraw only when you have coarse crumbs. Separate ½ of the cup bagel crumbs and transfer it into a shallow bowl, mix it with panko, cheese, and pepper flakes. You may retain or discard the other half of the bagel crumbs.
3. Get a shallow bowl that is safe for use in a microwave, heat microwave butter until it melts.
4. Sprinkle your chicken with salt and dip it in warm butter before coating it with crumb mixture. You may pat the chicken to ensure it retains the crumb.
5. After spraying the air fryer basket with cooking spray, transfer the chicken to form a single layer in the basket.
6. You may divide the chicken into batches. Cook each batch for seven minutes before turning over to the other side. Cook until the pink appearance of the chicken is replaced by the golden brown coating (for about seven to eight minutes).
7. Serve immediately.

Buffalo Chicken Strips

Prep + Cook Time: 35 minutes | Servings: 3

Ingredients:

- ¾ cup panko crumbs or bread crumbs
- ¼ cup flour
- 1 egg, beaten
- Garlic salt and ground black pepper to taste
- Cooking spray
- 12 oz chicken breast strips
- Buffalo sauce (I used about ½ cup)

Directions:

1. Get three separate bowls. In each bowl, place the panko crumbs, flour and egg. You may mix the panko alongside some pepper, garlic, and salt.
2. The bottom of the air fryer should be sprayed with a little cooking spray.
3. Place the chicken in the flour, egg, and the panko respectively. 35Ensure that the chicken is entirely coated.
4. Transfer the coated chicken into the air fryer while spraying the top with a little cooking spray again.
5. Set your Air Fryer to 375 F and fry for 10 minutes. At the same temperature, flip and cook for further 3-5 minutes or until the pink color disappears completely.
6. Transfer the chicken into the cooked chicken into a mixing bowl.
7. Immerse in a buffalo sauce until the whole chicken is well coated.
8. Serve alongside carrots, ranch, and celery.

Flourless Chicken Cordon Bleu

Prep + Cook Time: 35 minutes | Servings: 2

Ingredients:

- 2 chicken breasts
- 1 tbsp tarragon
- Salt and ground black pepper to taste
- 1 tsp parsley
- 1 tsp garlic puree
- 1 tbsp soft cheese

- 1 slice ham
- 1 slice cheddar cheese
- 1 small egg, beaten
- 1 oz oats
- 1 tbsp thyme

Directions:

1. Ensure that your air fryer is preheated to 365 F.
2. Using a chopping board, chop your chicken breasts at a side angle to the right, near the corner. This is to ensure that they can be folded over easily while adding the ingredients to the middle.
3. Using a mixture of tarragon, pepper, and salt, sprinkle the sides of your chicken very well.
4. Get a clean mixing bowl and make a mixture of parsley, garlic, and soft cheese.
5. Add a layer of the cheese mixture in the middle, plus half a slice each of the ham and cheddar cheese.
6. With the filling inside, press down the chicken till it appears almost sealed.
7. Add your egg and blended oats in another bowl, alongside thyme. Mix well.
8. Roll the chicken in the oats first, and in the egg. Roll in the oats again.
9. Transfer the rolled pieces of chicken on a baking sheet inside your air fryer.
10. Cook for 30 minutes. After the first 20 minutes of cooking, turn the chickens over to ensure that the crispiness is present on both sides.
11. Serve alongside new potatoes.

Jamaican Chicken Meatballs

Prep + Cook Time: 25 minutes | Servings: 10

Ingredients:

- 2 chicken breasts
- 1 large onion peeled and diced

Jamaican seasonings:

- 3 tbsp soy sauce
- 2 tbsp honey
- 1 tbsp cumin
- 1 tsp chilli powder
- 1 tbsp mustard powder

- 1 tbsp thyme
- 1 tbsp basil
- Salt and ground black pepper to taste
- 2 tsp jerk paste, optional

Directions:

1. Blend your chicken in the blender until it appears like chicken mince.
2. Blend the onion in the blender as well.
3. Place the Jamaican seasonings and blend again for the third time.
4. Make ten medium-sized meatballs from the blended products.
5. Transfer the medium-sized meatballs into your Air Fryer and allow them to cook at 360 F for 15 minutes.
6. After cooking, place them on sticks before spooning some of the sauce over them.
7. You can get the source from the sides of your blender. This gives the sticky meatballs a great taste sensation.
8. Sprinkle with fresh herbs. Serve.

Chicken Fried Rice

Prep + Cook Time: 35 minutes | Servings: 4-6

Ingredients:

- 3 cups cooked white rice cold
- 6 tbsp soy sauce
- 1 tbsp vegetable oil
- ½ cup onion diced
- 1 cup cooked chicken diced
- 1 cup frozen peas and carrots

Directions:

1. Get a mixing bowl and place the cold cooked white rice into it.
2. Add the soy sauce alongside the vegetable oil and mix thoroughly.
3. Add the diced onion, diced chicken, and the frozen carrots and peas before mixing well again.
4. Now, transfer the rice mixture into the nonstick pan.
5. In the case of aluminum pan, spray the inside with a non-stick cooking spray before adding the rice.
6. Transfer the pan into the air fryer, and with the temperature set at 360 F, cook for 20 minutes.
7. Withdraw the pan as soon as the air fryer timer goes off.
8. Serve the cooked rice only, or alongside your favorite meat.

Crispy Fried Spring Rolls

Prep + Cook Time: 30 minutes | Servings: 4

Ingredients:

- 4 oz cooked chicken breast
- 1 oz carrot
- 1 oz mushrooms
- 1 celery stalk
- 1 tsp chicken stock powder
- 1 tsp sugar
- ½ tsp finely chopped ginger
- 1 egg, beaten
- 1 tsp corn starch
- 8 spring roll wrappers

Directions:

1. Cut the breasts into shreds.
2. Cut the carrot, mushroom, and celery into long thin strips.
3. Transfer the shredded chicken into a bowl before mixing it with the mushroom, carrot and celery strips.
4. Add the chicken stock powder, sugar, and ginger. Stir the entire contents evenly to make the spring roll filling.
5. Add cornstarch to the whisked egg, and stir to create a thick paste. Keep the paste separately.
6. Add some filling into each spring roll wrapper and roll them up. Seal the ends of each roll with the egg mixture. It is recommended that you brush the spring rolls with oil to achieve a crispy result.
7. Ensure your Air Fryer is preheated to 390 F before placing the rolls into its basket.
8. With the timer at 4 minutes, cook the rolls.
9. Serve alongside sweet chili sauce.

Spicy Rolled Meat

Prep + Cook Time: 60 minutes | Servings: 4

Ingredients:

- 1 lb turkey breast fillet
- ½ tsp chili powder
- 1 tsp cinnamon
- 1½ tsp ground cumin
- 1 tsp salt
- 2 tbsp olive oil
- 1 small red onion, finely chopped
- 3 tbsp flat-leafed parsley, finely chopped
- 1 clove garlic, crushed
- String for rolled meat

Directions:

1. To create a long piece of meat, ensure that the meat is positioned on the cutting board, such that the short side is facing towards you, then slit it horizontally along the full length, i.e., about a 1/3 of the way from the top and stopping 1-inch from the edge. With this part folded open, slit it again from this side and open it.
2. Prepare a mixture of chili powder, pepper, cinnamon, cumin, one teaspoon salt in a big bowl.
3. After adding the olive oil, take away one tablespoon of the mixture into a new small bowl. Add onion and parsley in the mixture in the big bowl.
4. Ensure that your air fryer is preheated to 360 F.
5. Use the onion mixture to coat the meat. Coat by rolling the meat firmly and start from the short side. Ensure that the string is tied firmly around the meat, such that each tie is 1-inch away from another. Then rub the outside of the rolled meat with the herb mixture.
6. Cook for 40 minutes. After the first 25 minutes of cooking, turn the roll over to ensure that the crispiness is present on both sides. Serve.

Sizzling Turkey Fajitas Platter

Prep + Cook Time: 30 minutes | Servings: 2-3

Ingredients:

- 1 large avocado
- ½ small red onion
- 1 large green pepper
- 1 large yellow pepper
- 1 large red pepper
- 4 oz leftover turkey breast
- 6 tortilla wraps
- 2 tbsp mexican seasoning
- 1 tsp cumin
- 3 tbsp cajun spice
- Fresh coriander
- Salt and ground black pepper to tatse
- 5 tbsp soft cheese

Directions:

1. The first step is to slice up your salad. Cut your avocado into little wedges. Also, dice the red onion and slice the peppers into thin slices.
2. Cut the turkey breast into small little chunks.
3. Transfer the turkey, onions, and peppers into a separate bowl and mix.
4. Then add all seasonings and the soft cheese and mix again.
5. Place all the contents into a silver foil and air fry at 390 F for about 20 minutes. Serve.

Turkey Breast with Maple Mustard Glaze

Prep + Cook Time: 45 minutes | Servings: 6

Ingredients:

- 2 tsp olive oil
- 5-lbs whole turkey breast
- 1 tsp salt
- ½ tsp freshly ground black pepper
- ½ tsp smoked paprika
- 1 tsp dried thyme
- ½ tsp dried sage
- 2 tbsp Dijon mustard
- 1 tbsp butter
- ¼ cup maple syrup

Directions:

1. Ensure that your air fryer is preheated to 350 F.
2. Apply the olive oil all over the turkey breast.
3. Prepare a mixture of salt, pepper, paprika, thyme, and sage. Rub the mixture on the outside of the turkey breast.
4. Place the seasoned turkey breast into the basket of your air fryer and air fry for 25 minutes at 350 F. After 25 minutes, change the position of the turkey breast such that the other side is facing up, and then air fry for another 12 minutes.
5. Measure with an instant-read thermometer – once you have about 165 F as the internal temperature of the turkey breast, it means it is fully cooked.
6. While the turkey is still in the air fryer, prepare a mixture of mustard, butter, and maple syrup in a clean saucepan.
7. Once the turkey is done, apply the glaze on every part of the turkey while it stands in an upright position. Air fry again for five minutes, by which the skin will be crispy and nicely browned. Allow the turkey to cool for about five minutes, while covering it slightly with a foil.
8. Slice and serve.

Brazilian Mini Turkey Pies

Prep + Cook Time: 15 minutes | Servings: 8

Ingredients:

- 1 oz turkey stock
- 2 oz whole milk
- 2 oz coconut milk
- 8 oz homemade tomato sauce
- 1 tsp oregano
- 1 tbsp coriander
- Salt and ground black pepper to taste
- 2 oz turkey, cooked and shredded
- Flour
- 8 slices filo pastry
- 1 small egg beaten

Directions:

1. Get a clean mixing bowl and put all your wet ingredients, except the egg. Mix well.
2. The result should be a pale-looking sauce – the stock for your pie. Now add the seasoning and turkey before mixing again. Finally, set the mixture aside.
3. To each of your little pie cases, line them with a bit of flour before the filo pastry. This prevents them from sticking. Each pie should use up one sheet of filo, and it should be centrally positioned such that you can easily fold over the extra pastry for the top of the pie.
4. Add the mixture to every mini pie pot until they are ¾ full.
5. Cover the top with the remaining pastry before brushing the egg along the top.
6. Transfer the mini pie pot into the air fryer, set the temperature to 360 F and allow to cook for 10 minutes. Serve

Thanksgiving Turkey Sandwich Recipe

Prep + Cook Time: 20 minutes | Servings: 1

Ingredients:

- 1 tbsp leftover turkey gravy
- 3 slices wholemeal bread
- Handful fresh lettuce leaves
- 4 slices turkey breast skin still on
- 1 oz cranberry sauce
- 2 oz leftover turkey stuffing

Directions:

1. Use ½ of your leftover gravy in spreading two slices of your bread.
2. The third slice should be transformed into breadcrumbs, and then mixed with the unused gravy.
3. Layer your bread with lettuce, breadcrumbs, turkey, cranberry sauce, and turkey stuffing. While placing the second slice of bread on top, push it down to ensure that it all fits in. Add some small skewers into the sandwich to keep it in place.
4. Transfer into the air fryer and allow to cook at 360 F for 5 minutes, or until nicely warm.
5. Detach the skewers before serving.

Turkey Curry Samosas

Prep + Cook Time: 10 minutes | Servings: 2

Ingredients:

- 2 oz shredded turkey wing meat
- 1 tsp coriander
- 1 tsp turmeric
- 1 tsp garam masala
- Salt and ground black pepper to taste
- Coconut milk
- 1 small egg beaten
- 2 pastry sheets

Directions:

1. Get a clean mixing bowl and combine the turkey and all the seasonings. Mix well.
2. To get a soft and creamy mixture that would not dry out, put a little coconut milk to the mixture.
3. Transfer the contents onto your pastry sheets. Fold the sheet over to appear like samosa in shape.
4. Beat your eggs into a bowl, and brush the folded sheets until they have a golden glow.
5. Set your Air Fryer to 320 F and allow to cook for 3 minutes.
6. Serve.

Leftover Turkey Spring Rolls

Prep + Cook Time: 40 minutes | Servings: 1

Ingredients:

- 1 oz leftover turkey breast shredded
- 1 tbsp Chinese five spice
- 1 tsp coriander
- Salt and ground black pepper to taste
- 1 tsp Worcester sauce
- 1 tbsp soy sauce
- 1 tbsp honey
- 2 tortilla wraps get our recipe here
- 2 large eggs, beaten

Directions:

1. Get a clean mixing bowl and place your leftover turkey plus all the seasonings listed above. Use your hands to ensure that the turkey is coated very well.
2. Your tortilla wraps should be rolled out well to give the best possible thin sheets without breaking.
3. Brush the sheets first with a little water on either side and then with the egg.
4. Transfer the brushed sheet into the fridge for about 30 minutes. This ensures that the egg is adequately absorbed.
5. Withdraw from the fridge after 30 minutes and then cut them into eight different spring roll sheets.
6. Before rolling into a spring roll, put the turkey filling into each sheet.
7. Brush the rolls with another layer of the egg mix before placing them into the air fryer.
8. Set the air fryer to 360 F and allow to cook for 5 minutes.
9. Serve.

Turkey Stuffed Bread Recipe

Prep + Cook Time: 45 minutes | Servings: 2

Ingredients:

- 2 oz butter
- 11 oz plain flour
- 1 tsp yeast
- 1 oz shredded turkey wing meat
- 7 oz whole milk
- Salt and ground black pepper to taste
- Handful cooked spinach
- 4 oz soft cheese
- 4 oz white cheddar cheese

Directions:

1. Rub the butter into the plain flour so that it appears like breadcrumbs. Then mix in the yeast and the turkey, and finally the warm milk.
2. The next is mixing in pepper and salt. The mixing should be intensive such that the mixture gives a good dough. Then knead the dough for about 10 minutes. Finally, get a clean floury worktop and roll your dough on it.
3. Get a clean mixing bowl and make a mixture of spinach and soft cheese. Layer the top of the bread with the mixture.
4. Then cover it with the cheddar cheese before rolling up the bread. When rolling, the spinach and cheese should form as the center of the bread.
5. Transfer the rolled bread into your Air Fryer, precisely on the baking mat. Set to 360 F and allow to bake for 20 minutes. Reduce the temperature to 320 F and allow to cook for 8 minutes, to ensure that the bread is fully cooked at the center.
6. Serve alongside nice chili dip.

Leftover Turkey Muffins

Prep + Cook Time: 25 minutes | Servings: 8

Ingredients:

- Handful spinach
- 2 oz sweet potato
- ½ red onion
- 2 oz brown turkey meat
- 1 large egg
- 1 tbsp soft cheese
- 4 oz cheddar cheese grated
- 1 tsp parsley
- 1 tsp oregano
- 1 tsp garlic puree
- 1 tsp mustard
- Salt and ground black pepper to taste
- 4 oz plain flour

Directions:

1. The first step is to gather your vegetables in a bowl. Using your hands, mash up the vegetables. The result should be a few small lumps that can easily form into meatballs if there is the need to.
2. Make a mixture of all the ingredients, except the flour. The mixture should be wet, due to the presence of the egg.
3. Add the flour gradually to the mixture, so that it looks like average meatballs.
4. To ensure that the balls don't stick to your hands, flour your hands. Now, mold the mixture into eight medium-sized balls.
5. Transfer the balls onto a baking mat inside your Air Fryer, set it to 360 F and allow the balls to cook for 15 minutes. Then, turn them over and cook for an additional 5 minutes, but at 320 F.
6. Remove and serve.

Leftover Turkey and Cheese Calzone

Prep + Cook Time: 25 minutes | Servings: 4

Ingredients:

- Homemade pizza dough
- 1 tsp basil
- 1 tsp oregano
- 1 tsp thyme
- Salt and ground black pepper to taste
- 1 tbsp tomato puree
- 4 tbsp homemade tomato sauce
- Leftover turkey brown meat shredded
- 1 oz mozzarella cheese, grated
- 4 oz cheddar cheese, shredded
- 1 oz back bacon, diced
- 1 large egg, beaten

Directions:

1. Ensure that your Air Fryer is preheated to 360 F.
2. The first step is to roll out your pizza dough so that they have the size of small pizzas. Get a small mixing bowl, and in it, combine all the seasonings including the puree and the tomato sauce.
3. Add a layer of the tomato to your pizza bases with the aid of a cooking brush. Ensure that the layer doesn't touch the edge. Leave 1/2 -inch space.
4. Now layer up your pizza on one side with the turkey, cheese, and bacon.
5. With ½ - inch gap around your pizza base, use your cooking brush to brush the space with beaten egg. Then fold your pizza base over to look like an uncooked Cornish pasty and brush every area that is visible on the pizza dough with more egg.
6. Transfer to the air fryer and cook for 10 minutes at 360 F.
7. Serve.

Turkey Goujons and Sweet Chilli Dip

Prep + Cook Time: 25 minutes | Servings: 4

Ingredients:

Turkey goujons:

- 2 oz breadcrumbs
- 1 oz gluten free oats
- 1 oz cheddar cheese
- 1 tsp thyme
- 1 tsp parsley
- Salt and ground black pepper to taste
- 1 large egg beaten
- 2 oz plain flour
- 4 oz leftover turkey breast cut into strips

Sweet chilli dip:

- 4 oz white sugar
- 1 small red chilli finely chopped and seeds removed
- 2 tbsp garlic puree

Directions:

1. Ensure that your air fryer is preheated to 360 F.
2. Prepare a mixture of breadcrumbs, oats, thyme, parsley and cheese in a clean bowl and season to taste.
3. Place your egg in a different bowl, and your flour into another bowl.
4. While laying your turkey on your worktop, cover it in salt and pepper. Be generous with the salt to ensure that the turkey is adequately flavored.
5. Transfer each of the turkey strips into the flour, egg, and the breadcrumbs respectively.
6. The coated turkey strips should be transferred into your air fryer and allowed to cook for 7 minutes (7 turkey goujons). The next seven goujons should be cooked for another 7 minutes and continue like this till all the turkey strips are cooked.
7. While the turkey is in the air fryer, prepare your sweet chili dip.
8. Combine sugar and cold water into a medium pan, and allow to boil on high heat. Add the other ingredients and lower the heat to a simmer for about 10 minutes or until it has reduced. Let the mixture cool and then transfer it into the fridge for another 10 minutes.
9. Serve.

Airfryer Turkish Cheese and Leek Koftas

Prep + Cook Time: 30 minutes | Servings: 2

Ingredients:

- Leek 1-inch in length
- 1 tsp garlic puree
- 1 tbp parsley
- 1 tbsp mint
- 1 tbsp cumin
- 1 mixed spice
- Salt and ground black pepper to taste
- Feta cheese, broken up
- 11 oz minced beef

Directions:

1. After cleaning your leeks, dice them into very thin slices.
2. Get a small ceramic dish that can fit into your air fryer, and in it, add your leeks and the garlic puree. Mix thoroughly.
3. Set your Air Fryer to 360 F and allow the mixture to cook for 10 minutes.
4. Get a mixing bowl and in it, place all your seasonings alongside the cheese. Add minced beef and mix well.
5. Now add the leeks, and mix well again.
6. Make the mixture into kofta shapes and place them onto sticks.
7. Let the sticks cook in the air fryer for 15 minutes at a temperature of 360 F.
8. Serve alongside ketchup and mayonnaise.

Steak in the Air Fryer

Prep + Cook Time: 10 minutes | Servings: 2

Ingredients:

- 2 rump steaks
- Salt and ground black pepper to taste

Directions:

1. With the aid of a tenderizer, pound your steak so that it appears and feel tenderer.
2. Using salt and pepper, season the grill plan of your air fryer.
3. Transfer the steaks to the top of the seasoning before seasoning the top of the steak in salt and pepper as well.
4. Set your Air Fryer to 400 F.
5. Allow the steaks to cook for 12 minutes, but flip the steak at 6.
6. Withdraw and serve immediately.

Steak in the Airfryer

Prep + Cook Time: 10 minutes | Servings: 2

Ingredients:

- Steak with a thickness of 1-inch
- Olive oil
- Salt and ground black pepper to taste

Directions:

1. Withdraw the steak from the fridge.
2. Insert your baking tray into the air fryer, and preheat it for about 5 minutes at 390 F.
3. Use your olive oil to coat the steak at either side generously.
4. Use your salt and pepper to season the steak at either side.
5. Transfer the steak into the air fryer's baking tray.
6. Allow cooking for 3 minutes.
7. Once the timer goes off, flip the steak to the other side and cook for another 3 minutes.
8. Transfer the cooked steak to a plate.
9. Let it cool for 3 minutes more before serving.

<u>Note</u> that when the meat is cooling down, the meat fibers are in turn resting. Thus, some of the loose juices are absorbed, and subsequently, the cooled meat is more tender and juicier.

Rib Eye Steak

Prep + Cook Time: 20 minutes | Servings: 3-4

Ingredients:

- 2 lbs rib eye steak
- 1 tbsp steak rub
- 1 tbsp olive oil

Directions:

1. Ensure that your air fryer is preheated to 400 F and adjust the cooking time to 14 minutes and the mode to French Fries.
2. After seasoning the steak on either side, rub with olive oil too.
3. Transfer the steak into the basket of the air fryer.
4. Allow to cook for the first 7 minutes, then remove and flip the steak.
5. After 14 minutes, withdraw the steak and allow it to rest for 10 minutes.
6. Slice and serve.

Country Fried Steak

Prep + Cook Time: 40 minutes | Servings: 1

Ingredients:

- 1 tsp garlic powder
- 1 tsp onion powder
- 1 tsp salt
- 1 tsp ground black pepper
- 1 cup Panko bread crumbs
- 6 oz sirloin steak-pounded thin
- 1 cup flour
- 3 eggs, beaten

Sausage Gravy (optional):

- 6 oz ground sausage meat
- 2 tbsp flour
- 2 cups milk
- 1 tsp ground black pepper

Directions:

1. Using the spices as seasoning, season the panko.
2. Dip the steak in flour, egg, and seasoned panko respectively.
3. Transfer the dredged steak into the air fryer basket and close. Set the temperature to 370 F and allow to cook for 12 minutes.
4. Withdraw the steak after 12 minutes and serve alongside sausage gravy or mash potatoes.

Notes:

To prepare your sausage gravy, get a clean pan and cook your sausage in it until it is well cooked.

Then drain the fat and reserve about 2 tbsp in the pan.

Add flour to the sausage in the pan, and mix until the flour is well mixed with the sausage.

Add the milk and mix slowly.

Stir the mixture over medium heat until the milk thickens.

Finally, season with pepper and allow to cook for 3 minutes.

Air Fryer Herb and Cheese-Stuffed Burgers

Prep + Cook Time: 45 minutes | Servings: 4

Ingredients:

- 2 green onions, thinly sliced
- 2 tbsp minced fresh parsley
- ¼ cup cheddar cheese, cubed
- 3 tsp Dijon mustard, divided
- 2 tbsp ketchup
- ½ tsp salt

- ½ tsp rosemary, dried and crushed
- ¼ tsp sage leaves, dried
- 3 tbsp dry bread crumbs
- 1 lb lean ground beef (90% lean)
- 4 hamburger buns, split

Optional toppings:

- lettuce leaves and tomato slices

Directions:

1. Ensure that your air fryer is preheated to 375 F.
2. Get a small bowl, and in it, make a mixture of green onions, parsley, cheddar cheese, and one teaspoon mustard.
3. Get another clean bowl and make a mixture of ketchup, unused mustard, seasonings, and breadcrumbs, and beef. Mix thoroughly but lightly.
4. Portion the mixture into eight thin patties. Using a spoon, add a little out of the cheese mix to the center of the four patties. Top with the remaining patties, while pressing edges together firmly to seal completely.
5. Transfer the burger into the air fryer basket, arranging them in a single layer. If you have several burgers, you may work in batches.
6. Air fry each batch for 10 minutes, then flip and continue cooking for about 8-10 minutes again (until you have a reading of 160 F on your instant-read thermometer).

Bunless Burgers

Prep + Cook Time: 35 minutes | Servings: 3-4

Ingredients:

- Handful lettuce
- Handful fresh basil
- Handful fresh thyme
- 1 medium avocado
- 1 small red onion
- 3 medium tomatoes
- 1 tbsp parsley, dried

- Salt and ground black pepper to taste
- 1 lb minced beef
- 1 tbsp tomato puree
- Handful green beans
- 1 tbsp olive oil
- 4 slices back bacon

Directions:

1. Ensure that your air fryer is preheated to 360 F.
2. Dice your clean, fresh herbs. Peel and get rid of the stones in the avocado before slicing it. Also, peel and dice the red onion as well as the fresh tomato.
3. Get a clean mixing bowl and make a mixture of all the seasonings, the minced beef, 1/5 of the red onion, and the tomato puree. Then mix well and shape the mixture into four burger shapes.
4. Place the baking mat at the bottom of your air fryer.
5. Transfer the burgers onto your baking mat and cook for 10 minutes. After 10 minutes, place the green beans in the olive oil and place it inside the air fryer alongside the burgers. Cook for extra 5 minutes before adding the slices of bacon. Then cook for an additional 5 minutes.
6. Serve the burgers alongside the avocado, bacon, green beans and salad garnish.

Air Fryer Meatloaf

Prep + Cook Time: 45 minutes | Servings: 4

Ingredients:

- 1 lb lean ground beef
- 1 small onion, finely chopped
- 1 tbsp chopped fresh thyme
- 3 tbsp dry bread crumbs
- 1 egg, lightly beaten
- 1 tsp salt
- Ground black pepper to taste
- 2 mushrooms, thickly sliced
- 1 tbsp olive oil, or as needed

Directions:

1. Ensure that your air fryer is preheated to 390 F.
2. Get a clean bowl and make a mixture of ground beef, onion, thyme, bread crumbs, egg, salt, and pepper. Knead the mixture and mix thoroughly.
3. Get a clean baking pan and transfer the beef mixture in it and smooth the top, while pressing the mushrooms into the top and coating with olive oil.
4. Transfer the pan into the air fryer basket and slide into the air fryer.
5. Roast the meatloaf inside the air fryer for 25 minutes or until you have a nice brown color.
6. Allow the roasted meatloaf to cool for at least 10 minutes.
7. Slice into wedges and serve.

Meatloaf Flavoured with Black Peppercorns

Prep + Cook Time: 40 minutes | Servings: 6

Ingredients:

- 4 lbs minced beef
- 3 tbsp tomato ketchup
- 1 tbsp mixed herbs
- 1 tbsp oregano
- 1 tbsp parsley
- 1 tbsp basil
- 1 large onion peeled and diced
- 1 tsp Worcester sauce
- Breadcrumbs made from one slice of wholemeal bread
- Salt and ground black pepper to taste

Directions:

1. Get a large mixing bowl and place the mince in it alongside the tomato ketchup, herbs, onion, and Worchester sauce. Mix all the ingredients well.
2. Massage and mix the ingredients thoroughly for about five minutes to ensure that the slice is evenly distributed in the meatloaf slice.
3. Add the breadcrumbs, salt and pepper to the mixture and mix thoroughly again.
4. Get a small dish and place the mixture in it.
5. Slide the dish into your air fryer and cook for 25 minutes at 360 F.
6. Withdraw and serve.

Fried Meatballs in Tomato Sauce

Prep + Cook Time: 20 minutes | Servings: 2

Ingredients:

- 1 small onion
- 1 egg, beaten
- 11 oz minced beef
- 1 tbsp fresh thyme leaves, chopped
- 1 tbsp fresh parsley, chopped
- 3 tbsp bread crumbs
- ¾ cup of your favourite tomato sauce
- Salt and ground black pepper to taste

Directions:

1. Ensure that your air fryer is preheated to 390 F.
2. Chop your onion into fine pieces and transfer it, alongside all other ingredients, into a clean mixing bowl. Mix well and shape the mixture into 10 to 12 balls.
3. Separate the balls into two batches and transfer each batch into the air fryer basket.
4. Fry each batch for 7 minutes.
5. Transfer the meatballs into an oven dish, put the tomato sauce and place the oven dish into the air fryer basket. Then set the temperature to 320 F and allow to cook for 5 minutes.
6. This will warm everything through before you finally serve.

Roasted Stuffed Peppers

Prep + Cook Time: 40 minutes | Servings 2

Ingredients:

- 1 tsp olive oil
- ½ medium onion, chopped
- 1 clove garlic, minced
- 1 tsp Worcestershire sauce
- ½ cup tomato sauce
- 8 oz lean ground beef
- ½ tsp salt
- ½ tsp black pepper
- 2 medium green peppers, stems and seeds removed - cooked in boiling salted water for 3 minutes
- 4 oz cheddar cheese, shredded

Directions:

1. Ensure that your air fryer is preheated to 390 F or your convection toaster oven to 400 F.
2. Get a small nonstick skillet and pour some olive oil into it. Then stir-fry your onion and garlic in it until you have a golden appearance. Withdraw from the burner and allow to cool.
3. Combine your Worcestershire, ¼ cup tomato sauce, cooked garlic and onion, beef, salt, and pepper. Blend the mixture alongside half the shredded cheese and transfer the blended mixture into a medium bowl.
4. Divide the peppers into halves and top each with the remaining cheese and tomato sauce. Arrange them into the air fryer basket or in a small baking dish that has been sprayed with cooking oil.
5. Air fry or bake for about 15 to 20 minutes, or until the meat is well cooked.
6. Withdraw and serve.

Air Fryer Party Meatballs

Prep + Cook Time: 25 minutes | Servings: 24 meatballs

Ingredients:

- 2 ½ tbsp worcester sauce
- ¾ cup tomato ketchup
- 1 tbsp lemon juice
- 1 tbsp Tabasco
- ½ tsp dry mustard
- ¼ cup vinegar
- 3 gingersnaps crushed
- ½ cup brown sugar
- 1 lb mince beef

Directions:

1. Get a large mixing bowl and mix all your seasonings thoroughly to ensure even coating.
2. Toss the mince into the bowl and mix well again.
3. Create medium sized meatballs from the mixture and transfer them into the air fryer.
4. Set the timer to 15 minutes and temperature to 400 F.
5. Allow to cook, and when done, you will have a nice, crispy, and well-cooked meatballs. If not, cook for a few minutes more.
6. Place the cooked meatballs on sticks.
7. Serve.

Beef Wellington (medium rear)

Prep + Cook Time: 55 minutes | Servings: 4

Ingredients:

- 2 lb beef fillet
- Salt and ground black pepper to taste
- Homemade shortcrust pastry
- Homemade chicken liver pate
- 1 medium egg, beaten

Directions:

1. Clean out your beef fillet, remove any visible fat, and season with pepper and salt. Then seal it up using cling film and fridge it for an hour.
2. Create your homemade shortcrust pastry and your chicken liver pate.
3. With your shortcrust pastry rolled out, use your pastry brush to coat all around the edges with beaten egg. This ensures that it is sticky for sealing.
4. Right inside the outer egg line, place a thin layer of the homemade pate until the white pastry is no longer visible.
5. Withdraw the cling film from the meat and put the meat in the middle, on the top, of the pate and apply a little force to push it down a bit.
6. Seal the pastry around the pate and the meat.
7. Ensure that you score the top of the pastry to ensure that the meat is not entirely devoid of air.
8. Transfer into the grill plan of the air fryer.
9. Allow cooking for 35 minutes at 320 F.
10. Remove after 35 minutes and allow to rest for some minutes.
11. Slice and serve alongside roast potatoes.

Easy Spring Rolls

Prep + Cook Time: 55 minutes | Servings: 3-4

Ingredients:

- 2 oz rice noodles, dried
- 1 tbsp sesame oil
- 3 cloves garlic, crushed
- 1 small onion, diced
- 1 cup frozen mixed vegetables
- 7 oz ground beef
- 1 tsp soy sauce
- 1 (16 oz) package egg roll wrappers
- 1 tbsp vegetable oil, or to taste

Directions:

1. Ensure that your air fryer is preheated to 350 F.
2. Get a clean bowl and pour some hot water in it. Then soak your noodles in hot water for about 5 minutes. Cut the soaked noodles into shorter strands.
3. Heat your sesame oil in a suitable cooking pan and over medium-high heat. Add the garlic, onion, mixed vegetables, and ground beef.
4. Cook the mixture until you have a browned beef – this takes about 6 minutes. Withdraw from heat. Stir in the noodles, and allow it to cool for a while so that the juices are well absorbed. Add soy sauce to the filling.
5. Get a flat work surface and lay one egg roll wrapper. Then place a diagonal strip of filling across the wrapper. Fold the top corner over the filling, and fold in the two side corners. Then brush the center with cold water and roll over the spring rolls to seal finally.
6. Do the same for the other wrappers and filling.
7. Brush the tops of the spring rolls using vegetable oil. Arrange the rolls in batches into the air fryer basket.
8. Cook each batch until the rolls are crispy and lightly browned – this takes about 8 minutes.
9. Repeat the process until all the rolls are cooked. Serve.

Mustard Honey Beef Balls

Prep + Cook Time: 35 minutes | Servings: 4

Ingredients:

- 11 oz beef, minced
- 1 tsp garlic, minced
- 2 oz onion, peeled and diced
- 1 tbsp cheddar cheese, grated
- 1 tsp honey
- 1 tsp mustard
- Handful basil, fresh and chopped
- Salt and ground black pepper to taste

Directions:

1. Get a large, clean bowl and make a mix of all the ingredients above in it.
2. Form small balls from the mixture.
3. Transfer the balls into the air fryer and cook for 15 minutes at 390 F.
4. Serve hot alongside egg fried rice.

Pork Tenderloin with Bell Pepper

Prep + Cook Time: 30 minutes | Servings: 2

Ingredients:

- 2 tsp Provençal herbs
- 1 red or yellow bell pepper, in thin strips
- 1 red onion, in thin slices
- Salt to taste
- Freshly ground black pepper to taste
- 1 tbsp olive oil
- 1 (15 oz) pork tenderloin
- ½ tbsp mustard
- Round 6-inch oven dish

Directions:

1. Ensure that your air fryer is preheated to 390 F.
2. Get a clean dish and make a mixture of the Provencal herbs, bell pepper strips, and onion. Add salt and pepper to taste, and finally a ½ tablespoon olive oil.
3. Cut the pork tenderloin into four pieces. Rub each piece with pepper, mustard, and salt. Coat each piece thinly using olive oil, and transfer them into the dish uprightly, on top of the pepper mixture.
4. Transfer the bowl into the air fryer basket. Allow the meat to roast for 15 minutes, alongside the vegetables.
5. Halfway into roasting, turn the meat and mix the peppers.
6. Withdraw after 15 minutes.
7. Serve with mashed potatoes and a fresh salad for the best taste.

Sticky BBQ Pork Strips

Prep + Cook Time: 25 minutes | Servings: 4-6

Ingredients:

- 6 pcs pork loin chops
- Freshly ground pepper
- 2 tbsp honey
- 2 tbsp soy sauce
- 1 tsp balsamic vinegar
- ¼ tsp ground ginger (or ½ tsp freshly grated ginger)
- 1 garlic clove, chopped

Directions:

1. Ensure that your Air Fryer is preheated to 360 F for 5 minutes.
2. Tenderize your chops using a meat tenderizer before seasoning it with some ground fresh pepper.
3. Prepare your marinade by combining honey, soy sauce, and balsamic vinegar in a clean bowl.
4. Toss ground ginger and chopped garlic into the marinade mixture, and stir well and thoroughly. Set the mixture aside.
5. Add the pork chops into the marinade mixture and allow the combination to marinate overnight or for 2 hours.
6. Transfer the chops into the air fryer baking tray and air bake alongside the marinade juice for 5 to 8 minutes on either side. You will have a golden brown color when it is cooked thoroughly.
7. Withdraw the well-cooked pork chops and cut it into strips and serve.
8. You can also serve as chops.

Air-Fried Pork Dumplings with Dipping Sauce

Prep + Cook Time: 1 hour 10 minutes | Servings: 6

Ingredients:

- 1 tsp canola oil
- 4 cups bok choy (about 12 oz), chopped
- 1 tbsp garlic (3 garlic cloves), chopped
- 1 tbsp fresh ginger, chopped
- 4 oz ground pork
- ¼ tsp crushed red pepper
- 18 (3 1/2-inch-square) dumpling wrappers or wonton wrappers

- Cooking spray
- 2 tbsp rice vinegar
- ½ tsp packed light brown sugar
- 1 tbsp finely chopped scallions
- 1 tsp toasted sesame oil
- 2 tsp lower-sodium soy sauce

Directions:

1. Get a clean large nonstick skillet and heat your canola oil in it over medium-high heat.
2. Add bok choy and cook while stirring consistently until the mixture is wilted and almost dry – this takes about 6 to 8 minutes.
3. Toss in garlic and ginger, and cook again for a minute, constantly stirring this time.
4. Remove the bok choy mixture and place in a plate for 5 minutes. Using a paper towel, pat the mixture dry.
5. Get a medium bowl and in it, stir the bok choy mixture, the ground pork, and crushed red pepper together.
6. Lay a dumpling wrapper on your work surface, and using a spoon, place one tablespoon filling into the center of the wrapper. Use your fingers or your pastry brush to moisten the edges of the wrapper lightly with water. Fold the wrapper over to give a shape of a half-moon, and press the edges to seal. Do the same for the other wrappers and filling.
7. Coat the air fryer basket lightly using the cooking spray. Arrange six dumplings in the basket, such that there is a little space between each. Spray the dumplings lightly with the cooking spray.
8. Set your Air Fryer to 375 F and allow to cook for 12 minutes until the dumplings are lightly browned. Turn the dumplings over halfway through cooking (at 6 minutes). Do the same for all the dumplings while keeping the cooked dumplings warm.
9. While cooking the dumplings, create a mixture of rice vinegar, brown sugar, scallions, sesame oil, and soy sauce in a small bowl. Stir together until the sugar is dissolved.
10. Serve by placing three dumplings on each plate alongside two teaspoons sauce.

Air Fryer Bacon

Prep + Cook Time: 25 minutes | Servings: 11 slices

Ingredients:

- 11 slices bacon (I am using Trader Joe's, and it is a thick cut)

Directions:

1. Divide the bacon into two equal amounts.
2. Transfer a half into the air fryer and cook for 10 minutes at 400 F. For thinner bacon, you may reduce the cooking time.
3. After 5 minutes of cooking, check and rearrange (if there is the need to). Use tongs here.
4. After rearranging, cook for another 5 minutes.
5. Once it is done, withdraw from the air fryer and serve.

Pork Chops (ver. 1)

Prep + Cook Time: 20 minutes | Servings:4

Ingredients:

- ½ cup Dijon mustard
- 4 pork loin chops (3/4-inch thick)
- ¼ tsp cayenne pepper
- ½ tsp black pepper
- ½ tsp salt
- 1 cup Italian bread crumbs
- Cooking spray

Directions:

1. Ensure that your Air Fryer is preheated to 400 F.
2. Spread the mustard on either side of the pork chops. Ensure it is evenly spread.
3. Get a shallow dish and combine the cayenne, black pepper, salt, and the bread crumbs. Dip the pork chops in the crumbs such that the two sides are well and evenly coated.
4. Arrange the chops in a single layer in the air fryer basket, and spray lightly with the cooking spray.
5. Place the sheet in the oven, leaving a space of about 4 inches between the heating element and the sheet.
6. Cook until you have a golden brown color of the chops, for about 10 mintes. Turn the pork chops to the other side after 5 minutes.
7. Once cooked, serve immediately.

Crispy Breaded Pork Chops (ver. 2)

Prep + Cook Time: 25 minutes | Servings: 2

Ingredients:

- Olive oil spray
- Kosher salt
- 6 (3/4-inch thick) center cut boneless pork chops, fat trimmed (5 oz each)
- ½ cup panko crumbs (check labels for GF)
- 2 tbsp parmesan cheese, grated
- ½ tsp garlic powder
- 1/3 cup crushed cornflakes crumbs
- ½ tsp onion powder
- 1/8 tsp black pepper
- 1¼ tsp sweet paprika
- ¼ tsp chili powder
- 1 large egg, beaten

Directions:

1. Ensure that your Air Fryer is preheated to 400 F for about 2 minutes. Also, spritz the air fryer basket with oil.
2. Use ½ tsp kosher salt to season the pork chops on either side.
3. Place the panko, parmesan cheese, garlic powder, ¾ tsp kosher salt, cornflake crumbs, onion powder, black pepper, paprika and chili powder in a large shallow bowl.
4. Get another large shallow bowl and beat the egg in it. Then dip the pork into the beaten egg and the crumb mixture respectively.
5. Transfer about 3 of the chops into the sprayed air fryer basket and sprinkle the top with cooking oil lightly.
6. Allow cooking for 12 minutes, while turning the chops to the other side after 6 minutes. Spritz either side of the chops with oil.
7. Withdraw the cooked chops after 12 minutes and cook the remaining chops.
8. Serve while warm.

Breaded Pork Chops (ver. 3)

Prep + Cook Time: 20 minutes | Servings: 5

Ingredients:

- 4 slices homemade bread
- Salt and ground black pepper to taste
- 5 pork chops bone in
- 2 tbsp olive oil
- 4 oz plain flour
- 1 tbsp pork seasoning
- 1 large egg
- 3 oz apple juice
- 3 tbsp parsley

Directions:

1. Ensure that your Air Fryer is preheated to 350 F for about 2 minutes.
2. Prepare your breadcrumbs by blending the bread.
3. Using salt and pepper, season your pork chops, and rub little olive oil into the meat.
4. Get a clean mixing bowl and place the plain flour, salt, pork seasoning, and pepper.
5. Get another clean bowl and beat an egg and add the apple juice.
6. Get a third bowl and mix the breadcrumbs with pepper, parsley, and salt.
7. Dredge the pork chops into the flour mixture and egg mixture respectively before coating it generously with the breadcrumbs.
8. Allow the coated pork chops to cook for 10 minutes at 350 F. Serve.

Garlic Butter Pork Chops

Prep + Cook Time: 1 hour 25 minutes | Servings: 2

Ingredients:

- 2 tsp parsley, dried
- Salt and ground black pepper to taste
- 2 tsp garlic cloves grated
- 1 tbsp coconut butter
- 1 tbsp coconut oil
- 4 pork chops

Directions:

1. Ensure that your air fryer is preheated to 350 F.
2. Combine all the seasonings in a clean mixing bowl, alongside the garlic, butter, and the coconut oil.
3. Apply the mixture to either side of the pork chops before sealing them in silver foil. Fridge the sealed pork chops for an hour.
4. After an hour, withdraw from the fridge and separate the silver foil from the chops. Rub the remaining marinade in the silver foil over the chops.
5. Transfer them into the grill pan of the air fryer.
6. Allow to cook for 7 minutes, then turn to the other side and allow to cook for another 8 minutes.
7. Serve cooked chops alongside the garden salad. You may drizzle with a bit of olive oil.

Balsamic Smoked Pork Chops

Prep + Cook Time: 35 minutes | Servings: 4

Ingredients:

- Cooking spray
- 2 large Nellie's Free Range Eggs, beaten
- ¼ cup 2% milk
- 1 cup finely chopped pecans
- 1 cup panko (Japanese) bread crumbs
- 4 smoked bone-in pork chops
- ¼ cup all-purpose flour

For sauce:

- 2 tbsp seedless raspberry jam
- 2 tbsp brown sugar
- 1/3 cup balsamic vinegar
- 1 tbsp thawed frozen orange juice concentrate

Directions:

1. Ensure that your Air Fryer is preheated to 400 F.
2. Spray the air fryer basket with the cooking spray.
3. Get a shallow bowl and whisk the eggs and milk together in it.
4. Get another shallow bowl and place the pecans alongside the breadcrumbs.
5. Coat the pork chops with flour, and shake to remove the excess flour.
6. Dip the coated pork chops into the egg mixture and the crumb mixture respectively. Pat occasionally to ensure that the mixtures do not fall off. You may work in batches if you have many pork chops.
7. Arrange the chops in a single layer in the air fryer basket, and spray lightly with the cooking spray.
8. Allow the pork chops to cook inside the air fryer for 12 to 15 minutes or until they appear golden brown. After 6-7 minutes, turn the chops and spray lightly again.
9. After cooking, withdraw and keep warm. Then cook the other chops.
10. While cooking, place the unused ingredients in a small saucepan and boil while stirring until the mixture is slightly thickened. This should take about 6 to 8 minutes.
11. Serve the chops alongside the sauce.

Tender Juicy Smoked BBQ Ribs

Prep + Cook Time: 1 hour 5 minutes | Servings: 1-2

Ingredients:

- 1 rack ribs (baby back or spare ribs)
- 1 tbsp liquid smoke
- 2-3 tbsp pork rub
- Salt and ground black pepper to taste
- ½ cup BBQ sauce

Directions:

1. There is always a thin layer, usually tough to remove, at the back of the ribs. Remove the membrane by cutting it and pulling it off. Then cut the ribs in half or almost half, such that each half fits conveniently in the air fryer.
2. Drizzle both sides of the ribs with the liquid smoke.
3. Combine the pork rub, pepper, and salt and season both sides of the ribs with the mixture.
4. Cover the ribs and leave it for 30 minutes at room temperature.
5. Transfer the ribs into the air fryer. You may stack the ribs if you want.
6. Allow cooking for 15 minutes at 360 F.
7. Flip the ribs to the other side after 15 minutes and allow to cook for an extra 15 minutes.
8. Withdraw the cooked ribs from the air fryer and drizzle with BBQ sauce.
9. Serve.

Chinese Take Out Sweet 'N Sour Pork

Prep + Cook Time: 30 minutes | Servings: 4

Ingredients:

- 1/8 tsp Chinese Five Spice
- ½ tsp sea salt
- ¼ tsp freshly ground black pepper
- 1 cup potato starch (or cornstarch)
- 2 large eggs
- 1 tsp pure sesame oil, optional
- 2 lbs pork cut into chunks
- 3 tbsp canola oil
- Cooking oil spray
- 1 prepared Simple sweet 'n sour sauce, optional

Directions:

1. Get a clean mixing bowl and mix the Chinese Five Spice, pepper, salt, and potato starch in it.
2. Get another clean mixing bowl and beat the eggs in it; add the sesame oil.
3. Dip the pork pieces into the potato starch mixture; shake to remove any excess starch. Then dip into the egg mixture, and shake again to get rid of excess. Finally, dip it into the potato starch mixture again.
4. Place the coated pork pieces into an already-coated air fryer basket (coated with oil).
5. Spray with oil and allow to cook at 340 F for about 8-12 minutes, or until you see that the pork is well cooked. Shake the basket a few times while cooking.
6. Combine the cooked pork with Simple Sweet 'N' Sour Sauce and serve.

Bourbon Bacon Cinnamon Rolls

Prep + Cook Time: 40 minutes | Servings: 8

Ingredients:

- 8 bacon strips
- 3/4 cup bourbon
- 1 tube (12.4 oz) refrigerated cinnamon rolls with icing
- 2 tbsp maple syrup
- ½ cup chopped pecans
- 1 tsp minced fresh gingerroot

Directions:

1. Get a clean shallow dish. In the dish, place the bacon and add bourbon. Seal the dish containing the mixture and refrigerate.
2. The next day, remove the bacon and pat dry, throw the bourbon away.
3. Get a large skillet and cook the bacon in it over medium heat. Stop cooking when you have nearly crisp but pliable bacon. You can cook in batches. Remove the cooked bacon and drain using paper towels. Discard all but one teaspoon drippings.
4. Preheat your Air Fryer to 350 F.
5. Create eight rolls out of the dough, while keeping the icing packet.
6. Unroll each spiral roll into a long strip, and pat the dough to form 6x1-inches strips. Put one bacon strip on each dough strip, while trimming the bacon as required. Reroll the strip to form a spiral and seal by pinching the ends. Do the same for the remaining dough.
7. Place four rolls into the basket of the air fryer and allow to cook for 5 minutes. After 5 minutes, turn over the rolls and cook the other side until you have a golden brown color (for about 4 minutes).
8. While cooking the rolls, make a mixture of maple syrup and pecans in a bowl. Stir the contents of the icing packet and ginger together in another bowl. Pour the remaining bacon drippings into the same skillet and heat over medium heat. Then add the pecan mixture and allow to cook until lightly toasted while frequently stirring (for about 2-3 minutes).
9. Drizzle half of the icing over warm cinnamon rolls and top them with half of the pecans. Do the same for the second batch. Serve.

Rosemary Sausage Meatballs

Prep + Cook Time: 30 minutes | Servings: 2

Ingredients:

- 2 tbsp olive oil
- 1 tsp curry powder
- 4 garlic cloves, minced
- ¼ cup fresh parsley, minced
- 1 tbsp fresh rosemary, minced
- ¼ cup dry bread crumbs
- 1 jar (4 oz) diced pimientos, drained
- 1 large egg, lightly beaten
- 2 lbs bulk pork sausage
- Pretzel sticks or toothpicks, optional

Directions:

1. Ensure that your air fryer is preheated to 400 F.
2. Grab a small skillet and place over medium heat. Heat the oil in the skillet, alongside curry powder and sauté garlic, until the mixture is tender. It takes about 1-2 minutes. Allow the mixture to cool slightly.
3. Get a clean bowl and make a mixture of parsley, rosemary, bread crumbs, pimientos, egg, and the garlic mixture. Add the sausage and mix thoroughly but lightly.
4. Make 1 to ¼ inches balls from the sausage mix. Transfer the balls into the air fryer basket, arranging them in a single layer. Cook for about 7-10 minutes until the balls are lightly browned and cooked through.
5. Withdraw the cooked balls and keep warm.
6. Do the same for the other meatballs.
7. Serve alone or alongside pretzels.

Sexy Air-Fried Meatloaf

Prep + Cook Time: 1 day 55 minutes | Servings: 4

Ingredients:

- ½ lb ground veal
- ½ lb ground pork
- ½ tsp Sriracha salt
- ½ tsp ground black pepper
- 2 medium spring onions, diced
- 1 large egg, beaten
- ¼ cup chopped fresh cilantro
- ¼ cup gluten-free bread crumbs
- 1 tsp blackstrap molasses
- 1 tsp olive oil
- 2 tsp gluten-free chipotle chili sauce
- ½ cup ketchup

Directions:

1. Ensure that your air fryer is preheated to 400 F.
2. Get a nonstick baking dish that can fit into the air fryer basket, then combine veal and pork in the dish. Mix well and add ½ teaspoon of Sriracha salt, black pepper, spring onions, egg, cilantro, and breadcrumbs. Now mix with your hands, and form a loaf inside the sizable baking dish.
3. Make a mixture of molasses, olive oil, chipotle chili sauce, and ketchup in a small bowl. Whisk the mixture well and set aside without refrigerating.
4. Allow the meatloaf to cook for 25 minutes in the air fryer without opening the basket. After 25 minutes, top the meatloaf with the ketchup mixture, ensuring that the top is entirely covered. Now transfer the covered meatloaf into the air fryer and bake until the internal temperature is 160 F – this takes about 7 minutes or more.
5. Turn off the air fryer with the meatloaf still inside. Allow to rest for 5 minutes and withdraw the meatloaf.
6. Let the baked meatloaf rest 5 minutes outside the air fryer.
7. Slice and serve.

Chinese Pineapple Pork

Prep + Cook Time: 45 minutes | Servings: 4

Ingredients:

- 1 lb pork loin, cut into cubes
- ½ tsp pepper
- ½ tsp salt
- 1 tsp fresh ginger, minced
- 1 clove garlic, minced
- 1 green pepper, cut into cubes
- ½ pineapple, cut into cubes
- 1 tbsp brown sugar
- 2 tbsp soy sauce
- 1 tbsp vegetable oil
- Toasted sesame seeds
- 1 small bunch fresh coriander leaves, chopped

Directions:

1. Season your pork with pepper and salt.
2. Combine the seasoned pork alongside ginger, garlic, green pepper and pineapple in the air fryer pan.
3. Get a clean bowl and in it, make a mixture of brown sugar and soy sauce as well as the ingredients. Drizzle the vegetable oil over the ingredients.
4. Ensure that your air fryer is preheated to 360 F.
5. Set the cooking time to 17 minutes. After 17 minutes, check and ensure all ingredients are well cooked.
6. Combine the sesame seeds and chopped coriander as a garnish for the pork.
7. Serve alongside white rice.

Chinese Kebabs and Rice

Prep + Cook Time: 15 minutes | Servings: 20 slices

Ingredients:
- 4 oz egg fried rice
- 1 tbsp Chinese five spice
- ½ small onion peeled and diced
- 6 oz minced pork
- 1 tsp garlic puree
- 1 tsp tomato puree
- 1 tbsp soy sauce
- Salt and ground black pepper to taste
- 1 slice wholemeal bread made into breadcrumbs

Directions:
1. Start by making your egged fried rice: boil the Chinese rice in a pan, add half the Chinese seasoning once it is cooked, then add a hard-boiled egg and mix thoroughly.
2. To make your kebabs, combine the remaining half of the Chinese seasoning, onion, minced pork, garlic and tomato puree, and soy sauce in a mixing bowl. Mix thoroughly and season with salt and pepper.
3. Toss in the breadcrumbs and shape into sausage shapes.
4. Allow the mixture to cook for 20 minutes at 360 F in the air fryer. Serve.

Drunken Ham with Mustard

Prep + Cook Time: 45 minutes | Servings: 4

Ingredients:
- 1 joint of ham (1½ lbs)
- 8 oz whiskey
- 2 tbsp French mustard
- 2 tbsp honey

Directions:
1. Withdraw the ham from the fridge 30 minutes before cooking – this ensures that the ham is at room temperature before cooking.
2. Make your marinade into a casserole dish that fits into your air fryer – mix the whiskey, mustard, and honey to get your marinade mixture.
3. Transfer the ham into the oven dish and turn it in the marinade.
4. Set your air fryer to 320 F and allow the ham cook for 15 minutes.
5. Withdraw the ham, add another shot of whiskey and turn in the marinade again. Allow the ham to cook for 25 minutes at 320 F (or until it is done).
6. Withdraw from the air fryer and serve immediately.
7. You can serve with potatoes and fresh vegetables.

Roasted Rack of Lamb with a Macadamia Crust

Prep + Cook Time: 45 minutes | Servings: 4

Ingredients:
- 1 garlic clove
- 1 tbsp olive oil
- 2 lbs rack of lamb
- Salt and ground black pepper to taste
- 3 oz macadamia nuts, unsalted
- 1 tbsp chopped fresh rosemary
- 1 tbsp breadcrumbs (preferably homemade)
- 1 egg, beaten

Directions:
1. Ensure that your air fryer is preheated to 210 F.
2. Chop your garlic into fine pieces, and mix them with oil to make the garlic oil. Season the rack of the lamb with salt and pepper alongside the garlic oil.
3. Chop your nuts finely and transfer the pieces into a bowl, add rosemary and breadcrumbs.
4. Get a clean bowl and whisk the egg in it.
5. Dredge the meat in the egg mixture and drain off any excess. Dip it in the macadamia crust again.
6. Transfer the coated lamb rack in the air fryer basket and allow to cook for 25 minutes.
7. Increase the temperature to 390 F after 25 minutes. Cook for 5 minutes at 390 F.
8. Withdraw from the air fryer and allow to rest for another 10 minutes while covering with aluminum foil.
9. Serve.

Note:
You can use hazelnuts, cashews, pistachios, or almonds instead of the macadamia nuts.

Meatballs with Feta

Prep + Cook Time: 20 minutes | Servings: 10

Ingredients:

- 6 oz lamb mince or lean minced beef
- 1 slice of stale white bread, turned into fine crumbs
- ½ tbsp lemon peel, grated
- 1 tbsp fresh oregano, finely chopped
- 2 oz Greek feta, crumbled
- Freshly ground black pepper
- Round, shallow oven dish, 6 - inch
- Tapas forks

Directions:

1. Ensure that your Air Fryer is preheated to 390 F.
2. Get a bowl and make a mixture of the mince, breadcrumbs, lemon peel, oregano, feta, and black pepper and knead everything together.
3. Create ten equal portions out of the mixture. With your damp hands, create ten smooth balls from the ten portions.
4. Transfer the balls into the oven dish and then into the basket.
5. Place the basket into the air fryer and allow to bake for 8 minutes. The balls are done when they are nicely brown.
6. Serve while hot in a platter alongside tapas forks.

The Ultimate Air Fryer Lamb Burgers

Prep + Cook Time: 25 minutes | Servings: 4

Ingredients:

Lamb burgers:
- 1 tsp harissa paste
- 2 tsp garlic puree
- 1 tbsp moroccan spice
- Salt and ground black pepper to taste
- 1¼ lamb, minced

Greek Dip:
- 3 tbsp greek yoghurt
- 1 small lemon juice only
- ½ tsp oregano
- 1 tsp moroccan spice

Directions:

1. Get a clean mixing bowl and combine your lamb burger ingredients alongside the lamb mince. Mix thoroughly until you are sure the lamb mince is evenly seasoned.
2. Make the mince into lamb burger shapes with the aid of your burger press.
3. Transfer the lamb burgers into your air fryer and set the temperature to 360 F.
4. Allow cooking for 18 minutes.
5. Meanwhile, prepare your Greek Dip by using your fork to mix the Greek dip ingredients.
6. Serve the cooked lamb burgers alongside the Greek dip.

Fish and Fries

Prep + Cook Time: 40 minutes | Servings: 4

Ingredients:

- 1 lb potatoes (about 2 medium)
- 2 tbsp olive oil
- ¼ tsp pepper
- ¼ tsp salt

Fish:

- ¼ tsp pepper
- 1/3 cup all-purpose flour
- 1 large egg
- 2 tbsp water
- 1/8 tsp cayenne pepper
- 1 tbsp Parmesan cheese, grated
- 1 lb haddock or cod fillets
- ¼ tsp salt
- 2/3 cup crushed cornflakes
- Tartar sauce, optional

Directions:

1. Ensure that your air fryer is preheated to 400 F.
2. Cut the peeled potatoes lengthwise into thick slices (of 0.5-inch thickness), and then cut the slices into thick sticks (of 0.5-inch thickness).
3. Get a large bowl, and combine the potatoes, oil, pepper, and salt in it. You may work in batches if required. Arrange the potatoes in the air fryer basket to form a single layer. Allow cooking until just tender (for about 5-10 minutes). Transfer the cooked potatoes into the basket to redistribute and continue cooking until they are crisp and lightly browned (for about 5-10 minutes longer).
4. While cooking the potatoes, get a shallow bowl and mix the pepper and flour in it.
5. Mix the whisked egg and water in a separate shallow bowl.
6. Combine the cayenne and cheese in a third bowl.
7. Sprinkle your fish with salt, and dip it into the flour mixture ensuring that the two sides are well coated while shaking off the excess.
8. Dredge in the egg mixture too, and finally in the cornflake mixture.
9. Withdraw the fries from the basket, and allow it to cool.
10. Transfer the fish into the air fryer basket, forming a single layer. Allow the fish to cook until it is lightly browned and flakes easily with a fork. Turn halfway through cooking (say after 8-10 minutes).
11. Endeavor not to overcook the fish. Replace the cooked fish with the fries and heat through.
12. Serve immediately alone, or alongside tartar sauce.

Fish and Chips (ver. 1)

Prep + Cook Time: 45 minutes | Servings: 4

Ingredients:

- 2 (10 oz) russet potatoes, scrubbed
- Cooking spray
- 1¼ tsp kosher salt, divided
- 1 cup (about 4¼ oz) all-purpose flour
- 2 large eggs
- 2 tbsp water
- 1 cup whole-wheat panko (Japanese-style breadcrumbs)
- 4 (6 oz) skinless tilapia fillets
- ½ cup malt vinegar

Directions:

1. By following the instructions of the manufacturer, use your spiralizer to cut the potatoes into spirals. Place each batch of the spiral potatoes into the air fryer basket. Spray with cooking spray generously such that every piece is well coated.
2. Set your air fryer to 375 F and cook for 10 minutes (or until they are crispy and golden brown). Turn the potatoes halfway through cooking. Once cooked, transfer them into a separate bowl and cover to keep warm. Do the same for the other batches. Sprinkle all the cooked potatoes with ¼ teaspoon salt.
3. While you cook the potatoes, get a shallow dish and place your flour and add ½ teaspoon of the salt. Whisk the eggs and water together lightly in another shallow dish. Get a third shallow dish and stir the panko and the unused ½ teaspoon salt together.
4. Cut each fish fillet lengthwise into two long strips, and dip each strip into the flour mixture, the egg mixture, and the panko mixture respectively. Use the cooking spray to coat the fish pieces on both sides.
5. Transfer the fish into the air fryer basket (in a single layer). Allow each batch to cook for 10 minutes at 375 F (or until golden brown). Remember to turn fish over halfway through cooking.
6. Serve by placing two pieces of fish alongside equal portions of potato spirals on each plate. Include two tablespoons of malt vinegar for dipping.

Fish and Chips (ver. 2)

Prep + Cook Time: 30 minutes | Servings: 2

Ingredients:

- 8 oz white fish filet (tilapia, cod, pollack)
- Salt and ground black pepper to taste
- ½ tbsp lemon juice
- 1 oz tortilla chips
- 1 egg
- 10 oz (red) potatoes
- 1 tbsp vegetable oil

Directions:

1. Ensure that your air fryer is preheated to 360 F.
2. Cut the fish into four equal pieces. Rub each piece with pepper, salt, and the lemon juice and allow to rest for 5 minutes.
3. While the fish is resting, grind the tortilla chips in your food processor. Place the ground tortilla chips in a plate. Get a clean deep dish and beat the egg in it.
4. Dredge each fish piece into the egg and roll it through the ground tortilla chips until it is entirely covered. Do the same for the other pieces of fish.
5. Cut the cleaned potatoes lengthwise into thin strips and soak them in water for not less than 30 minutes. After draining the water, pat them dry using your kitchen paper. Finally, coat them with oil in a boil.
6. Fix your separator in the air fryer basket. Arrange the potato strips and fish pieces on either side.
7. Place the basket into the air fryer and allow the potatoes and fish to try for 12 minutes (or until they have a crispy brown appearance).

Fish Fingers

Prep + Cook Time: 25 minutes | Servings: 2

Ingredients:

- 2 slices wholemeal bread made into breadcrumbs
- Salt and ground black pepper to taste
- 1 tsp parsley
- 2 oz plain flour
- 1 medium egg, beaten
- 2 white fish fillets skinned and boned
- 1 tsp mixed herbs
- 1 small lemon juice only
- 1 tsp thyme

Directions:

1. Ensure that your air fryer is preheated to 360 F.
2. To prepare your breadcrumbs, place it in a clean dish and mix it thoroughly with pepper, parsley, and salt. Transfer your beaten egg in a separate dish and the plain flour in another.
3. Place the fish in a food processor alongside mixed herbs, salt and pepper, lemon juice, and thyme. When the mixture is all mashed up like uncooked fishcakes, start making your fish fingers.
4. Bread your fish – roll it in the flour, the egg, and then in the breadcrumbs.
5. Transfer the rolled fish into the air fryer and allow to cook at 360 F for 8 minutes.
6. Serve the cooked rolled fish alongside potatoes and mayonnaise. You may also serve in a sandwich.

Slimming World Beer Battered Fish and Chips Recipe

Prep + Cook Time: 25 minutes | Servings: 4

Ingredients:

- 5 oz beer
- 1 tsp turmeric
- 1 tsp paprika
- 1 tsp cayenne pepper
- 1 tsp lemon juice
- 1 tsp garlic puree
- 4 oz plain flour
- 2 large potatoes, peeled
- 1 lb cod fillet
- Salt and ground black pepper to taste
- 1 tbsp olive oil

Directions:

1. The first step is to make the batter: combine the beer, seasoning and the plain flour. Mix thoroughly until you have a smooth mixture without any flour lumps. Fridge the batter for about an hour.
2. Slice the peeled potatoes into chip shapes.
3. Remove any excess moisture from the fish by squeezing, then season with pepper and salt.
4. Chop the fish into pieces and immerse in the batter until each piece is well coated.
5. Transfer the chips into the air fryer and drizzle olive oil over them.
6. Allow cooking for 6 minutes at 360 F.
7. Place the potatoes in the baking pan and cook alongside the fish for 7 minutes at the same temperature.
8. Serve alongside the dipping sauce.

Chili Lime Tilapia: Easy and Healthy

Prep + Cook Time: 30 minutes | Servings: 3-4

Ingredients:

- 1 lb tilapia
- Ground black pepper and salt to taste
- 1 cup panko crumbs
- 1 tbs chili powder (less if you're not into spice)
- ½ cup flour (i used trader joe's gluten free flour)
- 1 -2 eggs, beaten
- Juice of 1 lime

Directions:

1. Grab a plate wide enough to lay tilapia flat. In the plate, mix the pepper, panko, chili powder, and salt.
2. Place the flour in a bowl and the scrambled egg in another.
3. Spray the bottom of the air fryer using a little cooking spray.
4. Dredge both sides of the tilapia in the flour, then the egg, and finally press well into the panko mixture until the tilapia is evenly coated.
5. Transfer the coated tilapia into the air fryer and spray the top with a little cooking spray. You may work in batches if necessary.
6. Fry the fish for 7-8 minutes at 375 F, then flip to the other side and cook for an extra 7-8 minutes or until the fish has cooked through.
7. Withdraw the tilapia and squeeze lime juice over the top.
8. Serve alongside some pico de gallo, avocado, and lime wedges. Otherwise, you can serve with your favorite veggie.

---

3 Ingredient Fried Catfish

Prep + Cook Time: 1 hour 5 minutes | Servings: 4

Ingredients:

- 4 catfish fillets
- ¼ cup seasoned fish fry I used Louisiana
- 1 tbsp olive oil
- 1 tbsp chopped parsley optional

Directions:

1. Ensure that your air fryer is preheated to 400 F.
2. Pat the catfish dry after rinsing well.
3. In a large Ziploc bag, pour the fish fry seasoning, and add the catfish to the bag one after the other.
4. Seal the bag and shake well to ensure that all parts of the fillet are well coated with the seasoning.
5. Spray olive oil on the top of each fillet and transfer them into the air fryer basket.
6. Cook for about 10 minutes before flipping the fish. After flipping, cook for an extra 10 minutes.
7. Flip the fish again, and cook for about 2-3 minutes more (or until as crisp as desired).
8. Top with parsley and serve.

Air-Fried Crumbed Fish

Prep + Cook Time: 25 minutes | Servings: 4

Ingredients:

- 1 cup dry bread crumbs
- 4 flounder fillets
- 1 egg, beaten
- ¼ cup vegetable oil
- 1 lemon, sliced

Directions:

1. Ensure that your air fryer is preheated to 355 F.
2. Grab a clean bowl and mix the breadcrumbs and the oil in it. Stir until you have a crumbly and loose mixture.
3. Dip the fish fillets into the egg, and then into the bread crumb mixture. In either case, coat thoroughly and evenly.
4. Place the coated fillets gently in the preheated air fryer. Allow cooking until the fish flakes easily with a fork (it takes about 12 minutes).
5. Garnish with lemon slices and serve.

Five Ingredient Super Simple Fisherman's Fishcakes

Prep + Cook Time: 60 minutes | Servings: 4

Ingredients:

- 3 cups white fish boned and cooked
- 1 cup mashed potatoes
- 1 tsp parsley
- 1 tsp sage
- Salt and ground black pepper
- 3 tbsp butter
- 3 tbsp milk
- 3 tsp flour

Directions:

1. Grab a large mixing bowl, and in it, combine fish, potatoes, and the seasoning. Mix very well and add the butter and milk.
2. Mix again until you have a uniform mixture. You may need to add more milk to ensure a nice consistency.
3. Add a little flour to the mixture and make patty cakes from it.
4. Transfer the cakes into the fridge and leave for three hours. This solidifies the cakes.
5. Cook the cakes in the air fryer for 15 minutes at 390 F.
6. Serve.

Thai Fish Cakes with Mango Salsa

Prep + Cook Time: 35 minutes | Servings: 4

Ingredients:

- 1 ripe mango, peeled
- 3 tbsp fresh coriander or flat leaf parsley
- 1½ tsp red chili paste
- Juice and zest of 1 lime

- 1 lb white fish fillet (pollack, cod, pangasius, tilapia)
- 1 egg, beaten
- 1 green onion, finely chopped
- 2 oz ground coconut

Directions:

1. Ensure that your Air Fryer is preheated to 375 F.
2. Cut the peeled mangoes into small cubes, and mix them in a bowl alongside one tablespoon coriander, ½ teaspoon red chili paste, the juice, and zest of half a lime.
3. In the food processor, puree the fish and add one egg, one teaspoon salt, and the remaining lime zest, red chili paste, and the lime juice. Mix these with the remaining coriander, the green onion, and two tablespoons coconut.
4. Get a clean soup plate and transfer the remainder of the coconut in it. Make 12 portions out of the fish mixture, with each portion shaped into round cakes. Finally, coat each cake with the coconut,
5. Arrange six fish cakes into your air fryer basket and air fry the fish cakes for about 7 minutes, or until the golden brown color is visible. Do the same for the other fish cakes.
6. Withdraw the cooked fish cakes and serve alongside mango salsa. You may also combine with pandan rice and stir-fried pak choi.

Grilled Fish Fillet with Pesto Sauce

Prep + Cook Time: 20 minutes | Servings: 2

Ingredients:

- 2 white fish fillets (8 oz each)
- 1 tbsp olive oil
- Ground black pepper and salt to taste

Pesto sauce:

- 1 bunch fresh basil
- 1 tbsp pine nuts
- 2 garlic cloves

- 1 cup extra-virgin olive oil
- 1 tbsp grated Parmesan cheese

Directions:

1. Ensure that your air fryer is preheated to 360 F.
2. Grab each fish fillet and brush with the oil and season with salt and pepper. Transfer the coated fillet into the air fryer cooking basket and allow to cook for 8 minutes.
3. While cooking the fish fillet, pick the basil leaves and combine them with pine nuts, garlic, olive oil, and the Parmesan cheese. Transfer the mixture into a food processor or mortar and pestle. Pulse or grind the mixture until you have a sauce. Salt to taste.
4. Serve the cooked fish fillets drizzled with pesto sauce on a serving plate.

Sesame Seeds Fish Fillet

Prep + Cook Time: 40 minutes | Servings: 3-5

Ingredients:

- 5 frozen fish fillets (if it's not frozen, just cut the cooking time by roughly 3 minutes)
- 3 tbsp plain flour
- 1 egg, beaten

Coating:

- Handful of sesame seeds
- 3 tbsp oil
- Pinch of ground black pepper
- Pinch of sea salt
- 5-6 soda biscuit crumbs (or any plain biscuits you have or breadcrumbs)
- Pinch of rosemary herbs, optional

Directions:

Coating

Without adding oil to the pan, fry the sesame seed in it for 2 minutes while stirring consistently. Once they become brown, remove them from pan.

Get a large plate and make a mixture of all the coating ingredients.

Fish Fillet

1. Ensure that your Air Fryer is preheated to 360 F and lined with aluminum foil.
2. Proceed to arrange your ingredients to ensure efficiency following the order below.
3. Dip the fish in the flour, then the egg, and finally in the coating mixture.
4. Place the coated fish inside the air fryer.
5. Cook for 10 minutes if it's frozen fillet, flip the fish and cook for extra 4 minutes.
6. If the fillet is not frozen, cook the first side for 8 minutes and the second for 2 minutes
7. Serve!

Perfect Air Fryer Salmon

Prep + Cook Time: 30 minutes | Servings: 4

Ingredients:

- 2 wild caught salmon fillets with comparable thickness (1-1/12-inches thick)
- 2 tsp avocado oil or olive oil
- Salt and ground black pepper to taste
- 2 tsp paprika
- Lemon wedges, to serve

Directions:

1. Ensure that your salmon has no bone, and set it aside for about an hour.
2. Grab each fillet and rub with olive oil, and seasoning with pepper, paprika, and salt.
3. Transfer the rubbed fillets into the air fryer basket.
4. Set the temperature to 390 F and allow the fillet to cook for 7 minutes (for 1 – 1½ inch fillets).
5. After 7 minutes, check the fillets with a fork to ensure they are well cooked according to your taste.

Notes:

You can also check if the fillets are done while cooking without necessarily withdrawing the basket from the air fryer. This helps you monitor the fillets better to ensure they are not overdone.

Another helpful tip is to set your timer for a little less to enable you regularly check to avoid overcooking any item.

Salmon with Fennel Salad

Prep + Cook Time: 30 minutes | Servings: 4

Ingredients:

- 2 tsp fresh flat-leaf parsley, finely chopped
- 1 tsp fresh thyme, finely chopped
- 1 tsp kosher salt, divided
- 4 (6 oz) skinless center-cut salmon fillets
- 2 tbsp olive oil
- 1 garlic clove, grated
- 4 cups thinly sliced fennel (from 2 [15 oz] heads fennel)
- 2 tbsp fresh orange juice (from 1 orange)
- 2/3 cup 2% reduced-fat Greek yogurt
- 2 tbsp chopped fresh dill
- 1 tsp fresh lemon juice (from 1 lemon)

Directions:

1. Ensure that your air fryer is preheated to 350 F.
2. Get a small bowl and mix the parsley, thyme, and a ½ teaspoon of the salt in it.
3. Grab the salmon and brush with oil, while sprinkling the herb mixture evenly all over the fish.
4. Transfer two salmon fillets into the air fryer basket and allow them to cook at 350 F.
5. Withdraw the fillets when you are satisfied that they are well cooked (it takes about 10 minutes).
6. Transfer the cooked fillets to the preheated oven to keep them warm. Do the same for other fillets.
7. While you are cooking the salmon, prepare your fennel salad. Get a medium bowl and in it, mix the garlic, fennel, orange juice, yougurt, dill, lemon juice, and the other ½ teaspoon salt.
8. Serve the salmon fillets over the fennel salad.

Tandoori Salmon with Refreshing Raita

Prep + Cook Time: 30 minutes | Servings: 4

Ingredients:

- 11 oz grams salmon
- ½ tbsp tandoori spice powder
- 3 cups plain yoghurt, divided, or to taste
- Salt and ground black pepper to taste
- ½ tsp ground cumin
- 1 tbsp minced green chilli, or to taste
- 30 leaves fresh mint, chopped
- 1 small tomato
- ½ red onion
- ½ cucumber

Directions:

1. Shape the salmon into 12 cubes. Coat each cube with tandoori spice powder. Place in the fridge and allow to marinate.
2. Separate ¼ of the yogurt, and blend it with the pepper, cumin, chili, mint, and salt. Place in the fridge and allow to steep.
3. After peeling and removing the seeds, dice the tomato into small pieces. Chop the peeled onion into fine pieces. Peel the cucumber also, and cut lengthwise and use a small spoon to get rid of the seeds. Finally, dice the seedless cucumber.
4. Before you serve, cook the salmon in your air fryer at 350 F for about 6 minutes, alongside seasoning. Avoid fat.
5. While cooking the salmon, combine the remaining yogurt and the flavored yogurt, diced onion, cucumber, and tomato.
6. Transfer the sauce into small soup plates or glasses and add the salmon on top. If you want your salmon to be more cooked, you may have to cook for another 4-5 minutes. But you may serve like that if you prefer it half-cooked.

Air-Grilled Honey-Glazed Salmon

Prep + Cook Time: 25 minutes | Servings: 2

Ingredients:

- 1 tsp water
- 6 tsp soy sauce
- 6 tbsp honey
- 3 tsp hon mirin (alternatively you can use rice wine vinegar)
- 2 pcs salmon fillets (about 4 oz each)

Directions:

1. Combine water, soy sauce, honey and Hon-Mirin (sweet rice wine) in a mixing bowl.
2. Divide the mixture into two.
3. Transfer half or some of the mixture into another bowl and set aside (to be served alongside the salmon).
4. Combine the marinade mixture and the salmon. Allow the mixture to marinate for at least 2 hours.
5. Ensure that your air fryer is preheated to 360 F.
6. Air-grill the salmon for about 8 minutes. Turn the other side up after four minutes, and cook for an extra 5 minutes. Drizzle the salmon with the marinade mixture at intervals of 3 minutes.
7. Prepare the sauce by transferring the remaining sauce into a pan and allow it to boil for a minute.
8. Serve the sauce alongside the salmon.

Salmon Patties

Prep + Cook Time: 40 minutes | Servings: 8

Ingredients:

- 3 large russet potatoes (15 oz)
- Breadcrumbs to coat
- Fresh parsley, chopped
- 1 salmon (8 oz) portion
- A handful of frozen vegetables (parboiled and drained)
- Salt and ground black pepper to taste
- 2 sprinkles of dill
- 1 egg, beaten
- Olive oil spray

Directions:

1. Chop the peeled potatoes into small pieces. Boil enough water in a pot, transfer the chopped potatoes and allow to cook for 10 minutes (or till the potatoes are tender). Drain the water and let the potatoes continue cooking on low flame.
2. Once the water in the potatoes has evaporated (it takes about 2-3 minutes), mash the cooked potatoes with a whisk. Transfer the mashed potatoes into a large mixing bowl. Place in the fridge and withdraw only when it is no longer hot.
3. While cooling your potatoes, prepare your breadcrumbs (not necessary if you are using packaged panko). Blend 4 pieces of breadcrumbs till you have a fine blend and set aside.
4. Withdraw the mashed potatoes from the fridge, and combine them with chopped parsley, flaked salmon, parboiled vegetables, salt, and dill. You may taste and if the seasonings are not enough, add more. Add the egg to the mixture and stir together.
5. Using your dry hands, make 6-8 patties or smaller balls from the mixture and coat them with breadcrumbs. Spray some oil to ensure the color of the balls come out nice. Air fry the coated balls for about 10-12 minutes (or until golden) at 360 F. You may not line with an aluminum foil if you are working with the grill pan. If you are lining with foil, ensure that you flip halfway once the top of the balls are golden.
6. Serve alongside lemon, mayo, and salad on the side.

Grilled Cajun Salmon

Prep + Cook Time: 25 minutes | Servings: 2

Ingredients:

- 2 salmon steak
- 2 tbsp cajun seasoning

Directions:

1. Start by cleaning and patting the salmon steak dry. Then rub every part of the salmon with Cajun seasoning. Allow it to marinate for about 10 minutes.
2. Ensure that your air fryer is preheated to 390 F.
3. Transfer the salmon steaks to the grill pan and allow it to grill for 8 minutes.
4. After 4 minutes, flip the steaks over.
5. Grill for another four minutes.
6. Serve the grilled salmon.

Chili Tuna Puff

Prep + Cook Time: 25 minutes | Servings: 2

Ingredients:

- ½ cup chili tuna
- 1 sheet puff pastry (thawed)

Directions:

1. Ensure that your Air Fryer is preheated to 375 F.
2. Make four equal squares out of the pastry.
3. Spread the Chili Tuna on each square pastry, right at the center.
4. Fold the square pastry into a triangle or a rectangle, and press the edges with a fork to seal them off.
5. Transfer the pastry in the baking tray and allow to air bake for 10-12 minutes, or until you have the golden brown color.

Tuna Patties

Prep + Cook Time: 20 minutes | Servings: 2

Ingredients:

- 2 cans tuna packed in water
- 1½ tbsp almond flour
- 1 tsp garlic powder
- ½ tsp onion powder
- 1 tsp dried dill
- 1½ tbsp mayo
- Juice of ½ lemon
- Pinch of salt and ground black pepper

Directions:

1. Mix all the ingredients thoroughly in a bowl.
2. The tuna should be wet such that it can form into patties. If the dryness is not enough to form patties, add an extra tablespoon of almond flour.
3. Make four patties out of the tuna.
4. Ensure that your air fryer is preheated to 400 F.
5. Transfer the patties into the basket, in a single layer, and allow to cook for 10 minutes.
6. If your preference is the crispier patties, then cook for an extra 3 minutes.

Shrimp Spring Rolls with Sweet Chili Sauce
Prep + Cook Time: 40 minutes | Servings: 4

Ingredients:

- 2 ½ tbsp sesame oil, divided
- 1 cup julienne-cut red bell pepper
- 1 cup matchstick carrots
- 2 cups pre-shredded cabbage
- ¼ cup chopped fresh cilantro
- 2 tsp fish sauce
- ¼ tsp crushed red pepper
- 1 tbsp fresh lime juice
- ¾ cup julienne-cut snow peas
- 4 oz peeled, deveined raw shrimp, chopped
- 8 (8-inch-square) spring roll wrappers
- ½ cup sweet chili sauce

Directions:

1. Get a large skillet, pour in 1.5 teaspoons of the oil and let it heat over high heat until it smokes slightly. Now toss in the bell pepper, carrots, and cabbage. Allow it to cook while continually stirring until the mixture is lightly wilted (this takes 1 or 1.5 minutes). Spread on a rimmed baking sheet and allow to cool for 5 minutes.
2. Get a large bowl and combine cilantro, fish sauce, crushed red pepper, lime juice, snow peas, shrimps, and the cabbage mixture. Stir slightly.
3. Place the spring roll wrappers on the work surface such that one corner is facing you. Using your spoon, transfer ¼ cup filling into the center of each spring roll wrapper, while spreading it from left to right and into a 3-inch long strip.
4. Fold the bottom corner of each wrapper over the filling, while tucking the tip of the corner under the filling. Fold right and left corners over filling. Brush the remaining corner lightly using water, and roll the filled end of the wrapper towards the remaining corner. Finally, press gently to seal. Brush the spring rolls with the unused two teaspoons oil.
5. Transfer the first four spring rolls in the air fryer basket and allow them to cook for about 7 minutes at 390 F. After the first five minutes, turn the spring rolls. Do the same for the other spring rolls.
6. Serve the cooked spring rolls alongside sweet chili sauce.

Lemon Pepper Shrimp
Prep + Cook Time: 20 minutes | Servings: 2

Ingredients:

- 1 lemon, juiced
- ¼ tsp paprika
- ¼ tsp garlic powder
- 1 tsp lemon pepper
- 1 tbsp olive oil
- 12 oz uncooked medium shrimp, peeled and deveined
- 1 lemon, sliced

Directions:

1. Ensure that your air fryer is preheated to 400 F.
2. Make a mixture of lemon juice, paprika, garlic powder, lemon pepper, and olive oil in a bowl.
3. Toss in the shrimp and coat it with the mixture.
4. Transfer the shrimp into the air fryer and cook for about 8 minutes (until the shrimp is firm and pink).
5. Serve alongside lemon slices.

Coconut Shrimp and Apricot

Prep + Cook Time: 40 minutes | Servings: 6

Ingredients:

- 1-1/2 lb large shrimp, uncooked
- 1-1/2 cup sweetened shredded coconut
- ½ cup panko bread crumbs
- 4 large egg whites
- ¼ tsp salt

Sauce:
- 1 cup apricot preserves
- ¼ tsp crushed red pepper flakes
- 1 tsp cider vinegar

- ¼ tsp ground black pepper
- 3 dashes Louisiana-style hot sauce
- ½ cup all-purpose flour
- Cooking spray

Directions:

1. Ensure that your air fryer is preheated to 375 F.
2. Peel the shrimp, get rid of the veins, but retain the tails.
3. Get a shallow bowl, and combine coconut and breadcrumbs in it.
4. Get another shallow bowl and whisk your egg whites, salt, pepper, and hot sauce.
5. Get a third shallow bowl and place your flour in it.
6. Dip the shrimp into the flour to coat lightly. Remove any excess flour by shaking.
7. Dip the flour-coated shrimp into the egg white mixture and finally in the coconut mixture. Pat to ensure the coating adheres.
8. Spray the basket in your air fryer with cooking spray. You may work in batches if required.
9. Arrange the shrimps in the air fryer basket such that they form a single layer.
10. Allow cooking for 4 minutes.
11. Turn the shrimps to the other side and cook until the coconut is lightly browned and the shrimp turned pink (this takes about 4 minutes).
12. While cooking the shrimps, get a small saucepan and mix the sauce ingredients in it. Then cook and stir the mixture over medium-low heat until the preserves are melted.
13. Serve the sauce alongside the freshly cooked shrimps.

Air Fryer Shrimp a la Bang Bang

Prep + Cook Time: 40 minutes | Servings: 4

Ingredients:

- ¼ cup sweet chili sauce
- 1 tbsp sriracha sauce
- ½ cup mayonnaise
- ¼ cup all-purpose flour
- 1 cup panko bread crumbs

- 1 lb raw shrimp, peeled and deveined
- 1 head loose leaf lettuce
- 2 green onions, chopped, or to taste (optional)

Directions:

1. Ensure your Air Fryer is set to 400 F.
2. Make a mixture of chili sauce, sriracha sauce, and mayonnaise in a bowl. Mix until smooth. Keep some bang source aside in a separate bowl for dipping, if you want.
3. Place the flour on a plate, and the panko on another plate.
4. Dip the shrimp into the flour first, and then the mayonnaise mixture. Finally, dip it into the panko.
5. Transfer the coated shrimp on a baking sheet, then into the air fryer basket without overcrowding the basket.
6. Allow cooking for 12 minutes.
7. Do the same for the remaining shrimp.
8. Serve the cooked shrimp in lettuce wraps with green onions as garnish.

Coconut Shrimp and Lime Juice

Prep + Cook Time: 35 minutes | Servings: 4

Ingredients:

- 1½ tsp black pepper
- ½ cup all-purpose flour
- 2 large eggs
- 2/3 cup unsweetened flaked coconut
- 1/3 cup panko (Japanese-style breadcrumbs)

- 12 oz medium peeled, deveined raw shrimp, tail-on (about 24 shrimp)
- Cooking spray
- ½ tsp kosher salt

Sauce:

- ¼ cup lime juice
- 1 serrano chile, thinly sliced
- ¼ cup honey
- 2 tsp chopped fresh cilantro, optional

Directions:

1. Get a shallow dish – and make a mixture of the pepper and the flour.
2. In a second shallow dish, beat the eggs.
3. Get a third shallow dish and mix the coconut and panko in it.
4. Hold each shrimp by the tail and dip into the flour mixture without coating the tail. Shake to get rid of the excess flour.
5. Dip in the egg mixture and allow any excess to drip off.
6. Finally, dip in the coconut mixture and press to ensure adherence.
7. Coat the shrimp generously with the cooking spray.
8. Transfer half of the shrimp in the air fryer basket and allow to cook for 6 to 8 minutes at 400 F.
9. Halfway into cooking, turn the shrimp to the other side and season with ¼ teaspoon of the salt.
10. Do the same for the other shrimps and salt also.
11. In the meantime, get a small bowl and whisk the lime juice, Serrano chile, and the honey together.
12. Sprinkle the cooked shrimp with cilantro, and serve alongside the sauce (if desired).

Crispy Nachos Prawns

Prep + Cook Time: 25 minutes | Servings: 6

Ingredients:

- 18 large prawns, peeled and deveined, tails left on
- 1 egg, beaten
- 1 (10 oz) bag nacho-cheese flavored corn chips, finely crushed

Directions:

1. Rinse the prawns and dry by patting them.
2. Get a small bowl and whisk the egg in it. Transfer the crushed chips in a separate bowl.
3. Dip a prawn in the whisked egg and the crushed chips respectively.
4. Transfer the coated prawn into a plate and do the same for the remaining prawns.
5. Ensure that your Air Fryer is preheated to 350 F.
6. Transfer the coated prawns into the air fryer and allow to cook for 8 minutes.
7. Opaque prawns mean they are well cooked.
8. Withdraw from the air fryer and serve.

Scampi Shrimp and Chips

Prep + Cook Time: 25 minutes | Servings: 4

Ingredients:

- 2 medium potatoes
- Salt and ground black pepper to taste
- 1 tbsp olive oil
- 1 lb King prawns
- 1 small egg
- 5 oz gluten free oats
- 1 large lemon
- 1 tsp thyme
- 1 tbsp parsley

Directions:

1. After peeling the potatoes, cut them into chunky chips and season with pepper and salt. Drizzle little olive oil on the chips. Finally, cook for 5 minutes in the air fryer at 360 F.
2. Rinse the prawns and dry by patting them with a kitchen towel. Transfer them to the chopping board and season with pepper and salt.
3. Transfer the egg into a small bowl and mix using a fork until you have a beaten egg.
4. Place 80% of the gluten-free oats into the blender alongside the thyme and parsley. Blend until you have a mixture that appears like coarse breadcrumbs. Transfer the blend into a medium sized mixing bowl.
5. Add the unused 20% gluten-free oats into another separate bowl.
6. Place the prawns into the blended oats, the egg, and the blended oats respectively.
7. Finally, place the prawns in the non-blended oats.
8. Withdraw the chips from the air fryer and place them on the grill pan.
9. Place the prawns rest in the grill pan of the air fryer and allow them to cook at 360 F.
10. Season the cooked prawns and chips with fresh lemon juice. Serve.

Gambas 'Pil Pil' with Sweet Potato

Prep + Cook Time: 35 minutes | Servings: 3-4

Ingredients:

- 12 King prawns
- 4 garlic cloves
- 1 red chili pepper, de-seeded
- 1 shallot
- 4 tbsp olive oil
- Smoked paprika powder
- 5 large sweet potatoes
- 2 tbsp olive oil
- 1 tbsp honey
- 2 tbsp fresh rosemary, finely chopped
- 4 stalks lemongrass
- 2 limes

Directions:

1. Clean and gut the prawns.
2. Gut the garlic and red chili pepper finely, and chop the shallots.
3. Combine the red chili pepper, garlic, and olive oil alongside the paprika to form a marinade. Let the prawns marinate for about 2 hours in the marinade.
4. Make fine slices by cutting the sweet potato. Mix the potato slices with 2 tablespoons of olive oil, honey, and the chopped rosemary. Bake the potatoes in the air fryer at 360 F for 15 minutes.
5. While baking the potatoes, thread the prawns on the lemongrass stalks. Increase the temperature to 390 F and include the prawn skewers.
6. Allow the combination to cook for 5 minutes.
7. Serve alongside lime wedges.

Fried Hot Prawns with Cocktail Sauce

Prep + Cook Time: 20 minutes | Servings: 4

Ingredients:

- 1 tsp chilli powder
- 1 tsp chilli flakes
- ½ tsp freshly ground black pepper

For sause:

- 1 tbsp cider or wine vinegar
- 1 tbsp ketchup
- 3 tbsp mayonnaise

- ½ tsp sea salt
- 8-12 fresh king prawns

Directions:

1. Ensure that your Air Fryer is set to 360 F.
2. Get a clean bowl and combine the spices in it.
3. Coat the prawns by tossing them in the spices mixture.
4. Transfer the spicy prawns into the air fryer basket and place the basket in the air fryer.
5. Allow the prawns to cook for 6 to 8 minutes (how long depends on the size of the prawns).
6. Get another clean bowl and make a mixture of the sauce ingredients.
7. Serve the prawns while hot alongside the cocktail sauce.

Crispy Airfryer Coconut Prawns

Prep + Cook Time: 25 minutes | Servings: 2

Ingredients:

- 1 lb fresh prawns
- 3 oz granola
- 1 tbsp chinese five spice
- 1 tbsp mixed spice
- 1 tbsp coriander

- Salt and ground black pepper to taste
- 1 lime rind and juice
- 2 tbsp light coconut milk
- 3 tbsp desiccated coconut
- 1 small egg

Directions:

1. After cleaning your prawns, lay them out on a chopping board.
2. Blend the granola in a blender until it appears like fine breadcrumbs.
3. Before removing the granola blend from the blender, add all the seasonings, lime, and the coconut mix.
4. Whizz the blender around again.
5. Get a clean bowl and beat your egg in it, using a fork.
6. While holding each prawn by the tail, dip it into the egg and the batter one after another.
7. After dipping all the prawns, line the baking sheet at the bottom of the air fryer with your prawns.
8. Allow cooking at 360 F for 18 minutes.
9. Serve the cooked prawns.

King Prawns in Ham with Red Pepper Dip

Prep + Cook Time: 30 minutes | Servings: 10

Ingredients:

- 1 large red bell pepper, halved
- 10 (frozen) king prawns, defrosted
- 5 slices of raw ham
- 1 tbsp olive oil
- ½ tbsp paprika
- 1 large clove garlic, crushed
- Salt to taste
- Freshly ground black pepper to taste
- Tapas forks

Directions:

1. Ensure that the air fryer is preheated to 390 F.
2. Place the bell pepper in the air fryer basket and allow to roast for 10 minutes; withdraw when the skin is slightly charred.
3. Transfer the roasted bell pepper in a bowl, while covering it with a cling film or lid. Allow it to rest for about 15 minutes.
4. Peel your prawns and make a deep incision in the back to allow you to take out the black vein. Cut the ham into slices lengthwise, and wrap each prawn in each ham slice.
5. Coat each parcel using a thin film of olive oil and transfer into the basket. Return the basket into the air fryer and allow to fry for 3 minutes. Withdraw once the prawns appear crispy and just right.
6. While frying the prawns, peel off the skin of the bell pepper halves, and get rid of the seeds too. Then cut the pepper into pieces and puree the pieces in the blender alongside olive oil, paprika, and garlic. Transfer the sauce into a dish and add pepper and salt to taste.
7. Serve the prawns in harm in a platter alongside tapas forks. Include a small dish of red pepper dip.

Crispy Crabstick Crackers

Prep + Cook Time: 25 minutes | Servings: 2-3

Ingredients:

- 1 packet Crabstick Filament, thawed
- Cooking Spray

Directions:

1. Ensure that your Air Fryer is set at 360 F.
2. After detaching the plastic wrapper on each crabstick filament, peel and unroll them. Finally, separate them into little pieces, ½ - inch wide is good for thicker crackers.
3. Before transferring them into the frying basket, spray them with some cooking spray.
4. Transfer the crab sticks in batches into the air fryer.
5. Air fry each batch for 8-10 minutes.
6. In the 4th minute, remove the tray and stir the crabstick crackers with your kitchen tongs – this ensures that they do not stick together.
7. When air frying is completed, withdraw and allow to cool before storing them in an airtight container.

Wasabi Crab Cakes

Prep + Cook Time: 35 minutes | Servings: 2

Ingredients:

- 2 large egg whites
- 1 celery rib, finely chopped
- 1 medium sweet red pepper, finely chopped
- 3 green onions, finely chopped
- ¼ tsp prepared wasabi
- 3 tbsp reduced-fat mayonnaise
- ¼ tsp salt
- 1/3 cup plus ½ cup dry bread crumbs, divided
- 1-1/2 cups lump crabmeat, drained
- Cooking spray

Sauce:

- ½ tsp prepared wasabi
- 1 green onion, chopped
- 1 celery rib, chopped
- 1 tbsp sweet pickle relish
- ¼ tsp celery salt
- 1/3 cup reduced-fat mayonnaise

Directions:

1. Ensure that your Air Fryer is preheated to 375 F, and the air fryer basket spritzed with cooking spray.
2. Get a mixing bowl and make a mixture of the first seven ingredients, alongside 1/3 cup breadcrumbs. Fold gently in crab.
3. Get a shallow bowl and transfer the remaining bread crumbs in it. Then add heaping tablespoonfuls of crab mixture into the bowl. Coat and shape the crumbs into patties of ¾-inches thick.
4. You may work in batches if required – each batch of crab cakes should be arranged in the air fryer basket to form a single layer.
5. Only cook after spritzing the crab cakes with cooking spray.
6. The cooking should last for 8 to 12 minutes, or until the cakes turn golden brown. Halfway through cooking, turn the cakes, and spritz again with extra cooking spray.
7. Once cooked, withdraw and keep warm.
8. Do the same for the other batches.
9. While cooking the cakes, place the sauce ingredients in your food processor and blend to the preferred consistency.
10. Serve cooked crabs while hot, alongside the dipping sauce.

Flourless Truly Crispy Calamari Rings

Prep + Cook Time: 15 minutes | Servings: 2

Ingredients:

- 1 oz calamari
- 1 cup gluten free oats
- 1 large egg, beaten
- 1 tbsp paprika
- 1 tsp parsley
- 1 small lemon juice and rind
- Salt and ground black pepper to taste

Directions:

1. Ensure that your Air Fryer is preheated to 360 F.
2. Slice your calamari thinly to produce small rings of calamari.
3. Using a food processor or a blender, blend your oats until you have a consistency that looks like that of fine breadcrumbs.
4. Transfer the beaten egg in a separate bowl and the oats in another bowl.
5. Mix the oats with the paprika and parsley.
6. Get a chopping board, and coat your calamari rings on it using salt, lemon, and pepper.
7. Your hands may be sticky, thus, ensure you rub them in the oats.
8. Transfer the calamari rings into the oats first, then into the egg, then the oats, why ensuring that they are thoroughly coated at each stage.
9. Get rid of any excess oats and transfer the rings into the baking mat of your air fryer.
10. Allow cooking for 8 minutes at 360 F.
11. Serve!

Scallops Wrapped In Bacon

Prep + Cook Time: 25 minutes | Servings: 4

Ingredients:

- 8 scallops
- 8 bacon slices
- Toothpicks

Directions:

1. Wrap the bacon over the scallop.
2. Hold it in place with a toothpick.
3. Set your air fryer to 360 F and air fry the bacon.
4. Withdraw after 18 minutes or when a beautiful golden brown color is observed.

Hard Boiled Eggs

Prep + Cook Time: 22 minutes | Servings: 6

Ingredients:

- 6 eggs (right out of the fridge)

Directions:

1. Fix the wire rack of your air fryer inside the basket.
2. Arrange the eggs on top of the wire rack.
3. Allow the eggs to cook in the air fryer for 16 minutes and temperature to 250 F.
4. Withdraw the cooked eggs and place them into an ice water bath to stop the cooking.
5. Peel the cooked eggs and serve.

Breakfast Egg Rolls (ver. 1)

Prep + Cook Time: 40 minutes | Servings: 12

Ingredients:

- 12 egg roll wrappers

Filling ungredients:

- 6 eggs, scrambled
- 3 cups frozen hash browns
- 8 strips bacon
- 1 cup shredded cheese

For the sauce:

- ½ cup ketchup
- 1 tbsp hot sauce (Sriracha)
- ½ cup maple syrup

Directions:

1. Get a skillet and cook the eggs in it. Set aside the cooked eggs and allow to cool.
2. Get a skillet and brown the hash browns in it. Set aside and allow to cool too.
3. Crisp the bacon in another skillet or the oven and cut into small pieces.
4. Make your egg rolls by filling each wrapper with some of the filling ingredients (at the center). Brush the edges of the wrapper using a small amount of water to help it stick.
5. Set the heat to medium-high and heat a skillet containing about 3 inches of vegetable oil. Divide the egg rolls into batches, fry each batch while turning halfway through. Remove when they are crispy and golden brown on both sides. Line a plate with paper towels and place the fried egg rolls into it to catch the excess warm.
6. To prepare the dipping sauce, make a mixture of the ketchup and the hot sauce.
7. Serve warm alongside the dipping sauce or maple syrup.

Breakfast Egg Rolls (ver. 2)

Prep + Cook Time: 50 minutes | Servings: 16

Ingredients:

- 1 (4 oz) can diced green chiles, drained
- 4 green onions, sliced
- 1 cup sharp Cheddar cheese, shredded
- 1½ cups shredded jalapeno Jack cheese
- 1 (13.5 oz) can spinach, drained
- 2 cups frozen corn, thawed
- 1 (15 oz) can black beans, drained and rinsed
- 1 tsp salt
- 1 tsp ground cumin
- 1 tsp chili powder
- 1 (16 oz) package egg roll wrappers
- Cooking spray

Directions:

1. Combine the green chiles, green onions, cheddar cheese, jalapeno jack cheese, spinach, corn, beans, salt, cumin, and chili powder in a large mixing bowl, to be used as the filling.
2. Lay an egg roll wrapper at an angle, and use the finger to moisten the four edges with water, lightly.
3. Divide the filling into four, and add each half to the center of the wrapper. Fold one corner over the filling and tuck in the sides, thus creating a roll. Do the same for the other wrappers, while adding some cooking spray to mist the roll.
4. Ensure that your air fryer is preheated to 390 F.
5. Transfer the egg rolls in the basket, while leaving some space, and cooking in batches when necessary.
6. Allow the egg rolls to fry for 8 minutes, flip and cook for about 4 minutes extra or until you have crispy skins.

Breakfast Soufflé

Prep + Cook Time: 25 minutes | Servings: 2

Ingredients:

- Red chili pepper
- Parsley
- 2 eggs, beaten
- 2 tbsp cream (light)

Directions:

1. Chop your chili and parsley into fine pieces.
2. Get a bowl and place the eggs, alongside the cream, parsley, and pepper. Stir.
3. Pour the egg mixture into the dishes until half-filled. Allow baking for 8 minutes at 390 F.
4. If you prefer the Souffles Baveux soft, cook for only 5 minutes.

Scrambled Eggs

Prep + Cook Time: 12 minutes | Servings: 2

Ingredients:

4 large eggs

Salt and ground black pepper

2 slices wholemeal bread

Directions:

1. Ensure that your bread is harder like toast by warming it up for 3 minutes at 390 F.
2. Crack your eggs into a bowl, and stir before adding the seasoning. Transfer the mixture into the baking pan inside the air fryer.
3. Allow to cook at 360 F for 2 minutes, and then an additional 4 minutes at 360 F.
4. Pour the scrambled eggs over the wholemeal toast.
5. Serve.

Omelette with Onion and Cheese

Prep + Cook Time: 25 minutes | Servings: 1

Ingredients:

- 2 eggs
- Ground black pepper to taste
- Soy sauce to taste
- Cooking spray
- 1 medium onion, sliced
- Cheddar cheese, grated

Directions:

1. Get a clean bowl and crack open the eggs in it. Add the pepper and soy sauce (as seasoning).
2. Spritz some cooking spray lightly into the pan.
3. Transfer the sliced onions in the oiled pan at air fry for 8-10 minutes at 360 F. Withdraw when the onion is softened.
4. Transfer the egg mixture into the pan, and add bits of Cheddar Cheese. Air fry until the eggs are fully cooked – about 3 to 5 minutes.
5. Serve.

Air Fryer Egg in a Hole

Prep + Cook Time: 10 minutes | Servings: 1

Ingredients:

- 1 slice whole wheat bread
- 1 large egg
- Salt and ground black pepper to taste
- 2 oz avocado, optional

Directions:

1. With the aid of a cookie cutter, make a hole at the center of your slice of bread.
2. Transfer the slice of bread into the baking pan of the air fryer, and crack the egg into the hole.
3. Allow cooking for 7 minutes at 320 F.
4. Season the top of the cooked egg with pepper and salt.
5. Get a small bowl and make a mixture of avocado. Use a fork to mix well to get rid of lumps.
6. Spread the avocado around the bread edges.
7. Serve.

Bacon and Eggs

Prep + Cook Time: 15 minutes | Servings: 4

Ingredients:

- 8 back bacon
- 4 large eggs
- Salt and ground black pepper to taste
- Fresh chives optional
- 4 ramekins

Directions:

1. Eject the ramekins and add the bacon around the sides and the bottom, such that the overlapping is same as when making a pastry over an apple pie.
2. Crack an egg into the center of each of the ramekin.
3. Allow the ramekin to cook the air fryer for 360 F for 13 minutes.
4. Add pepper and salt as seasonings, alongside fresh chives.
5. Serve.

Super Crispy Bacon

Prep + Cook Time: 8 minutes | Servings: 4

Ingredients:

- 4 slices back bacon

Directions:

1. Ensure that your air fryer is preheated to 360 F.
2. Carefully put four slices of back bacon into the air fryer's basket.
3. Allow each side to cook for 2-3 minutes.
4. Serve.

French Toast

Prep + Cook Time: 10 minutes | Servings: 2

Ingredients:

- Butter
- 4 slices bread
- 2 eggs
- ½ tsp cinnamon

Directions:

1. After adding butter to both sides of the bread, cut it into sticks or strips.
2. Combine the cinnamon with whisked eggs.
3. Spritz some cooking oil into the basket of air fryer.
4. Dip the bread sticks into the egg mixture and transfer it into the basket of the air fryer.
5. Set the air fryer to 360 F and allow to cook for 3 minutes.
6. Change to the other side and cook for an extra 2 minutes.
7. Serve.

French Toast Sticks (ver. 1)

Prep + Cook Time: 25 minutes | Servings: 12

Ingredients:

- 1 tsp ground cinnamon
- 1 tsp vanilla extract
- 1 tbsp butter, melted
- 2 large eggs, beaten
- 1/3 cup milk
- 4 slices day-old bread, cut into thirds
- 1 tsp confectioners' sugar, or to taste

Directions:

1. Combine the cinnamon, vanilla extract, butter, eggs, and milk in a mixing bowl.
2. After lining the air fryer basket with parchment paper, dip each bread piece into the milk mixture and place in the basket.
3. Ensure that there are spaces between them, and divide into batches if there is the need to.
4. Ensure that your Air Fryer is preheated to 360 F, then place in the basket containing the bread.
5. Allow to cook for 6 minutes, and change to the other side, and cook for an extra 3 minutes.
6. Sprinkle each stick with confectioner's sugar.
7. Serve.

Easy French Toast Sticks (ver. 2)

Prep + Cook Time: 25 minutes | Servings: 2

Ingredients:

- 4 slices slightly stale thick bread, such as Texas toast
- 2 eggs, lightly beaten
- 1 tsp cinnamon
- 1 tsp vanilla extract
- 1 pinch ground nutmeg, optional
- ¼ cup milk

Directions:

1. Make sticks out of the slice of bread by cutting each slice into three. Trim a piece of parchment paper into a size that fits the base of the air fryer basket.
2. Ensure that your Air Fryer is preheated to 360 F.
3. In a mixing bowl, combine eggs, cinnamon, vanilla extract, nutmeg, and milk and mix thoroughly.
4. Dip each piece of bread into the mixture. Remove when the piece is well submerged and shake to get rid of the excess egg mixture.
5. Transfer the coated piece into the air fryer basket. Maintain a single layer in the basket, and divide into batches if necessary.
6. Allow each batch to cook for 5 minutes each per side.
7. Serve.

French Toast Soldiers

Prep + Cook Time: 20 minutes | Servings: 2

Ingredients:

- 4 slices wholemeal bread
- 2 large eggs, beaten
- 1 tsp cinnamon
- ¼ cup brown sugar
- ¼ cup whole milk
- 1 tbsp honey
- Pinch of nutmeg
- Pinch of icing sugar

Directions:

1. Make soldiers out of your slices of bread by chopping them – 4 soldiers from a slice.
2. Get a clean mixing bowl and combine all ingredients, except the icing sugar. Mix thoroughly.
3. Dip each soldier into the mixture, ensuring that it is well coated.
4. Transfer the coated soldiers into the air fryer while wet and allow the 16 soldiers to cook at 320 F for 10 minutes. Withdraw when they are crispy, nice, and dry like toast. Turn the soldiers over halfway during cooking to ensure that either side is well cooked.
5. Serve alongside a sprinkle of icing sugar and some fresh berries.

Cheese Toastie

Prep + Cook Time: 10 minutes | Servings: 4

Ingredients:

- 8 slices wholemeal bread
- 6 oz cheddar cheese

Directions:

1. Fill up the sandwiches with your bread and cheese.
2. Cook each batch of two sandwiches in the air fryer at 360 F, allowing each side to cook for 4 minutes.
3. Serve while warm.

Flax Seed French Toast Sticks With Berries

Prep + Cook Time: 1 hour | Servings: 4

Ingredients:

- 4 (1½ -oz) whole-grain bread slices
- 2 large eggs, beaten and wisked
- 1 tsp vanilla extract
- ¼ cup packed light brown sugar, divided
- ¼ cup 2% reduced-fat milk
- ½ tsp ground cinnamon
- 2/3 cup flax seed meal
- Cooking spray
- 2 cups sliced fresh strawberries
- 8 tsp pure maple syrup, divided
- 1 tsp powdered sugar

Directions:

1. Make four long sticks out of each bread slice.
2. Combine whisked eggs, vanilla, one tablespoon brown sugar, milk, and cinnamon into a shallow dish.
3. Get another shallow dish and combine flax seed meal alongside three tablespoons of brown sugar.
4. Dip the pieces of bread in the egg mixture until they are slightly soaked while allowing the excess to drip off.
5. Dredge the soaked piece in the flaxseed mixture, ensuring that the coating is uniform.
6. Apply some cooking spray to coat the bread pieces also.
7. Transfer the coated bread pieces into the air fryer basket, arranging them in a single layer and leaving space between each.
8. Allow to cook for 10 minutes at 375 F or until they are crunchy and golden brown. Turn them over halfway through cooking.
9. Place four sticks on each plate, topped with ½ cup strawberries, two teaspoons maple syrup, as well as a sprinkle of powdered sugar.
10. Serve immediately.

Traditional Welsh Rarebit

Prep + Cook Time: 30 minutes | Servings: 2

Ingredients:

- 3 slices bread
- 2 large eggs separated
- 1 tsp paprika
- 4 oz cheddar cheese
- 1 tsp mustard

Directions:

1. Heat the bread in the air fryer at a very light heat so that it is almost like toast – leave for about 5 minutes at 360 F.
2. Get a clean bowl, and in it, whisk the egg whites until you have soft peaks.
3. Combine the egg yolks, paprika, cheddsr cheese and mustard in a separate bowl.
4. Fold in the egg whites, and spoon it onto the partly toasted bread.
5. Return the bread into the air fryer and allow to cook for 10 minutes at 360 F.
6. Serve.

Breakfast Potatoes

Prep + Cook Time: 25 minutes | Servings: 4

Ingredients:

- 3 large white potatoes
- 1 medium white onion
- Salt and ground black pepper
- 2 tsp parsley, dried
- 6 slices back bacon
- ½ tsp olive oil

Instructions:

1. Shape the peeled potatoes into cubes and transfer the cubes into a large mixing bowl.
2. Dice the peeled onions, alongside the bacon.
3. Get a mixing bowl and in it, combine onion, seasoning and the bacon. Mix well.
4. Add the olive oil and mix thoroughly.
5. Transfer the mixture into the air fryer basket and allow to cook at 360 F for 15 minutes.
6. Shake halfway through cooking so that the potatoes will not stick.
7. Serve warm.

Breakfast Toad-in-the-Hole Tarts

Prep + Cook Time: 35 minutes | Servings: 4

Ingredients:

- 1 sheet frozen puff pastry, thawed
- 4 tbsp shredded Cheddar cheese
- 4 tbsp diced cooked ham
- 4 eggs, beaten
- Chopped fresh chives, optional

Directions:

1. Ensure that your Air Fryer is preheated to 390 F.
2. Having unfolded the pastry sheet on a flat surface, make four squared pieces out of the sheet.
3. Cook 2 pastry squares for 6-8 minutes in the air fryer.
4. Withdraw, and with the aid of a metal tablespoon, press the cooked square gently to form an indentation.
5. Fill the hole made with one tablespoon Cheddar cheese and one tablespoon ham. Finally, pour one egg on the top of each square.
6. Allow the filled square to cook again in the air fryer for about 6 minutes or more.
7. Remove from the basket once it is done and allow to cool for about 5 minutes.
8. Do the same for the other pastry squares, cheese, ham, and eggs.
9. Garnish the tarts with chives and serve.

Breakfast Bombs Are a Portable Healthy Meal

Prep + Cook Time: 30 minutes | Servings: 2

Ingredients:

- 3 center-cut bacon slices
- 3 large eggs, lightly beaten
- 1 tbsp chopped fresh chives
- 1 oz 1/3-less-fat cream cheese, softened
- 4 oz fresh prepared whole-wheat pizza dough
- Cooking spray

Directions:

1. Set the heat to medium and cook the bacon for about 10 minutes, or until very crisp. Withdraw from the pan and crumble.
2. Add eggs to the bacon drippings, and cook while stirring consistently in a pan. Stop cooking when the bacon is almost set but still lose, after about a minute. Get a bowl and pour the eggs in it, and stir in chives, cream cheese, and crumbled bacon.
3. Make four equal pieces out of the dough and roll each piece on a lightly floured surface to form a 5-inch circle.
4. Put about ¼ of the egg mixture in the center of each dough circle. Brush the outside edge of the dough with water. Form a purse by wrapping the dough around the egg mixture. While wrapping, pinch together the dough at the seams.
5. Arrange the dough purses to form a single layer in the air fryer basket, while coating generously with cooking spray.
6. Allow to cook for 5 to 6 minutes at 350 F; the golden brown color should start forming after 4 minutes.
7. Withdraw and serve.

Cheesy Garlic Bread

Prep + Cook Time: 20 minutes | Servings: 2

Ingredients:

- 2 dinner rolls
- ½ cup grated Parmesan cheese
- 2 tbsp butter, melted
- 2 tbsp garlic and herb seasoning, or more to taste

Directions:

1. Into each roll, cut a crisscross that almost reaches the base, while leaving the bottom crusts untouched. Fill all the holes with Parmesan cheese.
2. Use melted butter to paint the tops of the rolls, and sprinkle garlic seasoning also.
3. Ensure that your air fryer is preheated to 350 F.
4. Transfer the rolls in the air fryer basket, and allow to cook for 5 minutes, or until you have the cheese melted.

Green Tomato BLT

Prep + Cook Time: 35 minutes | Servings: 4

Ingredients:

- 2 medium green tomatoes (about 10 oz)
- ¼ tsp pepper
- ½ tsp salt
- 1 cup panko (Japanese) bread crumbs
- ¼ cup all-purpose flour
- 1 large egg, beaten
- 2 green onions, finely chopped
- 1 tsp snipped fresh dill or ¼ tsp dill weed
- ½ cup reduced-fat mayonnaise
- 8 slices whole wheat bread, toasted
- 8 cooked center-cut bacon strips
- 4 Bibb or Boston lettuce leaves

Directions:

1. Ensure that your air fryer is preheated to 350 F and spray the basket with some cooking spray.
2. Make eight slices out of your tomato, each slice with a thickness of ¼ inch. Finally, sprinkle salt and pepper on the tomato slices.
3. Get three separate shallow bowls and place the bread, flour, and egg in each. Dip the tomato slices in the flour, and shake to remove excess, then into the egg, and finally the crumb mixture.
4. You may divide the slices into batches.
5. Place the tomato slices in the air fryer basket to form a single layer, then spray with cooking spray.
6. Allow to cook for about 8-12 minutes, turning halfway, and spritzing with additional cooking spray. Remove when the golden brown color is consistent, and keep warm. Do the same for the other tomato slices.
7. While cooking the tomato slices, make a mixture of green onions, dill, and mayonnaise. On each of the four slices of bread, lay two bacon strips, one lettuce, and two tomato slices in it. Then spread the mayonnaise mixture over the remaining slices of bread, and place over the top.
8. Serve immediately.

Leftovers Bubble and Squeak

Prep + Cook Time: 30 minutes | Servings: 4

Ingredients:

- leftover vegetables (mash veggie bake, sprouts, cabbage, stuffing,
- 1 tbsp mixed herbs
- 1 tsp tarragon
- Salt and ground black pepper to taste
- 2 oz Cheddar cheese, shredded
- 1 medium onion, peeled and sliced
- 2 medium eggs, beaten
- 4 slices turkey breast

Directions:

1. Get a large mixing bowl, and in it, place the leftovers, breaking them into small bits to facilitate blending.
2. To the mixture, add the seasoning, cheese, onions, and eggs.
3. Chop up the turkey and add it to the bowl and mix thoroughly using the hands.
4. Transfer the mixture into ramekins or a baking dish and then into the air fryer.
5. Allow cooking for 25 minutes at 360 F. Remove when it is bubbling on top.
6. Serve.

Breakfast Frittata

Prep + Cook Time: 40 minutes | Servings: 2

Ingredients:

- 1 pinch cayenne pepper (optional)
- 1 green onion, chopped
- 2 tbsp red bell pepper, diced
- ¼ lb breakfast sausage, fully cooked and crumbled
- 4 eggs, lightly beaten
- ½ cup shredded Cheddar-Monterey Jack cheese blend
- Cooking spray

Directions:

1. Get a clean bowl and make a mixture of cayenne, onion, bell pepper, sausage, eggs, and Cheddar-Monterey Jack Cheese.
2. Ensure that your air fryer is preheated to 360 F. Get a 6x2-inch cake pan that can fit into the air fryer, and spray the same with a little cooking spray.
3. Transfer the egg mixture into the sprayed pan.
4. Allow the mixture to cook until it is set. It takes up to 18 or 20 minutes.

Spinach Frittata

Prep + Cook Time: 15 minutes | Servings: 2

Ingredients:

- 1 small red onion, minced
- 1/3 pack of spinach
- 3 eggs, whisked
- Salt and ground black pepper to taste
- Mozzarella cheese

Directions:

1. Ensure that your air fryer is preheated to 360 F.
2. Let the oil in the baking pan stay for a minute before adding minced onions. Allow staying for another 2-3 minutes or until the onions become translucent.
3. Add spinach and fry until it is half-cooked (for about 3-5 minutes). Do not worry if the spinach appears dry, just continue frying.
4. Season the whisked eggs and add cheese.
5. Finally, pour the seasoned mixture into the pan and bake until cooked – it takes about 8 minutes.

Whole 30 Airfryer Breakfast Muffins

Prep + Cook Time: 45 minutes | Servings: 2

Ingredients:

- 3 handfuls leftover cooked vegetables
- 3 oz plain granola
- 2 oz coconut milk
- 1 tbsp coriander
- Handful fresh thyme thinly diced
- Salt and ground black pepper to taste

Directions:

1. Get a mixing bowl and in it, add your cooked leftover vegetables.
2. Whizz your plain granola in a blender until you have an appearance of breadcrumbs.
3. Combine the vegetables with the granola, coconut milk, and the seasoning.
4. Mix thoroughly and shape into balls.
5. Allow cooking for 20 minutes in the air fryer at 360 F.
6. Serve.

Baked Mini Spinach Quiches

Prep + Cook Time: 40 minutes | Servings: 4

Ingredients:

- 4 cupcake moulds or small ramekins that fi t inside the air fryer

For the dough:

- 8 oz flour
- 3 oz butter
- 1 egg, beaten
- 2 tbsp milk
- Salt and ground black pepper to taste

Filling:

- 1 small onion
- 1 tbsp olive oil
- 8 oz spinach
- 1 egg, beaten
- 8 oz cottage cheese (unsalted)

Directions:

1. Combine all the ingredients for the dough in a food processor.
2. Add a pinch of salt and blend until you have a ball of dough.
3. Transfer the dough onto a worktop and using your hands, knead until the dough is smooth.
4. Allow the kneaded dough to refrigerate for 15 minutes.
5. Transfer the finely chopped onion into the pan containing the already-heated oil. Fry until the onion is translucent, then add the spinach and allow to fry for about 1 or 2 minutes or until when the spinach is wilted.
6. Get a clean bowl and whisk the egg, adding the cottage cheese.
7. Get rid of the excess water in the spinach by squeezing, then chop the squeezed spinach and add to the cheese mixture.
8. Make four halves out of the dough, and roll each into a round that is large enough to cover the base of the molds. Line the molds with the dough, and fill each with the spinach mixture.
9. Ensure that your air fryer is preheated to 360 F. Transfer the quiche(s) into the air fryer basket and slide it in. Allow cooking for 15 minutes.
10. Serve the quiches either cold or lukewarm.

Flourless Broccoli Cheese Quiche

Prep + Cook Time: 55 minutes | Servings: 2

Ingredients:

- 1 large broccoli
- 3 large carrots
- 1 tsp thyme
- 1 tsp parsley
- Salt and ground black pepper to taste
- 2 large eggs
- 5 oz whole milk
- 1 large tomato
- 4 oz cheddar cheese grated
- 1 oz feta cheese

Directions:

1. Chop up your broccoli into florets. Then dice your peeled carrots and combine it with the broccoli in a food steamer. Allow cooking until soft (for about 20 minutes).
2. Get a measuring cup, and in it, combine all the seasonings, and crack the eggs into it as well. Mix thoroughly before adding the milk gradually until the mixture is pale.
3. After steaming, drain the vegetables and use it to line the base of your quiche dish. Layer with the tomatoes and then add your cheese on top.
4. Pour the liquid over and then add a little bit more cheese on top.
5. Transfer the liquid into the fryer and allow to cook for 20 minutes at 360 F.
6. Serve.

Fried Ravioli

Prep + Cook Time: 12 minutes | Servings: 6

Ingredients:

- 1 (9-oz) box cheese ravioli, store-bought or meat ravioli
- 1 cup buttermilk
- 2 cups Italian-style bread crumbs
- 1 tsp olive oil
- 1 (14-oz) jar marinara sauce
- ¼ cup Parmesan cheese, shredded

Directions:

1. Dip the ravioli in buttermilk.
2. Combine breadcrumbs and the olive oil, and press the ravioli into the breadcrumbs.
3. Transfer the breaded ravioli into a preheated air fryer or baking paper.
4. Allow cooking for 5 minutes at 200 F.
5. Serve while warm alongside marinara sauce for dipping and cheese for topping.

Fast Food

Hot Dogs

Prep + Cook Time: 12 minutes | Servings: 2

Ingredients:

- 2 hot dogs
- 2 hot dog buns
- 2 tbsp of grated cheese, optional

Directions:

1. Ensure that your air fryer is preheated at 390 F for about 4 minutes.
2. Cook the two hot dogs in the air fryer for about 5 minutes, and remove.
3. Transfer the hot dog into a bun, and you may add cheese.
4. Return the dressed hot dog into the air fryer, and allow to cook for an extra 2 minutes.

Taco Dogs

Prep + Cook Time: 17 minutes | Servings: 2

Ingredients:

- 2 jumbo hot dogs
- 1 tsp taco seasoning mix
- 2 hot dog buns
- 1/3 cup guacamole
- 4 tbsp salsa
- 6 pickled jalapeno slices

Directions:

1. Ensure that your air fryer is preheated at 390 F for at least four minutes.
2. Make five slits into each hot dog, and rub ½ teaspoon taco seasoning over each hot dog.
3. Allow the hot dogs to cook in the air fryer for about 5 minutes, before placing them in bus and back into the air fryer basket.
4. This time around, cook until the buns are toasted and hot dogs crisp. This takes about 4 minutes or more.
5. Top the hot dogs with guacamole, salsa, and jalapenos – all in equal amounts.

Pizza Dogs

Prep + Cook Time: 17 minutes | Servings: 2

Ingredients:

- 2 hot dogs
- 4 slices pepperoni, halved
- ½ cup pizza sauce
- 2 hot dog buns
- ¼ cup shredded mozzarella cheese
- 2 tsp sliced olives

Directions:

1. Ensure that your air fryer is preheated to 200°C.
2. Cut four slits into each hot dog, and place them into the basket of the air fryer.
3. Allow cooking for 3 minutes before withdrawing onto a cutting board using tongs.
4. Put a pepperoni half in each of the slits in the hot dogs. Divide the pizza sauce between the buns, and fill with the olives, hot dogs, and mozzarella cheese.
5. Place the hot dogs in the basket of the air fryer and allow to cook, again.
6. Remove when the cheese is melted, and the buns appear crisp – this takes about 2 minutes.

Pizza with Salami and Mushrooms

Prep + Cook Time: 30 minutes | Servings: 1

Ingredients:

- 4 oz flour
- 1 tsp instant yeast
- Salt to taste
- ½ tbsp olive oil
- 2 oz tomato sauce
- ½ ball of mozzarella, sliced thinly
- 2-3 mushrooms, sliced
- 2 oz salami, in strips
- 2 tsp dried oregano
- 2 tbsp Parmesan cheese, grated
- Freshly ground black pepper
- Handful of arugula
- Small pizza pan, 7 – inch diameter, buttered

Directions:

1. Combine the flour and yeast with a pinch of salt, water (2-3 oz), and olive oil. Mix to form a smooth dough ball, and knead until you have an elastic and flexible dough.
2. Ensure that your air fryer is preheated to 390 F.
3. Flour your work surface, and on it, roll out the dough to an 7 - inch round, and put the same in the pizza pan. Form a crust by folding the excess edge of the dough inward.
4. Spread the tomato sauce evenly over the dough, and on top of the sauce, add the mozzarella slices.
5. Ensure even distribution of the mushrooms and the salami over the cheese. Add some sprinkles of oregano, Parmesan cheese, pepper, and arugula on the pizza.
6. Transfer the pizza pan into the air fryer basket, and bake the pizza until golden brown – it takes about 12 minutes.
7. You may use ready-to-use pizza dough for faster but same results.

Amazing XXL burger

Prep + Cook Time: 15 minutes | Servings: 1

Ingredients:

- 2 burgers (beef)
- 2 burger buns
- Mayonnaise to taste
- Ketchup to taste
- Lollo rosso lettuce
- 1 tomato, sliced
- 1 red onion, chopped
- 2 slices cheddar cheese
- Garden cress

Directions:

1. Ensure that your air fryer is preheated when cooking the meat. Set the burgers in the air fryer and allow to cook at 390 F for five minutes. Cut the bread buns along the center to produce the needed two bottom halves and a top half.
2. Add some mayonnaise on one bottom half, and some ketchup on the other.
3. Combine the lettuce, the sliced tomatoes, and the chopped onions, and add the mixture to the bottoms. Open the air fryer, and add the cheddar cheese on the burgers. Allow cooking for 2 minutes at 390 F.
4. After putting the hamburger together, and strengthen it with a cocktail stick.

Quick Blend Mexican Chicken Burgers

Prep + Cook Time: 40 minutes | Servings: 4

Ingredients:

- 3 tbsp smoked paprika
- 1 tbsp mustard powder
- 1 jalapeno pepper
- 1 tsp cayenne pepper
- 1 tbsp thyme, dried
- 1 tbsp oregano, dried
- Salt and ground black pepper to taste
- 1 small cauliflower
- 1 large egg, beaten
- 4 chicken breasts skin and bones removed

Directions:

1. Ensure that your air fryer is preheated to 360 F.
2. Combine your seasonings and the cauliflower in a blender and blend until you have the appearance of breadcrumbs.
3. Take away ¾ of the blended cauliflower mixture and add it to the mixing bowl. Set aside.
4. Get a separate bowl and add your beaten egg. Set aside also.
5. Now add the chicken breasts into the blender, and alongside ¼ of the cauliflower and seasoning mixture, add some extra pepper and salt and blend.
6. Remove the mixture from the blender and make it into burger shapes. You may add some extra cauliflower crumbs if the binding is not strong enough.
7. Roll each burger in the cauliflower crumbs, roll in the egg, and the cauliflower crumbs again.
8. After rolling and dipping all the burgers, arrange them on a baking mat and allow to cook in the air fryer at 360 F for 2 minutes.
9. After 2 minutes, change the sides and allow to cook for an extra 10 minutes. This is to ensure that both sides are tasty and crispy.
10. Serve the burger alongside pickles, crisps, and coleslaw.

Chicken Spiedie Recipe

Prep + Cook Time: 40 minutes | Servings: 4

Ingredients:

- 2 chicken breasts
- 1 large lemon
- 4 garlic cloves, thinly-sliced
- 1 tbsp basil
- 2 tbsp oregano
- Fresh mint
- Salt and ground black pepper to taste
- 1 tbsp olive oil
- Homemade bread rolls
- Homemade mayonnaise
- Skewers

Directions:

1. The first step is to marinate your chicken. To marinate, dice your chicken into big-sized chunks and set them aside in a mixing bowl. Squeeze the juice from the lemon into the same bowl, and the peeled and thinly-sliced garlic also. Then add seasoning and the olive oil. Mix thoroughly with the hands and ensure the chicken is well coated. Now fill the skewers with the chicken and keep them in the fridge overnight.
2. The next step is to make the bread. Gather four bread rolls into the air fryer and allow them to cook at 365 F for 15 minutes.
3. Withdraw the cooked bread rolls and cook the chicken too, at 365 F for 15 minutes.
4. Fill the bread rolls with the stewed chicken, adding some homemade mayonnaise in the process.
5. Serve.

Chicken Quesadillas

Prep + Cook Time: 40 minutes | Servings: 4

Ingredients:

- Cooking spray
- Soft taco shells
- Mexican cheese, shredded
- Chicken fajita strips
- ½ cup onions, sliced
- ½ cup green peppers, sliced
- Sour cream, optional
- Salsa, optional

Directions:

1. Ensure that your air fryer is preheated to 370 F for 3 minutes and spray the pan with some vegetable oil.
2. Get a pan and place one soft taco shell in it, add the shredded cheese on the shell.
3. Arrange the fajita chicken strips to form a single layer and add the onions and green peppers on the strips.
4. Add extra shredded cheese.
5. Now place another soft taco shell on the top and spray with some vegetable oil. To hold the shell in place, put the rack that came with the air fryer on the top.
6. Set the air fryer timer for 4 minutes, and then change to the other side using a large spatula.
7. Spray again with vegetable oil and place the rack on the top of the shell to hold it in place.
8. Set the timer for four minutes.
9. If you want it to be crispier, let it stay a couple of additional minutes in the air fryer.
10. Withdraw when you are satisfied with the crispiness.
11. Cut into four or six slices.
12. Serve alongside sour cream and Salsa (not compulsory).

Chick-fil-A Chicken Sandwich

Prep + Cook Time: 30 minutes | Servings: 2

Ingredients:

- 2 boneless/skinless chicken breasts, pounded
- ½ cup dill pickle juice
- 2 eggs
- ½ cup milk
- ½ tsp garlic powder
- 2 tbsp powdered sugar
- 1 tsp paprika
- ¼ tsp ground celery seed ground
- 1 tsp sea salt
- ½ tsp freshly ground black pepper
- 1 tbsp extra virgin olive oil extra virgin
- 1 cup all purpose flour
- 1 oil mister
- 4 hamburger buns toasted/buttered
- 8 dill pickle chips or more
- Homemade mayonnaise
- ¼ tsp cayenne pepper for spicy sandwiches

Directions:

1. Put the chicken into a Ziploc Baggie and pound. This is to ensure an even thickness – of about 0.5 inches thick.
2. Depending on how big your chicken is, you may cut into two or three pieces.
3. Transfer the cut chicken back into the Ziploc bag and pour the pickle juice in the bag. Allow resting in the refrigerator for 30 minutes to ensure that it marinates.
4. Get a medium-sized bowl and in it, beat the egg and add milk.
5. Get another bowl, and in it, mix the spices and the flour.
6. With the aid of tongs, coat the chicken generously with the egg mixture; dip it into the flour mixture while also ensuring that it is well coated. Shake off excess flour.
7. Spray the base of the air fryer with the cooking coil.
8. Transfer the coated chicken into the air fryer, and spray again with the cooking oil.
9. Allow the chicken to cook for 6 minutes at 340 F. Use your silicone tongs to flip the chicken gently, then spray with oil and cook for an extra 6 minutes.
10. After this, increase the temperature to 400 F and cook for two minutes extra on each side.
11. Serve on toasted and buttered buns, alongside two pickle chips and possibly a small dollop of mayonnaise.

Sandwich

Prep + Cook Time: 25 minutes | Servings: 1

Ingredients:

- 3 tbsp half and half
- ¼ tsp vanilla extract
- 1 egg
- 2 slices sourdough, white or multigrain bread
- 2½ oz sliced Swiss cheese
- 2 oz slices deli ham
- 2 oz sliced deli turkey
- 1 tsp butter, melted
- Powdered sugar
- Raspberry jam, for serving

Directions:

1. Mix the half and half, vanilla extract and the egg in a shallow bowl.
2. Build your sandwich by putting your bread on the counter, and then add a slice of Swiss cheese, the ham, the turkey, and then the second slice of Swiss cheese on one slice of the bread. Finally, top with the other side of the bread. To flatten the combination, simply press down slightly.
3. Ensure that your air fryer is preheated to 350 F.
4. Brush an aluminum foil (almost the same size as the bread) with melted butter. Dip the two sides of the sandwich in the egg batter, one after the other. Allow the batter soak into either side of the bread for 30 seconds each.
5. Transfer the soaked sandwich on the greased aluminum foil and transfer it to the air fryer basket. You can get an extra brown sandwich by brushing the top with melted butter.
6. Set the air fryer temperature to 350 F and timer to 10 minutes.
7. After 10 minutes, flip the sandwich over, and brush again with butter.
8. Now, air-fry for an extra 8 minutes.
9. Finally, place the air-fried sandwich on a serving plate and add sprinkles of powdered sugar. Serve alongside raspberry or blackberry preserves.

Simple Grilled American Cheese Sandwich

Prep + Cook Time: 12 minutes | Servings: 1

Ingredients:

- 2-3 slices cheddar cheese
- 2 slices sandwich bread
- 2 tsp Butter

Directions:

1. With the cheese between the bread slices, spread the butter to the outside of both slices of bread.
2. Transfer the buttered bread into the air fryer and allow to cook for 8 minutes at 370 F.
3. After 4 minutes, flip the bread, and allow to cook for the next 4 minutes.
4. Note that you can use any type of cheese you want and may stuff with tomatoes if that's your preference.

Fried Pizza Sticks

Prep + Cook Time: 15 minutes | Servings: 6

Ingredients:

- 12 egg roll wrappers
- 36 slices pepperoni
- 12 pieces string cheese
- Oil for frying
- Marinara sauce for dipping

Directions:

1. The first step is to lay an egg roll wrapper out flat.
2. On the wrapper, lay three pieces of pepperoni, towards the center on the diagonal.
3. Now, lay a mozzarella stick on top of the pepperoni.
4. Fold the corners of the egg wrapper down over the cheese, and then fold one or both larger corners down over the cheese. Once folded, start rolling the folded cheese until you have used up the entire wrapper.
5. Add drops of water to hold the edges shut. Do the same for the other 11 mozzarella sticks.
6. Transfer the wrapped mozzarella sticks into a deep frying pan containing an already heated oil.
7. Now fry the wrapped cheese for about a minute or until there is a golden brown color on both sides.
8. Serve while hot, alongside marinara sauce for dipping.

Five Cheese Pull Apart Bread

Prep + Cook Time: 20 minutes | Servings: 2

Ingredients:

- 1 oz goats cheese
- 1 oz Cheddar cheese
- 1 oz Mozzarella cheese
- 1 oz Edam cheese
- 1 oz soft cheese
- 4 oz butter
- Salt and ground black pepper to taste
- 2 tsp chives
- 2 tsp garlic puree
- 1 large bread loaf

Directions:

1. The hard cheese should be grated into four separate piles and set aside.
2. Get a clean saucepan and place it on medium heat. Melt the butter in the saucepan, and add the pepper, salt, chives, and the garlic. Allow the mixture to cook for another 2 minutes while mixing. Set aside.
3. Make little slits into the bread with the aid of a sharp bread knife. Cover each slit wholes with garlic butter until every slit is well covered. Then cover all the slits with soft cheese – to ensure the lovely creamy taste in the end.
4. Add a little goat's cheese and a little cheddar into every other slit.
5. Add the Edam and Mozzarella to those that have not been filled.
6. Transfer them into the air fryer and allow to cook for 4 minutes at 360 F or until you have melted cheese and warm bread.
7. Serve.

Grilled Cheese

Prep + Cook Time: 15 minutes | Servings: 1

Ingredients:

- 2 slices of bread I used GF bread
- Butter
- 1 slice of cheese

Directions:

1. Add butter generously to one side of each of the slices of bread, however, avoid too much butter.
2. Add the folded cheese in-between the bread slices, while ensuring that the buttered side is facing out. Avoid letting the cheese hang outside the bread; otherwise, it will burn in the air fryer.
3. If you want to grill, set the air fryer temperature to 360 F and the timer to 8 minutes.
4. Flip the bread after 5 minutes.
5. Allow to cool and serve.

Juicy Lucy Cheese Burger

Prep + Cook Time: 25 minutes | Servings: 2

Ingredients:

- 1 onion
- 0.5 lb minced beef
- 1 tsp mixed herbs
- Salt and ground black pepper to taste
- 4 oz cheddar cheese

Directions:

1. Ensure that your air fryer is preheated to 360 F.
2. Dice the onion and set it aside.
3. Get a large mixing bowl, and in it, combine minced beef, seasoning, and the onion. Mix the combination thoroughly.
4. Roll the mixture into four even-sized balls and transfer them to the chopping board.
5. Squash the burgers until you have very thin pieces.
6. In-between two of the burgers, add half of the cheese and merge them so that there is a burger, then the cheese and then the second burger.
7. Repeat the process for the third and fourth burger, ensuring that the cheese is well hidden in each.
8. Transfer the burgers (two at a time) into the air fryer and allow cooking for 15 minutes at 360 F. Withdraw the burgers from the air fryer and see if the cheese has melted in the center. Also, place a knife or cake tester through it to confirm if they are well cooked. If the juices run clear, it means the burgers are cooked, and if not, return them into the air fryer and cook for an extra 10 minutes at 360 F
9. Serve the cooked burger in a burger bun alongside garnish.

Chicken Burgers

Prep + Cook Time: 25 minutes | Servings: 4

Ingredients:

- 1 lb chicken, minced
- Salt and ground black pepper to taste
- 1 tbsp oregano
- 4 oz wholemeal breadcrumbs
- 2 oz mozzarella cheese

Directions:

1. With the minced chicken in a mixing bowl, add salt, pepper, and oregano, alongside ¾ of the breadcrumbs. Mix thoroughly to ensure that the seasoning is well coated.
2. Mold the mixture into burger shapes.
3. Roll each burger in the remaining breadcrumbs first, then in the cheese. In each case, ensure that the bottom, top, and the sides are entirely coated.
4. Transfer the coated burger into the air fryer and allow cooking at 360 F for 18 minutes.
5. Withdraw cooked burger and serve in bread buns alongside salad and mayonnaise.

Veggie Burgers

Prep + Cook Time: 35 minutes | Servings: 6

Ingredients:

- 7 oz carrots
- 2 lb cauliflower
- 1 lb sweet potato
- 1 cup warm water
- 1 cup chickpeas
- 2 cups wholemeal breadcrumbs
- 1 tbsp basil
- 1 tbsp mixed herbs
- Salt and ground black pepper to taste
- 1 cup grated mozzarella cheese

Directions:

1. Chop the peeled vegetables. Then transfer them into the bottom of the Instant Pot. Add a cup of warm water and close the lid on the instant pot. Set the valve to sealing and allow the vegetables to cook for 10 minutes on manual.
2. After 10 minutes, withdraw the vegetables and squeeze out the excess water after draining with the aid of a tea towel. Ensure that the vegetables are very dry.
3. Combine the chickpeas and the vegetables. Mash together.
4. Add the breadcrumbs and mix thoroughly, and add the seasonings.
5. Make the mixture into veggie burger shapes.
6. Roll the burgers in the grated cheese, ensuring that the cheese covers everywhere.
7. Transfer the veggie burgers into the air fryer and allow cooking at 360 F for 10 minutes.
8. After this first round of cooking, change the temperature to 390 F and cook again for 5 minutes extra. This ensures that the veggie burger gets that crusty texture.
9. Serve while warm, in bread buns or alongside a salad, or both.

Cauliflower Veggie Burger Recipe

Prep + Cook Time: 50 minutes | Servings: 8

Ingredients:

- 2 lbs cauliflower
- Salt and ground black pepper to taste
- 1 tsp mustard powder
- 2 tsp garlic puree
- 1 tsp mixed spice
- 2 tsp thyme
- 2 tsp chives
- 2 tsp parsley
- 3 tsp coconut oil
- ½ cup oats
- 1 cup bread crumbs
- ¼ desiccated coconut
- 3 tbsp plain flour
- 1 small egg beaten
- 2 cups herby bread crumbs

Directions:

1. Chop up the cauliflower into florets. Steam the florets for 25 minutes in the soup maker. Drain the cauliflower and retain it in the soup maker. With the aid of a vegetable knife, dice the cauliflower so that you have very tiny pieces of cauliflower.
2. To the diced cauliflower, add salt, pepper, mustard and a teaspoon of garlic puree. Blend this mixture for a couple of minutes and drain the blend over the sink. Transfer the cauliflower into a tea towel, and use the same in squeezing out any excess water. You may stop when it appears like a bread dough.
3. Get a clean bowl and in it, combine the cauliflower with salt, pepper, the remaining seasoning, extra garlic puree, and coconut oil. Mix them thoroughly.
4. Then add the oats, a cup of bread crumbs and the desiccated coconut. Again, mix thoroughly.
5. Dip your hands in flour to ensure that you don't sick to the burgers. Now, shape the mixture above into burgers. Roll the shaped burgers in the flour, and then the egg, and finally the herby breadcrumbs.
6. Transfer the rolled burgers into the air fryer.
7. Set the temperature to 360 F and allow to cook for 10 minutes.
8. Flip and cook the other side for an extra 10 minutes.
9. Withdraw and serve alongside salad garnish and a burger bun.

Chicken Avocado Burgers

Prep + Cook Time: 15 minutes | Servings: 2

Ingredients:

- 14 oz avocado, peeled
- 14 oz chicken, minced
- 1 tbsp mexican seasoning

Directions:

1. Slice the peeled avocado and cut three slices into small cubes. Keep the rest aside as whole slices.
2. Transfer the minced chicken into a mixing bowl, and add the chunks of avocado alongside the Mexican seasoning.
3. After mixing the contents of the bowl above thoroughly, form the mixture into chicken burger patty shapes.
4. Transfer the burger into the air fryer and allow to cook for 12 minutes at 360 F for 12 minutes.
5. To get that ideal Mexican meal, serve the burger alongside potato wedges.

Falafel Burger

Prep + Cook Time: 20 minutes | Servings: 2

Ingredients:

- 1 tbsp oregano
- 1 tbsp parsley
- 1 tbsp coriander
- Salt and ground black pepper to taste
- 1 tbsp garlic puree
- 1 small lemon
- 14 oz can chickpeas
- 1 small red onion
- 4 tbsp soft cheese
- 1 oz hard cheese
- 1 oz feta cheese
- 5 oz gluten free oats
- 3 tbsp greek yoghurt

Directions:

1. Combine all the seasonings, garlic, lemon rind, drained chickpeas, and red onion in the food processor or blender. Blend until you have a coarse mixture – don't allow them to smoothen up.
2. Transfer the blended mixture into a bowl, add half of the soft cheese, the hard cheese, and the feta.
3. Mold the mixture into burger shapes.
4. Roll the burgers in the gluten-free oats until the chickpea mixture isn't visible anymore.
5. Transfer the rolled burgers into the air fryer's baking pan and allow to cook at 360 F for 8 minutes.
6. To make the burger sauce, combine the soft cheese, salt, pepper, and the Greek Yoghurt in a clean mixing bowl. Mix thoroughly until you have a fluffy mixture, then add the juice of the last lemon and mix again.
7. Place the falafel burger inside the homemade buns with garnish. Then load it up with your burger sauce.
8. Serve and enjoy.

Vegan Lentil Burgers

Prep + Cook Time: 45 minutes | Servings: 4

Ingredients:

- 10 oz gluten free oats
- 4 oz black beluga lentils
- 4 vegan burger buns
- 4 oz white cabbage
- 1 large onion peeled and diced
- 1 large carrot peeled and grated
- 1 tsp cumin
- 1 tbsp garlic puree
- Salt and ground black pepper to taste
- Handful fresh basil cleaned and chopped

Directions:

1. The first step is to transfer the gluten-free oats in the blender and blend until it appears like a flower.
2. Get a clean saucepan and place the lentils in it. Pour water until the lentils are submerged. Then cook on medium heat for about 45 minutes.
3. While cooking put the vegetables into the Instant Pot and allow to steam for 5 minutes with the steam function.
4. Remove the water from the lentils and transfer them in a bowl alongside the oats, steamed vegetables, and seasonings.
5. Make the mixture into burger shapes.
6. Transfer the burgers into the air fryer, set the temperature to 360 F and the timer to 30 minutes.
7. Serve the cooked burgers alongside vegan mayonnaise and salad garnish.

Spanakopita Bites

Prep + Cook Time: 50 minutes | Servings: 8

Ingredients:

- 1 (10-oz) pkg. baby spinach leaves
- 2 tbsp water
- 1/8 tsp cayenne pepper
- ¼ tsp kosher salt
- ¼ tsp black pepper
- 1 tsp dried oregano
- 1 large egg white
- 1 tsp lemon zest (from 1 lemon)
- 2 tbsp finely grated Parmesan cheese
- ¼ cup 1% low-fat cottage cheese
- 1 oz feta cheese, crumbled (about 1/4 cup)
- 4 (13- x 18-inch) sheets frozen phyllo dough, thawed
- 1 tbsp olive oil
- Cooking spray

Directions:

1. In a large cooking pot, combine spinach and enough water and cook over high heat. Stir often while cooking, for 5 minutes, or until wilted. Drain the spinach and allow cooling for 10 minutes. To get rid of excess moisture, press firmly using a paper towel.
2. Get a clean medium bowl, and in it, mix the cayenne pepper, salt, black pepper, oregano, egg white, zest, Parmesan cheese, spinach, cottage cheese, feta cheese until you have a smooth mixture.
3. Spread one phyllo sheet on the work surface and brush lightly with oil using a pastry brush. Add another sheet of phyllo and brush with oil again. Following the same procedure, add two more layers of oiled sheets to make four.
4. Start working from the long side, cut the stack of phyllo sheets into eight strips, each with 2¼ inches of width. Cut the eight strips into a half, crosswise, giving 16 x 2¼ inches of width strips. Place each tablespoon of filling onto one short end of each strip. Fold one corner over the filling, thus creating a triangle. Keep folding back and forth until you get to the end of the strip, and by then, you must have created a triangle-shaped phyllo packet.
5. Coat the air fryer basket mildly using the cooking spray.
6. Arrange eight packets of the phyllo, seam side down, in the basket.
7. Spray the tops with cooking oil and allow cooking till 375 F for about 12 minutes or until you have crispy and deep golden brown phyllo packets.
8. Turn the packets to the other side halfway through cooking.
9. Do the same for the uncooked phyllo packets.
10. Serve at room temperature or while warm.

Fried Calzones

Prep + Cook Time: 30 minutes | Servings: 2

Ingredients:

- 1 tsp olive oil
- ¼ cup red onion, finely chopped
- 3 cups baby spinach leaves
- 1/3 cup shredded rotisserie chicken breast
- 1/3 cup lower-sodium marinara sauce
- 6 oz fresh prepared whole-wheat pizza dough
- 1½ oz pre-shredded part-skim mozzarella cheese (about 6 tbsp)
- Cooking spray

Directions:

1. Get a medium-sized non-stick skillet and in it, heat the oil over medium-high. Toss in the onions, and cook while stirring occasionally. Stop cooking when the onions are tender – this takes about 2 minutes.
2. Now toss in the spinach, and allow to cook until wilted, while covering the skillet. This takes about 1.5 minutes. Withdraw the pan from the heat and stir in the chicken and the marinara sauce.
3. Halve the dough into four and roll each piece on a lightly floured surface to form a circle of 6 inches. Place 1/4th of the spinach mixture over half of each dough circle, and top with 1/4th of the cheese. Form half-moons by folding the dough over the filling, and crimp the edges to seal.
4. Transfer the calzones into the air fryer basket and allow cooking for 12 minutes at 325 F, or until you have the golden brown dough. Turn the calzones to the other side after the first 8 minutes.
5. Serve.

Reuben Calzones

Prep + Cook Time: 30 minutes | Servings: 6

Ingredients:

- Cooking spray
- 1 tube (13.8 oz) refrigerated pizza crust
- 4 slices Swiss cheese
- 1 cup sauerkraut, rinsed and well drained
- ½ lb sliced cooked corned beef
- Thousand Island salad dressing

Directions:

1. Ensure that your air fryer is preheated to 400 F.
2. Drizzle some cooking spray over the air fryer basket.
3. Prepare a lightly floured surface, and on it, unroll the pizza crust dough while patting into a 12-inches square.
4. Cut the dough into four squares. Layer a slice of the cheese, 1/4th of the sauerkraut, and the corned beef diagonally over half of each square to within 0.5 inches of edges.
5. Form a triangle by folding one corner over filling to the opposite corner. Seal by pressing the edges with your fork.
6. Arrange two calzones in a single layer in the sprayed air fryer basket.
7. Allow cooking for about 8-12 minutes or until the calzones are golden brown. Turn the sides after 4-6 minutes of cooking.
8. When fully cooked, withdraw and keep warm while preparing the other calzones.
9. Serve alongside salad dressing.

Pigs In a Blanket

Prep + Cook Time: 25 minutes | Servings: 16

Ingredients:

- 1 can (8 oz) of crescent rolls
- 1 pack (12 oz) of cocktail franks or mini smoked sausages

Directions:

1. Withdraw and drain the cocktail franks from the package. To get rid of any remaining moisture, dry with a paper towel.
2. Remove the crescent rolls dough from the can, and form eight triangles from it. Make two thin triangles from each of the eight triangles. In the end, you will have 16 triangles.
3. Place one frank on the triangle (on the widest part) and roll up. Do the same for the other franks and triangles.
4. Transfer about 8 "Pigs in a Blanket" into the air fryer basket, and air fry for 8 minutes at 330 F.
5. Do the same for the other 8.
6. Serve the fried Pigs in a Blanket alongside hot ketchup, gesso dip, salsa, or mustard.

Popcorn

Prep + Cook Time: 30 minutes | Servings: 6

Ingredients:

- 3 tbsp corn kernels, dried
- Spray avocado oil (Substitutes: safflower oil; coconut oil; peanut oil)
- Sea salt and ground black pepper to taste

Garnish:

- 2 tbsp nutritional yeast
- Dried chives

Directions:

1. Ensure that your air fryer is set to 390 F.
2. In the air fryer basket, arrange the kernels gently and light-spray some coconut or avocado oil. You may line the tray sides with aluminum foil – this ensures that the popped popcorn does not escape the basket.
3. Return the air fryer basket into the air fryer and allow cooking for 15 minutes. Pay close attention to the cooking kernels to ensure that they do not burn.
4. At the sound of popping sounds, monitor closely until they do not pop anymore – or until the 15 minutes lapses.
5. Withdraw the basket immediately and transfer the contents into a large bowl.
6. Spray the cooked kernels with some avocado or coconut oil.
7. Dust with garnish according to your preference.
8. Serve warm or at room temperature.

Mexican-Style Corn on the Cob

Prep + Cook Time: 25 minutes | Servings: 4

Ingredients:

- 4 ears fresh corn (about 1½ lbs), shucked
- Cooking spray
- 1½ tbsp unsalted butter
- 1 tsp lime zest
- 2 tsp chopped garlic
- 1 tbsp fresh juice (from 1 lime)
- ½ tsp black pepper
- 2 tbsp chopped fresh cilantro
- ½ tsp kosher salt

Directions:

1. Coat your corn mildly with some cooking spray before placing in the air fryer basket following a single layer. Allow cooking at 400 F until the corn is tender or mildly charred – this takes about 14 minutes. Turn the corn over after the first 7 minutes of cooking.
2. While cooking the corn, get a small bowl that is suitable for microwaving and in it, combine the butter, lime zest, garlic, and lime juice.
3. Set the microwave to 'high' and microwave the mixture until the butter is melted and the fragrance of the garlic obvious – this takes about 30 seconds.
4. Transfer the corn on a platter, and pour the butter mixture on it.
5. Add sprinkles of pepper, cilantro, and salt to taste.
6. Serve immediately.

Salt and Vinegar Chickpeas

Prep + Cook Time: 55 minutes | Servings: 2

Ingredients:

- 1 (15 oz) can chickpeas, drained and rinsed
- 1 cup white vinegar
- ½ tsp sea salt
- 1 tbsp olive oil

Directions:

1. Get a clean small saucepan, and in it, combine chickpeas and vinegar. Bring to a simmer over high heat. Once simmering, withdraw and allow to stand for 30 minutes.
2. Drain the chickpeas and get rid of all loose skins.
3. Ensure that your air fryer is preheated to 390 F.
4. With the chickpeas spread evenly in the air fryer basket, allow cooking for about 4 minutes or until the chickpeas dry out.
5. Move the dried chickpeas into a heat-proof bowl. Drizzle with sea salt and oil and stir to coat evenly.
6. Place the coated chickpeas into the air fryer again and allow cooking for about 8 minutes. Endeavor to shake the basket at 2 or 3 minutes intervals. Withdraw once you have lightly browned chickpeas.
7. Serve instantly.

Curry Chickpeas

Prep + Cook Time: 35 minutes | Servings: 4

Ingredients:

- 1 (15-oz) can no-salt-added chickpeas (garbanzo beans), drained and rinsed (about 1½ cups)
- 2 tbsp olive oil
- 2 tbsp red wine vinegar
- ¼ tsp ground coriander
- ¼ tsp plus 1/8 tsp ground cinnamon
- ¼ tsp ground cumin
- 2 tsp curry powder
- ½ tsp ground turmeric
- Thinly sliced fresh cilantro
- ½ tsp Aleppo pepper
- ¼ tsp kosher salt

Directions:

1. Smash the chickpeas mildly in a medium bowl with your hands. Remove the chickpea skins.
2. Pour over the oil and vinegar into the chickpeas. Stir to coat evenly, and add coriander, cinnamon, cumin, curry powder and turmeric. Stir the mixture gently to combine.
3. In the air fryer basket, arrange the chickpeas in a single layer and allow cooking at 400 F for about 15 minutes or until the chickpeas are crispy. Ensure that you shake the chickpeas after the first 7 or 8 minutes of cooking.
4. Move the cooked chickpeas into a bowl, while sprinkling the cilantro, Aleppo pepper, and salt – toss to coat.

Buffalo-Ranch Chickpeas

Prep + Cook Time: 35 minutes | Servings: 2

Ingredients:

- 1 (15 oz) can chickpeas, drained and rinsed
- 2 tbsp Buffalo wing sauce
- 1 tbsp dry ranch dressing mix

Directions:

1. Ensure that your air fryer is preheated to 350 F.
2. After lining your baking sheet with paper towels, spread the chickpeas over the lined paper towels. Cover the chickpeas with another layer of paper towels, and press gently to drain any excess moisture.
3. Place the chickpeas in a bowl and pour in the wing sauce. Stir the mixture to combine.
4. Add ranch dressing powder and mix well to combine.
5. Arrange the air fryer in an even layer in the air fryer basket.
6. Allow cooking for 8 minutes. Stop, shake, and cook for an extra 5 minutes, shake again, and cook for 5 minutes more, and shake again for the last time, before cooking for the final 2 minutes.
7. Set aside the cooked chickpeas for about 5 minutes to allow cooling.
8. Serve immediately.

Baja Fish Taco Recipe

Prep + Cook Time: 40 minutes | Servings: 4

Ingredients:

- 1 red onion
- 1 large mango
- 7 oz fresh cod fillet
- Salt and ground black pepper to taste
- 2 tbsp coriander
- 1 tbsp cumin
- 8 tbsp mexican seasoning
- 2 medium eggs
- 1 tbsp garlic puree
- 2 tbsp quark
- 4 limes
- 5 oz gluten free oats
- 4 homemade tortilla wraps

Directions:

1. After peeling the red onion and mango, chop them into small pieces and set aside.
2. Clean and cut the fresh cod into pieces that can be bitten easily. Add salt and pepper generously, alongside half of the coriander.
3. Get a large mixing bowl, and in it, combine all the seasonings and the other half of the coriander. Also, add ¾ of the red onion chopped earlier, the eggs, and the garlic. Mix well to combine. Toss in the quark, and stir in the juice, and the rind of 3 out of 4 limes. Mix thoroughly again to form a smooth batter.
4. Place ¾ of the oats in a blender and blend until you have a mixture like fine breadcrumbs. Combine the blend with unblended oats and mix well before tossing in the fresh cod. Ensure that the fresh cod is well coated in the oats mixture.
5. Transfer the battered cod pieces into the air fryer grill pan, and allow cooking for 10 minutes at 365 F.
6. Withdraw and shake, before allowing to cook for an additional 3 minutes at 390 F.
7. Toss in the cooked fish into the just cooked wraps. Add the mango and red onion mixture as the toppings.
8. Add some lime juice from the remaining lime as seasoning, alongside salt and pepper.
9. Serve.

Whole-Wheat Pizzas

Prep + Cook Time: 20 minutes | Servings: 2

Ingredients:

- 2 whole-wheat pita rounds
- ¼ cup lower-sodium marinara sauce
- 1 cup baby spinach leaves (1 oz)
- 1 oz pre-shredded part-skim mozzarella cheese (about ¼ cup)
- 1 small garlic clove, thinly sliced
- 1 small plum tomato, cut into 8 slices
- ¼ oz shaved Parmigiano-Reggiano cheese (about 1 tbsp)

Directions:

1. Lay out your pita bread.
2. Spread the marina sauce evenly over the side facing upwards. Add half of the spinach leaves, cheeses, garlic, and tomato slices as toppings.
3. Transfer each pita into the air fryer basket, and allow cooking at 350 F for about 4-5 minutes or until you have melted cheese.
4. Do the same for other pitas.

Lighten up Empanadas

Prep + Cook Time: 50 minutes | Servings: 2

Ingredients:

- 1 tbsp olive oil
- 3 oz lean ground beef
- ¼ cup white onion, chopped
- 3 oz cremini mushrooms, chopped
- 6 pitted green olives, chopped
- ¼ tsp ground cumin
- 2 tsp garlic, chopped
- ¼ tsp paprika
- 1/8 tsp ground cinnamon
- ½ cup tomatoes, chopped
- 8 square gyoza wrappers
- 1 large egg, lightly beaten

Directions:

1. Get a clean medium skillet and pour in some oil.
2. Heat over medium-high.
3. Toss in beef and onion, and allow cooking while stirring to crumble. Stop cooking after 3 minutes or when the beef and onion start browning.
4. Add the mushrooms, and continue cooking while stirring occasionally. Stop cooking after 6 minutes or when the mushrooms are appearing brown.
5. Now toss in the olives, cumin, garlic, paprika, and cinnamon, cook until the mushrooms are very soft and devoid of moisture – this will take about 3 minutes.
6. Add the tomatoes and cook further for a minute while stirring intermittently.
7. Transfer the filling into a clean bowl and set aside to cool for about 5 minutes.
8. On your work surface, carefully arrange four gyoza wrappers. At the center of each wrapper, pour about 1.5 tablespoons filling. Now brush the wrapper's edges with egg and fold each over. Seal by pinching the edges.
9. Do the same for the other wrappers and filling.
10. Arrange four empanadas in your air fryer basket following a single layer. Allow cooking at 400 F for 7 minutes or until nicely browned.
11. Do the same for the other empanadas.

Baked Camembert Cheese with Soldiers

Prep + Cook Time: 20 minutes | Servings: 2

Ingredients:

- 1 camembert
- 2 slices bread

Directions:

1. Move your camembert, in a clean, sturdy container, into the air fryer.
2. Allow cooking for 15 minutes at 360 F while shaking at 5-minute intervals. This ensures that the cheese melts evenly.
3. With about 2 minutes to the completion of the cooking, make the toast and then cut them into soldiers.
4. Once the cheese is ready, rip the top layer off.
5. Serve.

Crunchy Corn Dog Bites

Prep + Cook Time: 45 minutes | Servings: 4

Ingredients:

- 2 uncured all-beef hot dogs
- 12 craft sticks or bamboo skewers
- ½ cup (about 2 1/8 oz.) all-purpose flour
- 2 large eggs, lightly beaten

- 1½ cups cornflakes cereal, finely crushed
- Cooking spray
- 8 tsp yellow mustard

Directions:

1. After slicing your hotdog in half, lengthwise, proceed to cut each half into three equal pieces. Find a bamboo skewer or a craft stick into one end of each piece of hot dog.
2. Get a clean shallow dish and place the flour in it.
3. In another shallow dish, place the lightly beaten eggs.
4. In the third shallow dish, place the crushed cornflakes.
5. Now dredge the hot dogs in the flour (shake to get rid of excess flour), then dip in the egg (allowing excess egg mixture to drip off), and finally dredge in cornflakes (press mildly to make the cornflakes adhere).
6. Coat your air fryer basket with little cooking spray.
7. Arrange six corn dog bites in the basket, and spray the top lightly with the cooking spray.
8. Allow cooking for 10 minutes at 375 F or until the corn dog bites over halfway through cooking.
9. Do the same for the other corn dog bites.
10. Serve immediately by placing three corn dog bites per plate, and adding two teaspoons of mustard.

Homemade Sausage Rolls

Prep + Cook Time: 50 minutes | Servings: 4

Ingredients:

- 4 oz butter
- 8 oz plain flour
- 1 tsp parsley, dried
- Salt and ground black pepper to taste

- 1 tbsp olive oil
- 1 tsp mustard
- 11 oz sausage meat
- 1 medium egg beaten

Directions:

1. The first step is to make your pastry. Combine the butter, flour, and the seasoning into a mixing bowl.
2. Using the rubbing-in method, rub the fat into the flour until the mixture looks like breadcrumbs. Stir in the olive oil and little water bit by bit, while mixing into a flaky dough. While incorporating the pastry together, knead it until it becomes very smooth.
3. On your worktop, roll out the smooth pastry and make a square shape. Rub the mustard into the pastry, either with your fingers or a teaspoon. Move the sausage meat to the center, before brushing the edges of the pastry with egg. Roll up the sausage rolls.
4. Divide the rolled up portions into portions.
5. Brush all sides and tops of the sausage rolls with more eggs.
6. Use a knife to cut off the top of the sausage rolls to allow some breathing space.
7. Allow cooking in the air fryer for 20 minutes at 320 F. Increase the heat to 390 F and allow cooking for an additional 5 minutes to ensure that you have a crunchy pastry.
8. Serve.

Crispy Veggie Quesadillas

Prep + Cook Time: 45 minutes | Servings: 4

Ingredients:

- 4 (6-inch) sprouted whole-grain flour tortillas
- 1 cup reduced-fat sharp Cheddar cheese, shredded
- 1 cup sliced red bell pepper
- 1 cup no-salt-added canned black beans, drained and rinsed
- 1 cup sliced zucchini
- Cooking spray
- 1 tsp lime zest plus 1 tbsp fresh juice (from 1 lime)
- 2 oz plain 2% reduced-fat Greek yogurt
- ¼ tsp ground cumin
- 2 tbsp chopped fresh cilantro
- ½ cup drained refrigerated pico de gallo

Directions:

1. With your tortillas on the work surface, sprinkle two tablespoons shredded cheese over half of each tortilla. Add cheese on each tortilla, alongside ¼ cup each red pepper slices, black beans, and zucchini slices. Sprinkle the unused ½ cup cheese evenly over the tortilla.
2. Now form half-moon shaped quesadillas by folding the tortillas. Use some of the cooking sprays to coat the quesadillas mildly. Finally, secure the coated quesadillas with toothpicks.
3. Into the already sprayed air fryer basket, add two quesadillas gently and allow cooking at 400 F until you have golden brown and slightly crispy tortillas. By then, the cheese will be melted and vegetables a bit tender. This should take about 10 minutes.
4. Ensure that you change the side after 5 minutes of cooking.
5. Do the same for the other quesadillas.
6. Meanwhile, combine the lime juice, yogurt, and cumin in a small bowl and stir together.
7. Serve by cutting each quesadilla into wedges, and sprinkle a little cilantro on it.
8. Finally, add a tablespoon of cumin cream alongside two tablespoons of pico de gallo.

Flourless Crunchy Cheese Straws

Prep + Cook Time: 50 minutes | Servings: 8

Ingredients:

- 4 oz gluten free oats
- 1 large cauliflower
- 1 large egg
- 6 oz cheddar cheese
- 1 red onion peeled and thinly diced
- 1 tsp mustard
- 1 tsp mixed herbs
- Salt and ground black pepper to taste

Directions:

1. Blitz your oats in a food processor until you have the appearance of fine breadcrumbs.
2. Place your cauliflower florets in the steamer and allow to steam for 20 minutes. Immediately after steaming, drain and allow the florets to cool. Get rid of all excess water by squeezing out using a clean pillowcase.
3. Divide the cauliflower into two, and move the half into a separate bowl, alongside the other ingredients. Mix well to form a dough and if necessary add some more cauliflower to ensure even combination.
4. Twist the mixture into straw strips and move them into the air fryer baking mat.
5. Allow cooking for 10 minutes at 360 F.
6. Switch sides and allow cooking for another 10 minutes at 360 F.
7. Serve.

Low-Fat Mozzarella Cheese Sticks

Prep + Cook Time: 30 minutes | Servings: 5

Ingredients:

- Salt and ground black pepper to taste
- 1 cup Italian breadcrumbs
- 1 egg
- ½ cup flour
- 10 pieces mozzarella string cheese
- 1 cup marinara sauce

Directions:

1. Add salt and pepper to the breadcrumbs to taste.
2. Into three different bowls, place the eggs, breadcrumbs, and the flour.
3. Now dip each string of cheese in the flour, egg, and breadcrumbs respectively.
4. To harden the sticks, freeze them for about an hour. This ensures that the cheese doesn't lose its stick shape while frying.
5. To avoid the items getting a stick, season your air fryer before every use. You may use the coconut oil and a cooking brush to apply the seasoning.
6. Set your air fryer to 400 F. Add the sticks to the fryer and allow cooking for 8 minutes.
7. Withdraw the basket and flip each stick using thongs, while avoiding distorting the shapes. You may use your hands if the sticks are not too hot.
8. Cook for 8 minutes more.
9. After the timer goes off, retain the sticks in the air fryer pan for 5 minutes before withdrawing them from the pan.
10. If any of the sticks leak some cheese on the outside, correct the shape of such sticks after it must have cooled. Serve with marinara sauce.

Homemade Mozzarella Sticks (ver. 1)

Prep + Cook Time: 8 minutes | Servings: 6

Ingredients:

- 3 oz gluten free oats
- 2 tbsp italian seasoning
- 1 tbsp garlic powder
- 1 tsp basil
- 4 oz mozzarella
- Salt and ground black pepper to taste
- 1 medium egg

Directions:

1. Combine the gluten free oats alongside all the seasonings in your blender and allow blending until you have a mixture like coarse breadcrumbs – this takes about 5 seconds.
2. Dry the mozzarella by patting it with a clean tea towel or kitchen towel.
3. Apply salt and pepper to season the mozzarella before cutting into stick pieces.
4. Get a clean small dish and beat the egg into it. Set aside.
5. Get a larger mixing dish and transfer the blended oat mixture into it.
6. Place the sticks of mozzarella in the oats mixture, then the egg, and finally into the oats mixture again.
7. Transfer the coated sticks into the air fryer's baking pan.
8. Allow cooking at 350 F for 3 minutes.
9. Add some ketchup before serving.

Fried Mozzarella Sticks (ver. 2)

Prep + Cook Time: 1 hour 40 minutes | Servings: 4

Ingredients:

Batter:

- ½ sp salt
- 1 tsp garlic powder
- ½ cup water
- ¼ cup all-purpose flour
- 5 tbsp cornstarch
- 1 tbsp cornmeal

Coating:

- 1 cup panko bread crumbs
- ¼ tsp onion powder
- ½ tsp garlic powder
- ½ tsp parsley flakes
- ½ tsp ground black pepper
- ½ tsp salt
- ¼ tsp oregano, dried
- ¼ tsp basil, dried
- 5 oz mozzarella cheese, cut into ½-inch strips
- 1 tbsp all-purpose flour, or as needed
- Cooking spray

Directions:

1. Get a clean shallow bowl and in it combine salt, garlic powder, water, flour, cornstarch, and cornmeal. Mix until you have the consistency of a pancake batter. You may add or remove ingredients to get the correct consistency.
2. Get another wide, shallow bowl, and in it, combine panko, onion powder, garlic powder, parsley, pepper, salt, oregano and basil. Stir thoroughly.
3. Coat the mozzarella sticks with flour, lightly one after the other. Place the coated stick in the batter and toss in the panko mixture. Remove when the stick is fully coated, and transfer to the baking sheet. With the sticks arranged in a single layer, allow them to freeze for at least an hour.
4. Ensure that your air fryer is preheated to 400 F. Arrange the mozzarella sticks in a row in the air fryer basket, and spray lightly with cooking spray. Allow cooking for 6 minutes.
5. After 6 minutes, flip the sticks using thongs, and resume cooking until the sticks are golden brown – or about 7-9 minutes.

Feta Triangles

Prep + Cook Time: 30 minutes | Servings: 3

Ingredients:

- 1 egg yolk
- 2 tbsp flat-leafed parsley, finely chopped
- 4 oz feta
- 1 green onion, finely sliced into rings
- Freshly ground black pepper
- 5 sheets of frozen filo pastry, defrosted

Directions:

1. Get a clean bowl and in it, beat the egg and combine it with parsley, feta, and green onion. Season to taste with pepper.
2. Make three strips out of each sheet of filo pastry.
3. Take a full teaspoon of the feta mixture and place on the underside of a strip of pastry. Form a triangle by folding the pastry over the filling, after which you fold the strip zigzag until you have all the filling wrapped up in a triangle of pastry. Do the same for other strips.
4. Ensure that your air fryer is preheated to 390 F.
5. With little oil, brush the triangles lightly, before arranging them in the basket – 5 at a time. With the basket in the air fryer, allow baking for 3 minutes or until the feta triangles are golden brown. Do the same for other feta triangles.
6. Serve the baked triangles in a platter.

Feta Cheese Dough Balls

Prep + Cook Time: 25 minutes | Servings: 8

Ingredients:

- Leftover pizza dough get the recipe here
- 1 tbsp Greek yoghurt
- 2 oz soft cheese
- 1 tsp mustard
- 1 tsp garlic puree
- 1 tbsp olive oil
- 2 tsp rosemary
- Salt and ground black pepper to taste
- 2 oz feta cheese

Directions:

1. After removing it from the fridge, allow the pizza dough acclimatize to the room temperature so that working with it is easy.
2. Combine the dough with some flour and knead for a while. This makes the dough soft and gives it the local dough feel. Set aside.
3. In a clean mixing bowl, combine all the ingredients, except the feta and the dough. Mix thoroughly to form a creamy paste.
4. Make eight equal sized pieces from the dough and flatten each piece out like a pancake.
5. Top each flat piece with about 1/3 teaspoon of the ingredients mix. Now, add a little square of feta and seal it up.
6. Repeat the same process for the other seven flatten pieces, so that you have 8 top nice little balls.
7. Now transfer them into the air fryer and allow cooking for 10 minutes at 360 F.

Reduce the heat to 320 F and allow cooking for an additional 5 minutes.

Cheese and Onion Nuggets

Prep + Cook Time: 20 minutes | Servings: 8

Ingredients:

- 2 spring onion
- 7 oz Edam cheese
- 2 tbsp kyle's mayonnaise
- Salt and ground black pepper to taste
- 1 tbsp thyme
- 1 tbsp coconut oil
- ¼ shortcrust pastry
- 1 small egg, beaten

Directions:

1. Dice the cleaned spring onion into thin pieces.
2. Grate the cheese.
3. Combine the onion, mayonnaise, salt, pepper, dried thyme, and coconut oil in a medium mixing bowl. Mix thoroughly and make the mixture into eight small balls. Keep the balls in the fridge for an hour.
4. Make eight nugget shapes out of your shortcrust pastry. Ensure that there are no gaps by sealing it up.
5. With the aid of a pastry brush, brush the egg over the pastry. This gives them an eggy glow when cooked.
6. Allow the egg to cook in the air fryer at 356 F for 12 minutes.
7. Serve warm with the cheese still melting.

Airfryer Cheese and Bacon Fries

Prep + Cook Time: 25 minutes | Servings: 2

Ingredients:

- 2 medium potatoes, peeled
- 2 tsp olive oil
- 4 bacon rashers
- Salt and ground black pepper to taste
- 1 oz cheddar cheese, grated

Directions:

1. Ensure that your air fryer is preheated to 360 F.
2. Dice the peeled potatoes and transfer them into the air fryer.
3. Sprinkle a teaspoon of olive oil over them.
4. Allow cooking at 360 F for 10 minutes.
5. Dice the fat-free bacon into bits, and add them to the cooked potatoes in the air fryer.
6. Allow the combination to cook for another 5 minutes.
7. Shake and add another teaspoon of olive oil. Resume cooking for another 2 minutes but at a higher temperature of 390 F.
8. Withdraw and sprinkle with pepper, salt, and the grated cheese.
9. Serve.

Mini Peppers with Goat Cheese

Prep + Cook Time: 20 minutes | Servings: 8

Ingredients:

- 8 mini or snack peppers
- 1 tsp freshly ground black pepper
- ½ tbsp olive oil
- 4 oz soft goat cheese, in eight pieces

Directions:

1. Ensure that your air fryer is preheated to 390 F.
2. Get rid of the membrane, seeds, and the caps of the mini peppers.
3. In a deep mixing dish, combine the Italian herbs, the olive oil, and the pepper.
4. Place the pieces of goat cheese in the mixture one after the other. Withdraw and transfer each piece into each of the mini pepper. Arrange the goat cheese-filled mini peppers in the basket, placing them next to each other. Return the basket into the air fryer.
5. Allow baking for 8 minutes, or until you have the cheese all melted.
6. Serve the mini peppers by placing them in small dishes.
7. They are best eaten as snacks or appetizers.

Mini Frankfurters in Pastry

Prep + Cook Time: 35 minutes | Servings: 3

Ingredients:

- 1 tin of mini frankfurters (approx. 20 frankfurters)
- 4 oz ready-made puff pastry (chilled or frozen, defrosted)
- 1 tbsp fine mustard

Directions:

1. Ensure that your air fryer is preheated to 390 F.
2. Drain the sausages very well, on a layer of kitchen paper before dabbing them dry.
3. Make strips of 2 x 0.5 inch out of the puff pastry, and coat each strip with a thin layer of mustard.
4. Roll each sausage into a strip of pastry, spirally.
5. Divide the rolled sausages into two. Transfer half into the air fryer basket and allow baking for 10 minutes or until they are golden brown. Do the same for the other half.
6. Serve the sausages in a platter, alongside a small dish of mustard.

Roasted Pepper Rolls

Prep + Cook Time: 40 minutes | Servings: 8

Ingredients:

- 2 medium-sized red, yellow and/or orange bell peppers, halved
- Filling as desired
- Tapas forks

Directions:

1. Ensure that your air fryer is preheated to 390 F.
2. In the air fryer basket, place the bell peppers and allow cooking for 10 minutes. The peppers will be roasted until they have slightly charred skin.
3. Divide the peppers into two by cutting lengthwise. Remove the skin and the seeds.
4. Apply your preferred filling in coating the bell pepper pieces.
5. Roll them up, starting from the narrowest end.
6. Use tapas forks to secure the rolls, before placing them in a platter.

Fillings:

Anchovy with Capers

Empty a tin of anchovy fillets, and chop the fillets into fine bits. Combine the anchovy fillets with one crushed clove of garlic, two tablespoons of finely chopped parsley, some freshly ground black pepper, and two tablespoons of finely chopped capers. Mix.

Feta with green onion

Combine the crumbled 100g Greek Feta cheese with one thinly sliced green onion, alongside two teaspoons finely chopped oregano, and mix well.

Tuna with Red Onion

Empty one tin of tuna in olive oil, and combine with freshly ground black pepper, salt, two tablespoons of capers, one tablespoon of grated lemon peel, and one finely chopped red onion. Mix.

Roasted Corn

Prep + Cook Time: 25 minutes | Servings: 2-3

Ingredients:

- 4 fresh ears of corn
- 2 t o 3 tsp vegetable oil
- Salt and ground black pepper to taste

Directions:

1. After getting rid of the husks from the corn, wash them and pat them dry. If your basket is too small for the corn, you would have to cut it.
2. Add some drizzles of vegetable oil over the corn until the oil covers the corn well.
3. Add some salt and pepper to season to taste.
4. Allow cooking for 10 minutes at 400 F.

Mini Quiche Wedges

Prep + Cook Time: 20 minutes | Servings: 6

Ingredients:

- 4 oz (frozen or chilled) ready-made pie crust dough (pâte brisée)
- ½ tbsp oil
- 3 tbsp whipping cream
- 1½ oz Parmesan cheese, grated
- 1 egg
- Freshly ground black pepper to taste
- Salt to taste
- Filling as desired
- 2 small pie moulds of 4 inch

Directions:

1. Ensure that your air fryer is preheated to 390 F.
2. Make two rounds of 6 inch from the dough.
3. Grease the molds lightly using oil and line them with the dough. Apply some force along the edges of the dough.
4. Combine the cream, cheese, and the beaten egg in a bowl. Season with pepper and salt to taste.
5. Transfer the mixture into the molds and add the filling.
6. Put only one mold in the air fryer basket and allow baking for 12 minutes or until it is golden brown. Do the same for the other quiches.
7. Withdraw the quiches from the molds and cut each into six wedges. Serve the pieces warm or at room temperature.

Airfryer Pizza Hut Bread Sticks

Prep + Cook Time: 30 minutes | Servings: 2

Ingredients:

- 1/3 homemade pizza dough
- 2 tbsp desiccated coconut
- 1 tsp garlic puree
- 1 oz cheddar cheese
- Bread seeds, optional
- 1 tsp parsley
- Salt and ground black pepper to taste

Directions:

1. Melt the coconut in a small pan until it becomes a liquid – preferably on medium heat.
2. Pour in your seasonings alongside the garlic puree. Mix well.
3. Shape your pizza dough into a thick rectangular shape. Coat it evenly with your garlic oil using a baking brush. Add some sprinkles of desiccated coconut oil on the top until it covers the garlic oil entirely. Add some additional sprinkles of cheddar cheese, and finally some bread seeds.
4. Allow cooking in the air fryer for 10 minutes at 355 F.
5. Set the temperature to 390 F and allow cooking for a further 5 minutes or until the pizza is crispy and nice on the outside, and hot in the middle.
6. Chop the well-cooked pizza into fingers and serve.

Frugal Family Cheesy Homemade Garlic Bread

Prep + Cook Time: 30 minutes | Servings: 4

Ingredients:

- 10 inch homemade pizza dough
- 5 oz cream cheese
- 5 oz butter
- 1 tsp garlic puree
- 1 tsp parsley
- Salt and ground black pepper to taste

Directions:

1. Roll out your pizza dough and prepare it for topping.
2. Add a layer of soft cheese on your base.
3. Melt your butter in a pan on medium heat. Stop when you have a nice and runny liquid. Pour the melted butter into the garlic puree, salt, parsley, and pepper.
4. Place the garlic butter mixture such that it forms a layer on top of the cream cheese.
5. Transfer the layered dough into the oven. Allow cooking for 20 minutes at 355 F.
6. Serve.

Budget Friendly Airfryer Mini Cheese Scones

Prep + Cook Time: 35 minutes | Servings: 10

Ingredients:

- 6 oz self raising flour
- 1 oz butter
- 1 tsp chives
- 1 tsp mustard
- Salt and ground black pepper to taste
- 3 oz cheddar cheese
- 1 medium egg
- 1 tbsp whole milk

Directions:

1. Ensure that your air fryer is preheated to 355 F.
2. Combine the flour and butter in a large mixing bowl. Mix until the mixture appears like fine breadcrumbs. Then toss in your seasonings, alongside 2 oz worth of the cheddar cheese. Mix thoroughly, again.
3. Add the egg and milk, and mix again, preferably with your hands. Continue until the mixture appears like soft dough. To achieve the desired softness, you may add some more milk.
4. Roll out until you have a thickness of ½ inch, then divide into ten equal pieces. Place some of the leftover cheese in the middle of each piece, and shape them into balls. You will have a lovely melted cheese center if done properly.
5. Transfer the mini scones into the air fryer. Allow cooking for 20 minutes at 355 F.
6. Slice the cooked scones in half, and place some butter in the center of each slice.
7. Serve.

Bruschetta Recipe

Prep + Cook Time: 10 minutes | Servings: 4

Ingredients:

- 1 medium tomato
- Salt and ground black pepper to taste
- 1 tbsp oregano
- 3 tbsp olive oil
- 1 tbsp garlic puree
- 1 oz Italian cheese
- Fresh basil
- Medium Ciabatta

Directions:

1. Dice the fresh tomato into thin small pieces. Season to taste with salt, pepper, and oregano.
2. Get a small mixing bowl and in it combine the olive oil and the garlic puree, alongside the seasonings. Mix and set aside.
3. Slice the ciabatta into medium-sized pieces and brush one side with the garlic mixture above with the aid of a pastry brush.
4. Allow the ciabatta pieces cook in the air fryer grill pan for 4 minutes at 360 F, with the oil sides facing down.
5. Turn the pieces to the other side using your thongs, and decorate the other side with cheese, tomatoes, and the fresh basil respectively.
6. Allow the pieces to cook again for 2 minutes but at 390 F.
7. Serve while warm.

Two Ingredient Croutons

Prep + Cook Time: 15 minutes | Servings: 8

Ingredients:

- 2 slices wholemeal bread
- 1 tbsp olive oil

Directions:

1. Cut your bread slices into chunks of medium sizes.
2. Transfer the chunks into the air fryer and add the olive oil.
3. Allow cooking for 8 minutes at 390 F.
4. Serve as a snack or over your soup.

Vegan Croutons

Prep + Cook Time: 15 minutes | Servings: 2

Ingredients:

- 2 heaping cups of cubed baguette (or your preferred bread), cut in 1 inch pieces
- 2 tsp extra virgin olive oil
- 2 tsp lemon juice
- ½ tsp dried basil
- ½ tsp granulated garlic
- ½ tsp dried oregano
- Salt and ground black pepper to taste

Directions:

1. Get a clean large mixing bowl, and in it, add the cubed baguette, drizzles of extra virgin olive oil, and lemon juice across the bread. Then sprinkle the dried basil, garlic granules, dried oregano, salt, and pepper.
2. With your hands, coat the cubed bread evenly by tossing it into the spices mixture. For easy coating, ensure that the spices are on the bread instead of being stuck on the sides of the bowl.
3. Transfer the bread into the air fryer, and allow cooking for 5 minutes at 400 F. Shake the basket once or twice within this cooking time.
4. Serve as toppings for your favorite salad.

Garlic Bread Recipe

Prep + Cook Time: 50 minutes | Servings: 4

Ingredients:

- 1 small egg
- 1 oz whole milk
- ½ french bread stick
- 2 tsp garlic puree
- 2 tbsp olive oil
- 1 tsp parsley

Directions:

1. Get a clean mixing bowl, and in it, combine the milk and egg. Beat until you have a smooth mixture.
2. Chop your French bread into garlic bread pieces. Submerge them in the egg and milk mixture until the pieces are entirely coated with the egg and milk. Shake off any excess coating.
3. Place the bread in the air fryer grill pan, spreading it out to ensure that the bread pieces do not overlap.
4. Get a small bowl, and in it, mix the garlic, olive oil, and parsley.
5. With the aid of your pastry brush, brush the garlic mixture over the top of the bread.
6. Return the grill pan into the air fryer and allow cooking for 2 minutes at 360 F.
7. After two minutes of cooking, turn the sides, and brush the other side too.
8. Cook for an extra 2 minutes.
9. Withdraw and serve immediately.

British Fish and Chip Shop Healthy Battered Sausage and Chips

Prep + Cook Time: 45 minutes | Servings: 2

Ingredients:

- 2 large potatoes, peeled
- 1 tbsp olive oil
- 2 slices wholemeal bread
- Salt and ground black pepper to taste
- 1 medium egg beaten
- 4 oz plain flour
- 4 medium thick sausages

Directions:

1. Ensure that your air fryer is preheated to 360 F.
2. Cut your peeled potatoes into chips, transfer them into the air fryer, and add a tablespoon of olive oil.
3. Prepare your breaded crust by transferring the whole wholemeal bread in the air fryer, right on the chips, and harden it for about 5 minutes. Withdraw the bread after 5 minutes and break into bread crumbs.
4. Combine the breadcrumbs with some salt and pepper, in a clean dish. Get another dish and add the egg. And in the third dish, add the flour.
5. Make the breaded sausage by placing each sausage into your hand and rolling it in the flour, and the egg, and finally in the bread crumbs mixture.
6. Repeat for all the sausage pieces or at least four battered sausages.
7. Transfer the battered sausages into the air fryer, on top of the potatoes.
8. Allow cooking for 10 minutes at 360 F. Withdraw the chips after 10 minutes and cook only the sausages for an extra 5 minutes. Serve.

Healthy Flapjacks Recipe

Prep + Cook Time: 20 minutes | Servings: 4

Ingredients:

- 4 oz butter
- 10 oz gluten free oats
- 4 oz brown sugar
- 2 tbsp honey

Directions:

1. Place the baking pan on top of the air fryer grill pan and ensure that it slots in place inside the air fryer.
2. Dice the butter into quarters and transfer them onto the baking pan. Allow cooking for 2 minutes at 360 F or until you have the butter melted.
3. Blend the gluten-free oats in the blender until they appear like breadcrumbs.
4. Combine the brown sugar and the honey, and finally the oats. Mix well with a fork until you have a smooth mixture.
5. Allow cooking for 10 minutes at 320 F.
6. Raise the temperature to 360 F and allow cooking for an extra 5 minutes.
7. Withdraw and serve.

Air Fryer Chewy Granola Bars

Prep + Cook Time: 20 minutes | Servings: 6

Ingredients:

- 10 oz gluten free oats
- 1 oz brown sugar
- 1 tsp vanilla essence
- 1 tsp cinnamon
- 1 tbsp olive oil
- 3 tbsp honey
- 2 oz melted butter
- 1 medium apple, peeled and cooked
- Handful raisins

Directions:

1. After blending the gluten-free oats into a smooth mixture, toss in the other dry ingredients.
2. Combine the wet ingredients into the baking pan of the air fryer. Stir well using a small wooden spoon.
3. Transfer the dry ingredients from the blender into the baking pan. Mix thoroughly with a fork.
4. Toss in the raisins and press down the mixture into the baking pan, until it is all level.
5. Allow cooking for 10 minutes at 320 F.
6. Raise the temperature to 360 F and cook for an extra 5 minutes.
7. Withdraw and transfer into the freezer for about 5 minutes or until it stiffens up.
8. Cut into chewy sizes.
9. Serve your granola bars.

Banana Chips

Prep + Cook Time: 35 minutes | Servings 2-3

Ingredients:

- 3-4 raw bananas
- ½ tsp salt
- ½ tsp turmeric powder
- 1 tsp oil
- ½ tsp chaat masala

Directions:

1. After peeling the bananas, keep them.
2. Combine salt, turmeric powder, and water, and in this mixture, cut the bananas into slices. This ensures that the banana doesn't turn black and retains its nice yellow color. Retain the banana slices in the mixture for about 5 to 10 minutes.
3. Withdraw the chips from the mixture and dry.
4. Then add some oil on the chips – this ensures that they do not stick while in the air fryer.
5. Ensure that your air fryer is preheated to 360 F for 5 minutes.
6. Place the chips in the air fryer basket and allow air frying for 15 minutes at 360 F.
7. Add chat masala and salt.
8. Keep the chips in an airtight jar, and serve instantly.

Corn Tortilla Chips

Prep + Cook Time: 10 minutes | Servings: 4

Ingredients:

- 8 corn tortillas
- 1 tbsp olive oil
- Salt and ground black pepper to taste

Directions:

1. Ensure that your air fryer is preheated to 390 F.
2. With the aid of your knife, make triangles out of your corn tortillas, and brush each triangle with olive oil.
3. Divide the whole tortillas into two – transfer the first batch into the wire basket.
4. Allow air frying for 3 minutes.
5. Do the same for the second batch.
6. Add sprinkles of salt and serve.

Bacon Cashews

Prep + Cook Time: 15 minutes | Servings: 12

Ingredients:

- 3 cups raw cashews
- 2 tbsp blackstrap molasses
- 3 tbsp liquid smoke
- 2 tsp salt

Directions:

1. Get a large bowl and in it, combine all the ingredients and coat the cashews generously and evenly with the mixture.
2. Transfer the coated cashews into the air fryer basket, and allow cooking for 8-10 minutes at 350 F.
3. While cooking, shake the basket at intervals of 2 minutes – this ensures that the cashews cook evenly. Be extra careful at the last 2 minutes and shake/check consistently to avoid burning the cashews.
4. Allow the cooked cashews to cool to room temperature – this takes about 15 minutes.
5. Then transfer the cool cashews into an airtight storage container and serve.

Pumpkin Seeds

Prep + Cook Time: 1 hour 15 minutes minutes | Servings: 1½ cups

Ingredients:

- 1½ cups pumpkin seeds from a large whole pumpkin
- Olive oil
- 1 tsp smoked paprika
- 1½ tsp salt

Directions:

1. After cutting the pumpkin open, use your spoon to scrape out the contents inside. Remove the seeds from the flesh, and rinse the seeds with cold water.
2. Boil two quarts of salted water, and toss in the pumpkin seeds. Allow the seeds to boil for 10 minutes. Then withdraw the seeds, drain them, and spread on paper towels for at least 20 minutes or until they are dry.
3. Ensure that your air fryer is preheated to 350 F.
4. Combine olive oil, smoked paprika and salt into a bowl. Toss the seeds into the mixture, before moving them into the air fryer basket.
5. Allow the seeds to air fry for 35 minutes, while shaking the basket consistently while cooking. Stop cooking when the seeds are crispy and slightly browned.
6. Do not serve or store the seeds in a bag or air-tight container until they are cool.
7. Serve as a snack or as toppings for yogurt or salad.

Spiced Nuts

Prep + Cook Time: 40 minutes | Servings: 8

Ingredients:

- 1 packet stevia
- Pinch cayenne pepper, optional
- ½ tbsp cinnamon
- 1 tbsp egg white
- 1 cup nuts (walnuts, pecans and almonds)

Directions:

1. Ensure that your air fryer is preheated to 300 F.
2. Get a small bowl and in it, combine the stevia, cayenne pepper, and cinnamon. Keep the mixture.
3. Get another bowl and in it, mix the egg whites with the nuts. Now, combine the spices mixture and the egg white mixture.
4. Transfer the new mixture into the air fryer basket.
5. Set the timer to 10 minutes and allow the mixture to bake.
6. After the first 10 minutes, stir and allow the mixture bake for an extra 10 minutes.
7. Serve the nuts when they are completely cool.

Salted Nuts

Prep + Cook Time: 15 minutes | Servings: 1 ½ cups

Ingredients:

- ½ cup whole almonds
- ½ cup whole cashews
- ½ cup fox nuts / makhana, optional
- 1 tsp ghee
- Vegans can use olive oil or canola oil
- Salt and ground black pepper to taste

Note:

You may choose the nuts of your choice like pecans or walnuts, or macademia etc. You may air fry these together as a mix or separate.

Directions:

1. Ensure that your air fryer is preheated to 350 F for 2 minutes.
2. Put all the nuts in a bowl, and add one teaspoon of melted ghee.
3. With your hands, rub the nuts with the melted ghee, and transfer them into the air fryer.
4. Allow them to air fry for 6 minutes. After 4 minutes, withdraw the basket and toss the nuts well. Return them into the basket and resume air frying for the remaining 2 minutes. In the end, you will have nice and pinkish nuts.
5. If your preference is a darker rich color, extend the air frying time by 2 minutes.
6. Withdraw the fried nuts and transfer them into a steel or glass bowl. Do not use plastic bowls, please.
7. Add sprinkles of black pepper and salt, then toss well. Serve.

Low Carb Roasted Nuts

Prep + Cook Time: 20 minutes | Servings: 2-3

Ingredients:

- 2 cups pecan halves
- 1 tbsp butter, ghee, or oil
- 1-2 tsp of ground pink Himalayan salt

Directions:

1. Ensure that your air fryer is preheated to 390 F for about 5 minutes.
2. Melt your ghee or butter, or oil. Add some salt.
3. Add some pecan halves into the melted butter and stir until the pecan are entirely coated.
4. Transfer into the air fryer and allow air-frying for 4-6 minutes at 390 F or until the nuts are toasty. While frying, toss at 2 minutes interval.
5. Withdraw and serve.

Cornish Pasty Recipe

Prep + Cook Time: 45 minutes | Servings: 4

Ingredients:

- 1 large carrot, peeled and sliced into small cubes
- 1 medium potato, peeled and sliced into small cubes
- 0.5 lb plain flour
- 4 oz butter
- 2 to 3 tbsp water (cold)

- 4 oz minced pork
- 1 tbsp olive oil
- 1 tsp mixed herbs
- Salt and ground black pepper to taste
- 1 tsp thyme
- 1 small egg, beaten

Directions:

1. Allow the carrot and potato to cook for 20 minutes or until soft in a food steamer. Set aside the cooked vegetables.
2. Make your pastry by rubbing the butter into the flour until you have an appearance of breadcrumbs. To achieve a nice soft dough, add little cold water intermittently. Roll out your pastry ready for the Cornish pasties.
3. Get a large pan, and in it, mix your mince alongside a little olive oil. Cook the mixture until it has browned through. Then add the seasoning, steamed potato, and carrot. Mix thoroughly again and keep separately.
4. Fill half of a side of the Cornish pastry with the cold filling, generously.
5. Brush the pastry with egg.
6. Transfer the pastry into your air fryer.
7. Allow to cook at 400 F for 25 minutes, or until the pastry is cooked to your satisfaction.
8. Remove and serve.

Flaky Buttermilk Biscuits

Prep + Cook Time: 20 minutes | Servings: 14

Ingredients:

- 4 oz butter
- 1.1 lbs self raising flour

- 20 oz buttermilk
- ½ small egg, beaten, optional

Directions:

1. Get a clean mixing bowl and transfer the butter and flour. Rub the fat into the flour until you have the appearance of coarse breadcrumbs.
2. Pour the buttermilk into the mixture and mix thoroughly with a fork.
3. Rub your hands with flour, and mold the mixture into a dough ball with your hands.
4. Roll out the dough. Make 16 medium-sized flaky biscuits from the dough by using the biscuit cutters.
5. Arrange the flaky biscuits in batches of four inside the air fryer grill pan, leaving a little space between them.
6. Cook each batch at 360 F for 4-8 minutes.
7. Withdraw and serve while warm.

Easy Pull Apart Bread

Prep + Cook Time: 2 hours 10 minutes | Servings: 6

Ingredients:

- 1 lb plain flour
- 3 oz butter
- 10 oz whole milk
- 1/3 tbsp yeast
- 1 tbsp coconut oil
- 1 tbsp olive oil
- Salt and ground black pepper to taste

Directions:

1. To prepare the bread, rub the butter into the flour until the butter is well mixed in.
2. Get a pan and pour in the milk and oils – warm until they are lukewarm.
3. Transfer the pan mixture into the bowl, add yeast, and form a dough by mixing with your hands.
4. Knead the bread for 5 minutes, and place a damp tea towel over the bowl while the bread dough is still in it. Place the bowl in a hot place. Wait for an hour and repeat the kneading and proving process, this time for 30 minutes.
5. Make the proved dough into bread roll shapes.
6. For the bread roll to become the "Easy Pull Apart" type, make them into medium-sized bread burns while leaving enough space to avoid contact and allow breathing. And ensure that you transfer the bread rolls straight into the air fryer.
7. If you follow all this, you will have the pull apart appearance in the end.
8. Lastly, allow cooking for 15 minutes at 365 F.

Pumpkin Bread

Prep + Cook Time: 25 minutes | Servings: 4

Ingredients:

- 6 tbsp banana flour
- 2 large eggs
- 8 tbsp pumpkin puree
- 2 tbsp vanilla essence
- Pinch of nutmeg
- 4 tbsp greek yoghurt
- 4 tbsp honey
- 6 tbsp gluten free oats

Directions:

1. In a clean mixing bowl; combine all the ingredients, except the oats, and mix with a hand mixer to form a creamy and smooth mix.
2. Mix in the oats using a fork.
3. Apply some extra banana flour to the sides and base of the baking pan before pouring in the pumpkin-bread mixture.
4. Use your spatula to smoothen the sides to ensure that lumps do not form.
5. Allow the mixture to cook for 15 minutes in the air fryer at 360 F.
6. To remove the baking pan, cut around the sides and edges of the pan.
7. Leave the cake to cool for about 2-3 minutes before slicing it.
8. Serve the slices alongside some butter.

Rock Buns

Prep + Cook Time: 15 minutes | Servings: 8

Ingredients:

- 4 oz butter
- 2 oz caster sugar
- 0.5 lb self raising flour
- 1 tbsp honey
- 3 oz mixed raisins
- 1 medium orange
- 1 medium lemon
- 1 medium egg
- Milk

Directions:

1. Get a mixing bowl and make a mixture of butter, sugar, and flour in it, while rubbing the fat into the flour. Include the honey and the raisins also.
2. With the aid of a good grater add the orange rind and the lemon as well. Squeeze the juice from the chopped lemon and orange into the mixing bowl.
3. Mix thoroughly with a fork.
4. Crack the egg in and mix thoroughly again.
5. Add little milk intermittently until the dough is soft enough.
6. Shape the dough into small to medium sized scones.
7. Transfer the shaped dough into the air fryer's grill pan.
8. Allow cooking for 10 minutes at 360 F.
9. Serve warm.

Buttery Dinner Rolls

Prep + Cook Time: 1 hour 15 minutes | Servings: 10

Ingredients:

- 1 cup fresh milk (room temperature)
- 4 oz butter, softened
- 2 oz sugar
- 2 eggs, beaten

Glaze:

- Some melted butter

- 1½ tsp salt
- 1 lb bread flour
- 2¼ tsp instant yeast

Directions:

1. Get a clean bread maker pan and add all the ingredients following the order listed above.
2. Select Dough setting, and at the end of the cycle, turn the dough onto a lightly floured surface and punch out the air.
3. Make 22 portions out of the dough, and shape each portion into a round ball.
4. Line your air fryer basket with baking sheet and oil the edges slightly. Then, transfer the shaped dough into the basket.
5. Cover with a damp cloth and allow to proof for until the dough is twice the original size – this takes about 30 minutes.
6. Ensure that your Air Fryer is preheated to 320 F.
7. Air bake the burns for 13-15 minutes at this temperature and withdraw when there is a visible golden brown color. Do the same for the other batches.
8. After baking, brush some melted butter on the buns. Serve.

Hot Cross Buns

Prep + Cook Time: 50 minutes | Servings: 6

Ingredients:

- 6 oz whole milk
- 1 tbsp olive oil
- 2/3 lb strong white bread flour
- ½ tbsp yeast
- 1 tsp mixed spice
- 1 tsp cinnamon

- 2 oz caster sugar
- 3 handfuls raisins
- 1 tsp nutmeg
- 2 oz butter
- 2 tbsp icing sugar
- 4 tbsp plain flour

Directions:

1. Ensure that your Air Fryer is preheated to 175 F or the lowest temperature possible.
2. Get a clean saucepan and place the milk and the olive oil. Warm the mixture until the milk is lukewarm.
3. While warming the milk, get a clean bowl and place the bread flour and yeast, alongside the seasonings. Rub the butter into the flour using the rubbing-in method.
4. Add the raisins and thoroughly mix until you have the appearance of a breadcrumb.
5. Put the saucepan ingredients, little at a time, until you have a soft bread dough.
6. Break the bread dough up into hot cross bun sizes and transfer them on the air fryer's baking mat.
7. Allow cooking for 12 minutes at 360 F.
8. Withdraw from the air fryer and allow it cool for 5 minutes before serving.
9. In the meantime, you can create the icing topping by mixing the icing sugar, plain flour, with a little water to form a thick paste. Use a spoon or piping bag to make a cross on each of the tops of the buns.
10. Serve the buns with butter.

Rich Fruit Scones

Prep + Cook Time: 15 minutes | Servings: 4

Ingredients:

- 0.5 lb self raising flour
- 2 oz butter
- 2 oz sultanas

- 1 oz caster sugar
- 1 medium egg
- Milk

Directions:

1. Get a clean mixing bowl and place the flour and butter and rub the fat into the flour.
2. Add the sultanas, followed by the caster sugar, and finally crack the egg into the mixture.
3. Mix thoroughly with a fork until you have a uniform mixture.
4. Add little milk intermittently until you have a smooth scone dough.
5. Shape the dough into scones.
6. Transfer the scones into the grill pan of the air fryer.
7. Allow cooking at 360 F for 8 minutes.
8. Withdraw and serve warm.

Strawberry Scones Recipe

Prep + Cook Time: 20 minutes | Servings: 4

Ingredients:

- 0.5 lb self raising flour
- 2 oz butter
- 2 oz caster sugar
- Vanilla essence
- 2 oz milk
- 4 tbsp whipped cream
- 1 tbsp homemade strawberry jam
- 2 oz fresh strawberries

Directions:

1. Get a clean mixing bowl and place the flour, butter, and sugar. Rub the butter into the sugar and flour until you have the appearance of breadcrumbs. Finally, add the vanilla essence and milk generously until you have a soft dough.
2. Shape the dough into four equal balls that look like scone shapes.
3. Transfer the shaped balls into the baking pan of your air fryer.
4. Allow cooking at 360 F for 10 minutes.
5. Withdraw cooked balls, place them on a cooling rack and allow to cool for some minutes.
6. Then cut in half, and fill the inside with whipped cream, strawberry jam, and fresh strawberries.
7. Serve.

Three Ingredient Shortbread Fingers

Prep + Cook Time: 20 minutes | Servings: 10

Ingredients:

- 0.5 lb plain flour
- 3 oz caster sugar
- 6 oz butter

Directions:

1. Ensure that your Air Fryer is preheated to 360 F.
2. Get a bowl and make a mixture of the flour and sugar and add the butter.
3. Rub the butter into the flour and sugar.
4. Knead the mixture to give a lovely and smooth mixture.
5. Shape the mixture into finger shapes and decorate with fork markings.
6. Allow cooking on the baking sheet of the air fryer for 12 minutes.
7. Serve.

Yorkshire Pudding Recipe

Prep + Cook Time: 25 minutes | Servings: 6

Ingredients:

- 2 oz plain flour
- Salt and ground black pepper ro taste
- 1 small egg, beaten
- 5 oz whole milk
- Olive oil

Directions:

1. Ensure that your Air Fryer is preheated to 390 F.
2. Get a bowl and make a mixture of the plain flour and seasoning.
3. Pour in the egg gradually, and stir continuously until you have all the egg in the mixture.
4. Add the milk gradually too, and stir consistently to get a mixture as thick as a batter.
5. Beat well until you have bubbles forming on the top.
6. Add a little olive oil in your Yorkshire pudding dish, and place it in the air fryer for about 5 minutes until it is smoking.
7. Now pour your mixture until it is halfway up the container, and place in the air fryer again.
8. Allow cooking for 15 minutes this time, at 390 F.

Crispy Risotto Balls

Prep + Cook Time: 3 hours 20 minutes | Servings: 4

Ingredients:

For risotto:

- 1 tbsp olive oil
- 1 cup onions, diced
- 1 cup arborio rice, dry
- 4 cups vegetable broth
- 1 cup parmesan cheese, grated
- 1 bunch of parsley, chopped
- Salt and ground black pepper to taste

Breading:

- 1.5 cups Bread Crumbs
- 2 eggs

Directions:

1. Place your frying or saute pan on the stove top and preheat it over medium heat. Then pour the olive oil and allow to heat.
2. Toss in the diced onions and saute, and stir regularly until the onions are soft.
3. Pour in the rice and allow to cook for an additional minute.
4. Add 2 cups of vegetable broth and allow to cook, while stirring regularly for 5 minutes.
5. Pour in the remaining 2 cups of broth.
6. Leave the rice to cook until the rice is soft and the broth is entirely absorbed – this takes about 15 minutes.
7. Combine the cheese and parsley using the risotto, adding season, pepper, and salt to taste.
8. Pour the risotto in a casserole dish, and leave in the fridge for 2 hours.
9. While the risotto is cooling, get a clean bowl and toss in the breadcrumbs.
10. Find another clean bowl, and beat the eggs in it.
11. Withdraw the rice mixture from the fridge and make it into 1-inch rice balls by rolling.
12. Dip the rice balls into the egg mixture before the breadcrumbs.
13. Transfer the coated rice balls back to the fridge, allow to cool for another 50miutes.
14. Ensure that your air fryer is preheated to 400 F.
15. With the rice balls in the air fryer, set the timer to 8-10 minutes and allow to cook until golden brown.
16. Withdraw and serve.

Sticky Mushroom Rice

Prep + Cook Time: 25 minutes | Servings: 6

Ingredients:

- 16 oz jasmine rice, uncooked
- 4 tbsp maple syrup
- 2 tsp Chinese 5 Spice
- 4 tbsp rice vinegar or white wine
- ½ cup soy sauce, you can use gluten free tamari
- ½ tsp ground ginger
- 4 cloves garlic, finely chopped
- 16 oz cremini mushrooms wiped clean, (any other mushrooms cut in half)
- ½ cup peas, frozen

Directions:

1. Keep the cooked rice separately.
2. Get a clean bowl and in it, mix the maple syrup, rice vinegar, soy sauce, ground ginger, garlic, and Chinese 5 spice.
3. Ensure that your air fryer is preheated to 350 F.
4. Allow the mushrooms to cook for 10 minutes in the air fryer.
5. After 10 minutes, open the air fryer and shake or stir the mushrooms.
6. Pour the liquid mixture over the cooked mushrooms, followed by the peas.
7. Stir and allow to cook for extra 5 minutes.
8. Finally, add the mushroom sauce to the cooked hot rice and stir well.
9. Serve.

Cool Green Beans

Prep + Cook Time: 15 minutes | Servings: 2

Ingredients:

- 1 lb green beens
- Oil cooking spray
- Salt and ground black pepper to taste
- Ranch seasoning to taste
- Lemon juice to taste

Directions:

1. Ensure that your air fryer is preheated to 400 F.
2. After spraying the green beans with the olive oil, add salt and pepper to taste.
3. Proceed to fry the seasoned green beans for about 9-10 minutes or until crisp.
4. Add sprinkles of ranch seasoning plus lemon juice to taste.
5. Serve.

Spicy Green Beans

Prep + Cook Time: 45 minutes | Servings: 4

Ingredients:

- 12 oz fresh green beans, trimmed
- 1 tsp rice wine vinegar
- 1 tsp soy sauce
- 1 tbsp sesame oil
- ½ tsp red pepper flakes
- 1 clove garlic, minced

Directions:

1. Ensure that your air fryer is preheated to 400 F.
2. Keep your green beans in a bowl.
3. Get a separate bowl and in it, combine the rice wine vinegar, soy sauce, sesame oil, red pepper flakes and garlic. Whisk the mixture and pour it over the green beans.
4. Toss to coat and allow marinating for 5 minutes.
5. Divide the green beans into two halves, and place the first batch in the air fryer basket.
6. Allow cooking for 12 minutes, while shaking the basket 6 minutes after cooking.
7. Do the same for the other half of the green beans.

Falafel

Prep + Cook Time: 1 d 1 h 45 m | Servings: 15

Ingredients:

- 1 cup dry garbanzo beans
- 1 clove garlic
- 1 small red onion, quartered
- 3/4 cup fresh flat-leafed parsley, stems removed
- 1 ½ cups fresh cilantro, stems removed
- 1 tbsp ground cumin
- 1 tbsp sriracha sauce
- 2 tbsp chickpea flour
- 1 tbsp ground coriander
- Salt and ground black pepper to taste
- ¼ tsp baking soda
- ½ tsp baking powder
- Cooking spray

Directions:

1. After soaking your chickpeas in water for 24 hours, loosen and remove the skins by rubbing them with your fingers. Rinse and drain the skin-less chickpeas, and spread them on a large, clean dish towel. This will enable them to get dry.
2. Combine the garlic, onion, parsley, cilantro and the chickpeas into a food processor and blend until you have a rough paste. Pour the mixture into a large bowl.
3. Into the bowl containing the blended mixture, toss in cumin, sriracha salt, chickpea flour, coriander, salt and pepper. Mix thoroughly before covering the bowl. Let the mixture rest for 1 hour.
4. Ensure that your air fryer is preheated at 375 F.
5. Add baking soda and baking powder to the chickpea mixture, before mixing thoroughly with your hands to ensure even combination. Mold the mixture into 15 balls of equal sizes, pressing each ball mildly to form patties. Spray the patties with cooking spray.
6. Arrange seven falafel patties in the air fryer basket, and allow cooking for 10 minutes.
7. Remove the cooked falafel and place them on a plate.
8. Do the same for the other eight falafels, cooking for 10-12 minutes.

Macaroni and Cheese Toasties in the Airfryer

Prep + Cook Time: 15 minutes | Servings: 1

Ingredients:

- 2 slices white bread
- 4 tbsp macaroni cheese
- 1 oz cheddar cheese
- 1 small egg, beaten
- Salt and ground black pepper to taste

Directions:

1. Make a sandwich by layering the bread alongside the macaroni cheese and the cheddar cheese.
2. With the second slice of bread on the top, slice the sandwich diagonally.
3. Apply the beaten egg to either side of the bread, followed by sprinkles of pepper and salt.
4. Ensure that your air fryer is preheated to 355 F.
5. Transfer the sandwich in the air fryer and allow to cook for 5 minutes.
6. Withdraw when the bread is crunchy, and the cheese melted.
7. Serve.

Macaroni and Cheese Mini Quiche Recipe

Prep + Cook Time: 30 minutes | Servings: 4

Ingredients:

- Shortcrust pastry
- 1 tsp garlic puree
- 2 tbsp Greek yoghurt
- 8 tbsp leftover macaroni and cheese
- 2 large eggs, beaten
- 12 oz whole milk
- Grated cheese, optional

Directions:

1. After preparing your ramekins, rub the bottom with some flour.
2. Transfer the shortcrust pastry on the bottom of the ramekins.
3. Get a clean small bowl, and in it, mix garlic, Greek yogurt and the unused macaroni.
4. Fill the ramekins with the yogurt and garlic mixture (up to ¾ full).
5. Get a separate bowl and mix the eggs and milk. Pour the mixture over the macaroni cheese.
6. Ensure that your air fryer is preheated to 355 F.
7. Pour the cheese as toppings on the ramekins and transfer them into the air fryer.
8. Allow cooking for 20 minutes.
9. Withdraw and serve.

Rosemary Potato Wedges (ver. 1)

Prep + Cook Time: 25 minutes | Servings: 4

Ingredients:

- 2 russet potatoes, sliced into 12 wedges each with skin on
- 1 tbsp extra-virgin olive oil
- 2 tsp seasoned salt
- 1 tbsp finely chopped fresh rosemary

Directions:

1. Ensure that your air fryer is preheated to 380 F.
2. Combine the potatoes in a large bowl add the olive oil. Add sprinkles of seasoned salt and rosemary. Mix to coat the potatoes very well.
3. Transfer the coated potatoes into the air fryer basket, maintaining an even layer arrangement. You may work in batches to ensure that all the potatoes are well fried.
4. Each batch should be air-fried for about 10 minutes at first, and then flip using tongs. The frying should resume after flipping and continue until done as desired – perhaps for an additional 10 minutes.

Rosemary Roast Potatoes (ver. 2)

Prep + Cook Time: 20 minutes | Servings: 4

Ingredients:

- 2 large potatoes
- 1 tsp rosemary
- 1 tbsp olive oil
- Salt and ground black pepper to taste

Directions:

1. After peeling the potatoes, quarter them into the shapes suitable for roasting.
2. Transfer the cut potatoes into the air fryer and add a tablespoon of olive oil. Then allow cooking for about 10 minutes at 360 F.
3. After cooking, place them in a mixing bowl. Sprinkle the cooked potatoes with salt, pepper, and rosemary.
4. Mix well and then serve.

Baked Potatoes

Prep + Cook Time: 1 hour 5 minutes | Servings: 2

Ingredients:

- 2 large russet potatoes, scrubbed
- 1 tbsp peanut oil
- ½ tsp coarse sea salt

Directions:

1. Ensure that your air fryer is preheated to 400 F.
2. Coat the potatoes with peanut oil, and sprinkle with salt.
3. Transfer the coated potatoes into the basket of the air fryer.
4. Allow cooking until the potatoes are done – perhaps for 1 hour.
5. Pierce the cooked potatoes to check if they are done.

Garlic and Parsley Baby Potatoes

Prep + Cook Time: 30 minutes | Servings: 4

Ingredients:

- 1 lb baby potatoes, cut into quarters
- 1 tbsp avocado oil
- ¼ tsp salt
- ½ tsp granulated garlic
- ½ tsp dried parsley

Directions:

1. Ensure that your air fryer is pre-heated to 350 F.
2. In a clean bowl, add the potatoes and oil.
3. Toss the potatoes to coat, and add ¼ teaspoon granulated garlic and ¼ teaspoon parsley. Toss the potatoes again to coat.
4. Add the remaining garlic, parsley, and salt and toss for the last time.
5. Transfer the potatoes into the air fryer basket and allow to cook, while tossing sometime, until you have a golden brown color. This may take about 20 or 25 minutes.

Airfryer Crispy Roasted Onion Potatoes

Prep + Cook Time: 25 minutes | Servings: 4-6

Ingredients:

- 2 lb baby red potatoes
- 2 tbsp olive oil
- 1 envelope Lipton onion soup mix

Directions:

1. Split the potatoes, and place the pieces into the olive oil placed in a medium bowl. In the same bowl, add the onion soup mix and stir coat all the potatoes very well.
2. Transfer the coated potatoes into the air fryer basket and cook for 17 to 20 minutes at 390 F. Withdraw until the potatoes are tender and golden brown. You may stir the potatoes halfway through.
3. Serve.

Patatas Bravas

Prep + Cook Time: 27 minutes | Servings: 4

Ingredients:

- 10 oz red potato, cut into 1-inch chunks
- 1 tbsp avocado oil (peanut oil; safflower oil; coconut oil)
- 1 tsp garlic powder
- Pinch of sea salt and ground black pepper

Seasoning:

- 1 tbsp smoked paprika
- Sea salt and ground black pepper to taste
- ½ tsp cayenne, optional

Garnish:

- Garlic aioli
- Dried chives

Directions:

1. Boil enough water in a pot.
2. Place the cut red potatoes into the water, and allow to cook for about 6 minutes.
3. With the aid of a filter, remove the potatoes instantly and transfer them to a kitchen towel to cool and pat dry.
4. Leave the potatoes for about 15 minutes, so that it cools to room temperature. Once they are dry, transfer them to a large bowl, and add avocado oil, garlic powder, pepper, and sea salt.
5. Coat the potatoes in the mixture and place them into the basket of your air-fryer. You may work in batches to avoid overcrowding and ensure proper frying.
6. Set your air fryer to 390 F and allow the potatoes air-fry for about 15 minutes. Withdraw the basket after 7 minutes and shake. You may spray the potatoes with the avocado oil one more time before frying. Once you have a golden brown layer on the outside, and crispy flakes, stop the frying.
7. Place the "fried" potatoes in a bowl. Spray again with avocado oil (lightly), and add the seasonings.
8. Coat the potatoes generously with the seasoned oil and serve immediately with your preferred condiment.

Potato Hay

Prep + Cook Time: 1 hour 10 minutes | Servings: 4

Ingredients:

- 2 russet potatoes
- 1 tbsp canola oil
- Kosher salt and ground black pepper to taste

Directions:

1. Make the potatoes into spiral shapes with the aid of the medium grating attachment on a spiralizer. Then cut the spirals after four or five rotations using kitchen shears.
2. Transfer the potato spirals into a bowl of water, and allow to soak for about 20 minutes. Remove the water and rinse thoroughly. Using paper towels, pat the potatoes dry, getting out as much moisture as possible.
3. Move the dried potato spirals into a large resealable plastic bag. Add salt, pepper, and oil into the bag and toss the spirals to coat them properly.
4. Ensure that your air fryer is preheated to 360 F.
5. Divide the potato spirals into two – transfer one half to the air fryer basket and cook for 5 minutes – until you have a golden color.
6. Then increase the temperature to 390 F. Remove the basket and toss the potato spirals with the aid of tongs, and return them into the fryer. Resume cooking, while sometimes stirring, for the next 10 – 12 minutes or until you have a golden brown color.
7. Reduce the temperature to 360 F and do the same for the other half of the spirals.

Super Easy Potato Gratin

Prep + Cook Time: 35 minutes | Servings: 4

Ingredients:

- 2 large potatoes
- 1 tbsp plain flour
- 4 oz coconut cream
- 2 eggs beaten
- 2 oz cheddar cheese

Directions:

1. Cut the potatoes into very thin slices while retaining the skin.
2. Transfer the potato slices into the air fryer – allow to cook for 10 minutes at 360 F.
3. While cooking the potatoes, prepare the sauce by combining flour, coconut cream, and two eggs and mixing till there is a consistent thickness.
4. Withdraw the potatoes from the air fryer, and line the bottom of four ramekins.
5. Cover with the cream mixture and some sprinkles of cheese.
6. Allow cooking for an extra 10 minutes on 390 F.
7. Serve.

Make Loaded Potatoes

Prep + Cook Time: 30 minutes | Servings: 2

Ingredients:

- 11 oz baby Yukon Gold potatoes (about 8 [2-inch] potatoes)
- 1 tsp olive oil
- 2 center-cut bacon slices
- 1/8 tsp kosher salt
- 2 tbsp reduced-fat sour cream
- ½ oz finely shredded reduced-fat Cheddar cheese (about 2 tbsp)
- 1½ tbsp chopped fresh chives

Directions:

1. Coat the potatoes in oil and transfer them into the air fryer basket.
2. Allow to cook at 350 F or until they are tender (check with a fork) while stirring sometimes.
3. While cooking the potatoes, get a medium skillet and cook the bacon in it over medium heat for about 7 minutes or until crispy.
4. Remove the bacon and crumble. Transfer the potatoes on a serving platter and split them by crushing them lightly.
5. Drizzle with bacon drippings. Combine crumbled bacon, salt, sour cream, cheese, and chives and top the potatoes with the mixture. Serve.

Small Jacket Potatoes with Rosemary

Prep + Cook Time: 30 minutes | Servings: 4

Ingredients:

- 1 lb small new potatoes, unpeeled
- ½ tbsp olive oil
- 1 tbsp fresh rosemary
- 2 cloves garlic, sliced
- Coarse sea salt
- Freshly ground black pepper to taste

Directions:

1. Ensure that the air fryer is preheated to 360 F.
2. Wash the small new potatoes thoroughly under running water.
3. When clean, pat-dry using a kitchen paper.
4. Get a clean bowl, and in it, combine olive oil, rosemary, and garlic.
5. Coat the small new potatoes with this mixture.
6. Transfer the coated potatoes into the air fryer and allow to air-fry for 24 minutes or until they are crispy and done.
7. Withdraw the fried potatoes and place them in a serving dish.
8. Add sprinkles of salt and pepper.
9. Serve alongside grilled fish or meat.
10. Another way to go about the potatoes is to slice them into blocks and submerge them under water for about 30 minutes. Then drain them thoroughly and dry them by patting with kitchen paper.

Stuffed Potatoes

Prep + Cook Time: 1 hour | Servings: 4

Ingredients:

- 4 baking potatoes, peeled and halved
- 3 tsp olive oil, divided
- ½ cup Cheddar cheese, divided
- ½ yellow onion, diced fine
- 2 slices bacon

Directions:

1. Ensure that your air fryer is preheated to 350 F.
2. Using a teaspoon of oil, brush the potatoes gently.
3. Transfer the brushed potatoes into the air fryer basket and allow cooking for 10 minutes.
4. Remove after 10 minutes and brush again with an extra teaspoon oil.
5. Resume cooking in the air fryer, for another 10 minutes.
6. Remove again and coat with the remaining oil.
7. Now cook until tender – for an additional 10 minutes.
8. Cut the cooked potatoes in half and spoon the insides into a bowl. Add ¼ cup Cheddar cheese and mix well.
9. Combine the bacon and onion in a skillet and cook over medium-high heat. Turn sometimes and withdraw once the bacon is evenly browned. This takes about 10 minutes.
10. Combine the potato-Cheddar cheese mixture with bacon and onion. Stuff the skins with the mix, and sprinkle the remaining cheese on top.
11. Put back the stuffed potatoes into the air fryer and allow to cook for about 6 minutes or until you have the cheese melted. Serve.

Potato-Skin Wedges

Prep + Cook Time: 55 minutes | Servings: 4

Ingredients:

- 4 medium russet potatoes
- 1 cup water
- ¼ tsp ground black pepper
- 1 tsp paprika
- ¼ tsp salt
- 3 tbsp canola oil

Directions:

1. In a large, clean pot, put the potatoes and cover them with salt water. Bring the water to a boil.
2. Once boiling, reduce the heat to medium-low and allow to simmer until the potatoes are tender – it takes about 20 minutes. Remove the water and transfer the potatoes into a bowl, and then into a refrigerator. Leave in the refrigerator for about 30 minutes or until completely cool.
3. Get a clean mixing bowl and make a mixture of black pepper, paprika, salt, and oil. Quarter the cooled potatoes and submerge them in the mixture made in the mixing bowl.
4. Ensure that the air fryer is preheated to 400 F.
5. Divide the potato wedges into two. Place one half into the air fryer basket gently, skin-side down. Avoid overcrowding.
6. Allow cooking for 13-15 minutes or until golden brown.
7. Do the same for the other half of the wedges.

Restaurant Style Garlic Potatoes

Prep + Cook Time: 25 minutes | Servings: 2

Ingredients:

- 6 small potatoes
- 3 rashers unsmoked bacon
- 1 tsp garlic puree
- 2 tsp olive oil
- Salt and ground black pepper to taste

Directions:

1. Chop the peeled potatoes into medium-sized cubes.
2. Transfer them into the air fryer and add a teaspoon of olive oil.
3. Allow cooking for 10 minutes in the air fryer at 360 F.
4. Meanwhile, dice the bacon and combine the bacon, garlic, extra teaspoon of olive oil, pepper and salt into a separate bowl.
5. Remove the cooked potatoes and toss them into the bowl containing the mixture. Mix thoroughly.
6. Get a big piece of silver foil. On the foil, place the potato and the bacon mixture. Make a small cut in the silver foil to create an avenue for breathing.
7. Return into the air fryer and allow to cook at the same temperature for an extra 10 minutes.
8. Withdraw and serve.

Roasted Paprika Potatoes with Greek Yoghurt

Prep + Cook Time: 55 minutes | Servings: 4

Ingredients:

- 1 and 2/3 lbs waxy potatoes
- 1 tbsp spicy paprika
- 2 tbsp olive oil
- Freshly ground black pepper to taste
- 5 oz Greek yoghurt

Directions:

1. Ensure that the air fryer is preheated to 360 F.
2. Chop the peeled potatoes into 1 - inch cubes, and allow them to soak in water for about 30 minutes.
3. Drain the water and pat the cubes dry using kitchen paper.
4. Get a medium-sized bowl, and combine paprika, one tablespoon olive oil, and pepper.
5. Coat the potato cubes in the mixture of spices and oil.
6. Transfer the coated potato cubes into the air fryer basket and allow to fry for 19 minutes or until the cubes are golden brown. Ensure that you turn them regularly during frying.
7. Combine the Greek yogurt with the remaining spoonful of olive oil, salt, and pepper in a small bowl. Add sprinkles of paprika.
8. Serve the potato cubes in a platter and sprinkle with salt, alongside the yogurt mixture as a dip. You may add kebabs or a ribeye.

Airfryer Spanish Spicy Potatoes (Patatas Bravas)

Prep + Cook Time: 35 minutes | Servings: 4

Ingredients:

- 3 large potatoes, peeled and chopped into chips
- 2 tbsp olive oil
- 4 oz homemade tomato sauce
- 1 small onion, peeled and diced
- 1 tomato, thinly diced
- 1 tsp rosemary
- 1 tsp paprika
- 1 tsp oregano
- 1 tsp chilli powder
- 2 tsp thyme
- 2 tsp coriander
- 1 tsp mixed spice
- 1 tbsp red wine vinegar
- Salt and ground black pepper to taste

Directions:

1. The first step is to put the chips in the air fryer, add olive oil, and allow to cook at 360 F for 15 minutes.
2. Meanwhile, prepare your sauce by combining the other ingredients in a mixing bowl.
3. Withdraw the cooked chips.
4. Place the tomato sauce in the baking dish of the air fryer and allow to cook for 8 minutes at 360 F.
5. Remove the sauce after 8 minutes and pour it over the potatoes.
6. Serve.

Hassleback Potatoes

Prep + Cook Time: 35 minutes | Servings: 4

Ingredients:

- 4 large potatoes
- Salt and ground black pepper to taste
- 1 tbsp parsley
- 1 tbsp fresh rosemary
- 1 tbsp olive oil
- 1 tbsp garlic puree
- 1 oz cheddar cheese, shredded

Directions:

1. On a clean chopping board, slice the four potatoes using the Hasselback potatoes method.
2. Add sprinkles of salt, parsley, and pepper on top of the potatoes, with some entering the gaps.
3. Transfer the sprinkled potatoes into the air fryer's grill pan.
4. Allow cooking for 15 minutes at 360 F.
5. Wear an oven glove and withdraw the potatoes from the air fryer. Transfer them onto the chopping board.
6. Get a clean mixing bowl and combine fresh rosemary, olive oil, and garlic.
7. Spread the mixture down the bottom, sides, and top of the potatoes with the fingers and thumbs. This ensures that the mixture goes down the slits while the potatoes cook.
8. Lastly, add sprinkles on top of cheddar cheese.
9. Allow cooking for an additional 10 minutes at 360 F.

Potato Latkes Bites

Prep + Cook Time: 35 minutes | Servings: 14 pieces

Ingredients:

- 4 large potatoes
- 1 large onion
- 4 large eggs, beaten
- 2 tsp kosher salt
- ½ tsp freshly ground black pepper

- 1/3 cup matzo meal
- 1 tbsp potato starch
- ½ tsp baking powder, optional
- Grapeseed oil

Tools:

- 1 (1.5 oz) silicone cheesecake bites mold
- 1 oil mister
- 1 air fryer

Directions:

1. Peel the washed potatoes, and grate them using the food processor. Transfer the grated potatoes into a bowl containing cold water. Keep the bowl somewhere safe.
2. Rinse the food processor and add onions. Grate.
3. Transfer the grated onions in a tea towel or paper towel to squeeze out all the liquid.
4. Get a medium mixing bowl and in it, combine the eggs, salt, pepper, matzo meal, potato starch, baking powder (optional) and finally, the grated onions.
5. Remove the potatoes from the water and save the starch left in the bowl. Squeeze all the water from the potatoes and transfer them into the onion mixture. Scoop out the starch from the potato bowl into the Latkes mixture.
6. Spray the silicone trays generously with oil. Fill each tray well with the latkes mixture and spray again with enough oil.
7. Transfer into the air fryer basket and allow to cook for 6 minutes at 350 F. Withdraw the air fryer basket and pop out bites into the air fryer. Spray generously and resume cooking for an extra 4 minutes but at 400°F.
8. Serve alongside sour cream and applesauce.

The Best Ever Air Fryer Fries

Prep + Cook Time: 35 minutes | Servings: 2

Ingredients:

- 4 medium potatoes
- 4 tbsp olive oil

- Salt and ground black pepper to taste

Directions:

1. Cut the peeled potatoes into fries.
2. Ensure that your air fryer is preheated to 360 F.
3. Transfer the fries into the air fryer basket and add the olive oil. Allow cooking for 2 minutes and shake.
4. Cook again for 8 minutes before shaking again.
5. Resume cooking and continue for another 15 minutes. If you want the fries to appear golden, cook for 20 minutes at 390 F instead.
6. Add salt and pepper. Serve.

Homemade Fries

Prep + Cook Time: 1 hour 25 minutes | Servings: 4

Ingredients:

- 1 and 2/3 lbs waxy potatoes, peeled
- 1 tbsp olive oil
- Salt to taste

Directions:

1. Slice the potatoes into long French fries – 8 mm thick each. You may use a French fry cutter too.
2. Soak the fries in water for not less than 30 minutes.
3. Drain and pat dry with kitchen paper.
4. Ensure that your air fryer is preheated to 320 F. Transfer the fries into a large bowl and add the oil. Toss the fries to coat them well and place the coated fries into the air fryer basket.
5. Allow cooking for 18 minutes.
6. Withdraw the basket after 18 minutes and shake the fries.
7. Return and allow to cook for an additional 12 minutes at 360 F.
8. Halfway during cooking, remove the basket and shake the fries again.
9. Resume cooking for the remaining 6 minutes or until the fries are golden brown.
10. Sprinkle the fries with salt to taste.
11. Serve on a platter.

Parmesan Truffle Oil Fries

Prep + Cook Time: 55 minutes | Servings: 6

Ingredients:

- 3 large russet potatoes peeled and cut lengthwise
- 1 tbsp olive oil
- 1 tbsp canola oil
- 2 tbsp white truffle oil
- Salt and ground black pepper to taste
- 1 tbsp parsley chopped
- 1 tsp paprika
- 2 tbsp parmesan shredded

Directions:

1. Pour cold water into a large bowl and soak the sliced potatoes in it for 30 minutes or an hour.
2. On a flat surface, coat the fries with olive oil, canola oil, one tablespoon of white truffle oil, alongside seasonings.
3. Divide the fries into two, transfer half into the air fryer basket. Set the temperature to 380 F and allow to cook for 15-20 minutes. Pause cooking after 10 minutes and shake the basket once.
4. If you want crispier fries, you may have to cook for more time, depending on your preference. And if the crispiness is obvious before 15 minutes, remove the fries.
5. Do the same for the other half.
6. Once you remove the fries from the air fryer, add the remaining parmesan and truffle oil.
7. Add shredded parsley as toppings. Serve.

Five Guys Cajun Fries

Prep + Cook Time: 35 minutes | Servings: 2

Ingredients:

- 1.5 lbs white potatoes, peeled into chips
- 2 tsp mexican seasoning
- 1 tbsp cajun spice
- Salt and ground black pepper to taste
- 1 tsp coriander
- 1 tsp mixed spice
- ½ tsp olive oil

Directions:

1. Transfer the peeled potatoes into a medium-sized bowl. Pour enough water until the potatoes are submerged. Leave in the fridge for 15 minutes.
2. Drain after 15 minutes and get rid of excess water. Pat the potatoes dry.
3. After seasoning the potatoes thoroughly, add olive oil and mix well using your hands. Ensure that the fries are well and evenly coated.
4. Transfer the French fries into the air fryer basket, and allow cooking for 10 minutes at 320 F.
5. Withdraw the basket and shake after 10 minutes.
6. Resume cooking for another 5 minutes, this time at 390 F to ensure crispiness of the fries.
7. Remove and serve.

Skin on French Fries

Prep + Cook Time: 20 minutes | Servings: 2

Ingredients:

- 2 large white potatoes
- 1 tsp olive oil
- 2 tsp chives, dried
- Salt and ground black pepper to taste

Directions:

1. While scrubbing the potatoes, get rid of any eyes.
2. Slice the washed potatoes into French fries and transfer the same into a bowl.
3. Add the olive oil and the entire seasoning in the bowl and mix well with your hands.
4. Transfer the coated slices into the air fryer basket, and allow cooking for 15 minutes at 360 F.
5. Shake after 7 or 8 minutes.
6. After 15 minutes, withdraw the fries and serve alongside mayonnaise or ketchup.

Flourless Mashed Potato Cakes

Prep + Cook Time: 30 minutes | Servings: 4

Ingredients:

- 4 lbs white potatoes, peeled and diced
- 9 oz vegetable stock
- 4 tbsp whole milk
- Salt and ground black pepper to taste
- 1 tbsp chives
- 4 oz cheddar cheese

Directions:

1. The first step is to prepare the mashed potatoes. Place the peeled and diced white potatoes into the Instant Pot. Pour in the vegetable stock too and place the lid on the Instant Pot. With the valve set to sealing, allow cooking for 25 minutes on manual.
2. After cooking, use the quick pressure release and drain the potatoes, but retain them in the Instant Pot. Use a masher or blender to mash the potatoes, while adding a little milk sometimes. Add salt and pepper to season to taste.
3. Transfer the mashed potato in the freezer until it becomes very cold and a bit hard – this is the perfect texture for making mashed potato cakes. You may decide to leave in the fridge overnight – it offers the same results.
4. Now you can prepare the mashed potato cakes by adding the seasoning and the cheese in the Instant Pot while mixing thoroughly with your hands. Mold the mixture into mashed potato cake shapes.
5. Inside the air fryer grill pan, arrange four mashed potato cakes – the first batch. Allow cooking for 12 minutes at 360 F. Do the same for other batches.
6. Serve the cooked mashed potato cakes while warm.

Super Easy Potato Gratin

Prep + Cook Time: 35 minutes | Servings: 4

Ingredients:

- 2 large potatoes
- 4 oz coconut cream
- 1 tbsp plain flour
- 2 eggs, beaten
- 2 oz cheddar cheese

Directions:

1. Slice the potatoes thinly while retaining the skin.
2. Transfer the slices into the air fryer and cook for 10 minutes at 360 F.
3. Meanwhile, prepare the sauce by combining coconut cream, flour, and two eggs. Mix until you have a consistent thickness.
4. Withdraw the crispy potatoes from the air fryer and line the bottom of four ramekins.
5. Cover with the cream mixture, and sprinkle with the cheese.
6. Now cook for an extra 10 minutes at 390 F.
7. Serve.

Poutine

Prep + Cook Time: 1 hour | Servings: 4

Ingredients:

- 1 ¾ lbs russet potatoes
- 4 tbsp vegetable oil, divided
- ½ tsp salt
- ½ tsp pepper
- 1 tbs all-purpose flour
- 1½ cups beef broth
- 1 dash Worcestershire sauce
- 1 cup part-skim mozzarella cheese, cubed

Directions:

1. Cut the scrubbed potatoes into fries of the same size – about 0.5-inch thick on all sides.
2. Rinsed the fries in water and drain. Remove the remaining water with a clean kitchen towel.
3. Transfer the fries into the air fryer's pan. Spray half of the oil and cook at 360 F for 25 minutes or until you have golden, crisp, and cooked through fries. Add half of the salt and pepper to season fries.
4. While cooking the fries, heat the remaining oil in a small saucepan over medium heat. Pour in the flour and cook, while stirring. Stop frying after a minute or until the flour is lightly browned. Whisk in broth and Worcestershire sauce and allow the mixture to boil.
5. Cook the mixture, while often stirring, until it is thick enough – this may take about 5 minutes. Add the remaining salt and pepper to taste.
6. Place the fries evenly in four serving plates, while topping each plate with an equal amount of cheese. Melt the cheese by drizzling with hot gravy.

Hash Brown Recipe

Prep + Cook Time: 35 minutes | Servings: 8

Ingredients:

- 4 large potatoes, peeled and finely grated
- 2 tsp vegetable oil
- 2 tsp chili flakes
- 1 tsp onion powder, optional
- 1 tsp garlic powder, optional
- Ground black pepper to taste
- Salt to taste
- 2 tbsp corn flour

Directions:

1. After the shredded potatoes have been soaked in cold water, drain the water and repeat the step to get rid of excess starch from the potatoes.
2. Get a non-stick pan, and in it, heat one teaspoon of vegetable oil. Saute the shredded potatoes until they are cooked slightly – it takes about 3 or 4 minutes.
3. Allow the potatoes to cool down before transferring into a plate.
4. Combine chili flakes, onion powder, garlic, pepper, salt, and corn flour and mix thoroughly.
5. Spread the mixture over the potatoes plate and pat firmly using the fingers.
6. Keep in the fridge for 20 minutes.
7. Ensure that your air fryer is preheated to 360 F.
8. Remove the refrigerated potato and halve it into pieces using a knife.
9. Using some oil, brush the wire basket of the air fryer gently.
10. Transfer the hash brown pieces into the basket and allow to air-fry for 15 minutes at 360 F.
11. Withdraw the basket and turn the hash browns to the other side after 6 minutes. This ensures even frying.
12. Serve while hot alongside ketchup.

Tex-Mex Hash Browns

Prep + Cook Time: 1 hour 10 minutes | Servings: 4

Ingredients:

- 1 ½ lbs potatoes, peeled and cut into 1-inch cubes
- 1 tbsp olive oil
- 1 red bell pepper, seeded and cut into 1-inch pieces
- 1 jalapeno, seeded and cut into 1-inch rings
- 1 small onion, cut into 1-inch pieces
- ½ tsp olive oil
- 1 pinch salt and ground black pepper to taste
- ½ tsp ground cumin
- ½ tsp taco seasoning mix

Directions:

1. After soaking the potatoes for 20 minutes in cold water, drain and dry with a clean towel, before placing them in a large bowl.
2. Ensure that your air fryer is preheated to 320 F.
3. Spread one tablespoon of olive oil over the potatoes and toss to ensure even coating.
4. Transfer the coated potatoes into the air fryer basket and set the timer for 18 minutes.
5. Meanwhile, combine bell pepper, the jalapeno, and onion in the bowl where the potatoes were initially kept. Add the ½ teaspoon olive oil, salt, pepper, ground cumin, and taco seasoning.
6. Withdraw the potatoes from the air fryer and transfer into the bowl containing the vegetable mixture.
7. With the empty basket back into the air fryer, set the temperature to 365 F.
8. Toss the contents of the bowl to ensure that the potatoes are well mixed with the seasoning and vegetables.
9. Return the mixture into the air fryer basket.
10. Allow cooking for 6 minutes, after which you withdraw and shake the basket.
11. Resume cooking until you have crispy and brown potatoes – this takes about 5 minutes or more.
12. Withdraw the crispy brown potatoes and serve immediately.

Sweet Potato Fries

Prep + Cook Time: 1 hour | Servings: 4

Ingredients:

- ¼ tsp garlic powder
- ¼ tsp fine sea salt
- 1 tsp chopped fresh thyme
- 1 tbsp olive oil
- 2 (6-oz) sweet potatoes, peeled and cut into 1/4-inch sticks
- Cooking spray

Directions:

1. In a clean medium bowl, combine the garlic powder, salt, thyme, and olive oil. Place the sweet potato in the mixture and toss well to coat thoroughly.
2. Apply some cooking spray as a coating for the air fryer basket. Transfer the sweet potatoes into the basket, ensuring they are arranged in a single layer. If necessary, work in batches.
3. Cook each batch at 400 F until the sweet potatoes are tender on the inside and lightly browned on the outside. This takes about 14 minutes.
4. After the first seven minutes, turn the fries.
5. Do the same for the other batches.
6. Serve the cooked sweet potatoes.

Spicy Sweet Potato Wedges

Prep + Cook Time: 30 minutes | Servings: 2

Ingredients:

- 2 large sweet potatoes, peeled
- 1 tsp chilli powder
- 1 tsp cumin
- 1 tsp mustard powder
- 1 tbsp mexican seasoning
- Salt and ground black pepper to taste
- 1 tbsp olive oil

Directions:

1. Chop the peeled sweet potatoes into the shape of wedges.
2. Ensure that your air fryer is preheated to 360 F for 5 minutes.
3. Get a clean mixing bowl and in it, combine your seasonings and mix thoroughly. Toss in the potato wedges until they are evenly coated.
4. Transfer the coated wedges into the air fryer, add some olive oil and allow cooking for 20 minutes. Shake the basket at 5 minutes' intervals until the cooking is complete.
5. Serve the cooked sweet potatoes alongside a thousand island dip and sprinkles of a little extra chili powder.

Crispy Crunchy Sweet Potato Fries

Prep + Cook Time: 30 minutes | Servings: 6

Ingredients:

- 2 large sweet potatoes peeled and cut lengthwise
- 1 tbsp olive oil
- 1 tbsp canola oil
- 2 tsp garlic powder
- 2 tsp paprika
- 1 ½ tbsp corn starch
- Salt and ground black pepper to taste

Directions:

1. Soak the sliced sweet potatoes in a large bowl containing cold water for an hour.
2. After an hour, transfer them into a Ziploc bag alongside the cornstarch.
3. Seal the bag and shake to ensure that the fries are thoroughly coated.
4. On a clean flat surface, spread the fries and coat them with the olive oil, canola, and seasonings.
5. Transfer the coated fries into the basket of the air fryer. With the temperature set to 380 F, allow cooking for about 25 minutes. Stop the cooking after every 10 minutes to shake the basket.
6. If your preference is the crispy type of fries, allow them to cook for more time while checking to ensure that they do not get burnt.
7. Serve when cool.

Garlic Sweet Potato Fries

Prep + Cook Time: 20 minutes | Servings: 2

Ingredients:

- 2 small sweet potatoes, peeled
- ½ tsp garlic powder
- 2 tbsp olive oil
- ¼ tsp salt

Directions:

1. Cut your potatoes into fries of desired thickness and transfer them into a food-safe plastic bag.
2. Add the other ingredients and toss to coat thoroughly.
3. Place the coated fries into the air fryer basket, while leveling them as much as you can.
4. Allow cooking for about 7 minutes at 350 F.
5. In the case of thicker fries, stir them after 7 minutes, and cook for an additional 7 minutes.
6. Do the same for all the fries until they are cooked to your taste.
7. Optionally, sprinkle extra salt when serving.

Sweet Potato Chips

Prep + Cook Time: 25 minutes | Servings: 2

Ingredients:

- 1 medium sweet potato, peeled and sliced crossways into 1/8-inch slices
- 1 tsp avocado oil
- ½ tsp Creole seasoning, or to taste

Directions:

1. Ensure that your air fryer is preheated to 400 F.
2. Get a large bowl, and place the sweet potato slices in it, add the avocado oil and stir well to ensure that each piece is well coated. Pour the creole seasoning and stir to make it mix with the potato.
3. Transfer the coated slices into a thin layer on the air fryer basket's base.
4. Allow cooking for 7 minutes, after which you turn and shake the fries to ensure even cooking.
5. Resume cooking until the fries are crisp according to your taste – this may take 6 minutes or more.
6. Place the cooked potato slices on a rack and allow to cool.
7. Serve.

Sweet Potato Hash

Prep + Cook Time: 30 minutes | Servings: 6

Ingredients:

- 2 slices bacon, cut into small pieces
- 2 tbsp olive oil
- 1 tbsp smoked paprika
- 1 tsp sea salt
- 1 tsp dried dill weed
- 1 tsp ground black pepper
- 2 large sweet potato, cut into small cubes

Directions:

1. Ensure that your air fryer is preheated to 400 F.
2. In a large bowl, combine the bacon, olive oil, paprika, salt, dill, and pepper. Toss the sweet potato in the mixture and then place it in the preheated air fryer.
3. Allow cooking for about 12 or 16 minutes. Check and stir after the first 10 minutes, and then at intervals of 3 minutes until you have browned and crispy potatoes

Sweet Potato Tots

Prep + Cook Time: 1 hour 10 minutes | Servings: 24

Ingredients:

- 2 sweet potatoes, peeled
- ½ tsp Cajun seasoning
- Olive oil cooking spray
- Sea salt to taste

Directions:

1. Toss sweet potatoes into a pot of boiling water and allow the potatoes to boil until they can be pierced with a fork without losing firmness. This should take about 15 minutes. Avoid excessive boiling as this may lead to messy potatoes.
2. Drain the cooked potatoes and leave to cool.
3. Grate the cool potatoes using a box grater and transfer into a bowl.
4. Combine the grated potatoes alongside Cajun seasoning.
5. Shape the mixture into tot-shaped cylinders.
6. After spraying the olive oil spray in the air fryer basket, transfer the tots in it – forming a single row while leaving space between the tots and the sides of the basket.
7. Spray the arranged tots with olive oil spray and add sprinkles of sea salt.
8. Allow the tots to cook for 8 minutes at 400 F. Withdraw the basket and turn the tots, then spray with more olive oil spray and add more sprinkles of sea salt.
9. Cook for an extra 8 minutes.
10. Allow to cool and serve.

Rosemary Sweet Potatoes

Prep + Cook Time: 25 minutes | Servings: 2

Ingredients:

- 6 sweet potatoes
- 2 tbsp olive oil
- Salt and ground black pepper to taste
- Handful fresh rosemary
- Paleo ranch dressing, optional

Directions:

1. Ensure that your air fryer is preheated to 360 F.
2. Divide the washed rosemary into two halves – put one half to one side and chop the other half into fine pieces.
3. Cut the sweet potato into medium slices while retaining the skins. Dip them in olive oil and season with pepper and salt.
4. Transfer the drizzled and seasoned slices into the air fryer, and sprinkle the small bits of rosemary over.
5. Allow cooking for 15 minutes at 360 F.
6. Withdraw the basket after 15 minutes and shake the slices.
7. Return the basket and allow to cook for an additional 5 minutes but at 390 F.
8. Stop cooking when the slices are crisp enough.
9. Season with fresh uncooked rosemary. You may serve alongside homemade Paleo ranch dressing.

Guilt Free Vegetable Fries

Prep + Cook Time: 25 minutes | Servings: 4

Ingredients:

- 5 oz sweet potato, peeled
- 5 oz carrots, peeled
- 5 oz courgette, peeled
- 2 tbsp olive oil
- 1 tsp thyme
- Pinch basil
- Pinch mixed spice
- Salt and ground black pepper to taste

Directions:

1. Chop your peeled sweet potato, carrots, and courgettes into chunks of chips with different shapes.
2. Gather them in the air fryer, alongside the olive oil.
3. Allow cooking for 18 minutes at 360 F.
4. Shake during the 5th and 12th minute to ensure even cooking.
5. Withdraw the cooked chips from the air fryer and transfer them into a bowl.
6. Add the seasoning and shake well to mix.
7. Serve.

Big Fat Veggie Fritters

Prep + Cook Time: 35 minutes | Servings: 2

Ingredients:

- 3 large carrots
- 1 small onion
- 1 large sweet potato
- 4 oz courgette
- 3 oz turmeric granola
- Salt and ground black pepper to taste
- 1 lime rind and juice

Directions:

1. Dice the peeled carrots, onion, and sweet potato alongside the courgette too.
2. Transfer everything into the Instant Pot and allow to steam for 5 minutes using the steam option.
3. After cooking for 5 minutes, remove the pressure and drain the vegetables.
4. Squeeze any excess moisture out of the vegetables using a tea towel. When completely drained, transfer into a mixing bowl.
5. Blend the turmeric granola in a blender. Pour the blend into the mixing bowl containing the drained vegetables, and add salt, pepper, as well as the juice and rind of one lime.
6. Mix thoroughly and mold the mixture into fritter-like shapes.
7. Fridge the shapes for about an hour, to harden them a bit.
8. Remove from the fridge after an hour and allow to cook for 15 minutes at 390 F.
9. Serve.

Airfryer Carrots Recipe

Prep + Cook Time: 20 minutes | Servings: 4

Ingredients:

- 6 large carrots, peeled
- 2 tbsp olive oil
- 1 tbsp oregano
- Salt and ground black pepper to taste
- Fresh parsley

Directions:

1. Make your peeled carrots into thick chips by slicing lengthways.
2. Sprinkle your air fryer basket with olive oil and arrange the sliced carrots in it.
3. Allow cooking at 360 F for 12 minutes.
4. Shake thoroughly and add the seasonings after 12 minutes.
5. Return the basket into the air fryer and allow to cook for an extra 2 minutes but at 400 F.
6. Withdraw and serve alongside extra fresh parsley.

Honey Roasted Carrots

Prep + Cook Time: 17 minutes | Servings: 2-3

Ingredients:

- 3 cups of baby carrots or carrots cut into large chunks
- 1 tbsp olive oil
- 1 tbsp honey
- Salt and ground black pepper to taste

Directions:

1. Get a clean bowl and combine the carrots alongside the olive oil and honey.
2. Immerse the carrots in the mixture.
3. Add salt and pepper to taste.
4. Allow cooking in the air fryer at 395 F for 12 minutes.
5. Serve while hot.

Shoestring Carrots

Prep + Cook Time: 25 minutes | Servings: 1-2

Ingredients:

- 1 bag (10 oz) of julienned carrots (sold for cole-slaw)
- 1 tbsp olive oil
- Salt and ground black pepper to taste
- 1 tsp orange zest
- Apple cider vinegar in a spray bottle

Directions:

1. Get a clean medium bowl and combine the carrots and the olive oil, while coating the carrots lightly. Ensure that all the pieces of carrots are well coated, and then season with salt and pepper.
2. Transfer the coated carrots in the air-fryer preheated at 390 F.
3. Set the timer to 13 or 16 minutes, and allow the carrots to cook, while mixing them around after every few minutes.
4. Withdraw the carrots from the air fryer when they are becoming nicely brown. Be observant so that the pieces will not get too dark very quickly.
5. Transfer the cooked carrots into a serving bowl.
6. Add some orange zest, little apple cider vinegar sprays, and season to taste with more pepper and salt.
7. Serve while hot.

Slimming World Carrot Fritters

Prep + Cook Time: 25 minutes | Servings: 8

Ingredients:

- 6 large carrots peeled and diced
- 1¼ oz gluten free oats
- 1 tbsp thyme
- 1 tbsp parsley
- 1 tsp mustard powder
- Salt and ground black pepper to taste
- 1 large egg

Directions:

1. Put your carrots into your food processor and blitz them until they appear like grated carrots.
2. Season the oats and mix until the oats become blended.
3. After removing the lid of your food processor, withdraw the blade as well and crack your egg into the mixture.
4. After mixing with a fork, make the mixture into shapes of small cakes.
5. Open your air fryer and place the baking mat in the bottom, before layering the fritters on top of it. You may have to work in batches if your air fryer is small.
6. Allow cooking for 15 minutes at 360 F, while turning at the halfway point.
7. Serve the cooked carrots warm.

Oil Free Pumpkin French Fries

Prep + Cook Time: 25 minutes | Servings: 2

Ingredients:

- 10 oz pumpkin
- Salt and ground black pepper to taste
- 1 tbsp mustard
- 1 tsp thyme
- Tomato ketchup, optional

Directions:

1. Remove the seeds from the peeled pumpkin before slicing into French fries.
2. Transfer them into the air fryer; set to 395 F and allow cooking for 15 minutes.
3. After 7 minutes, shake and season with salt, pepper, mustard, and thyme.
4. Serve hot alongside tomato ketchup.

Oil Free Sticky Pumpkin Wedges

Prep + Cook Time: 30 minutes | Servings: 2

Ingredients:

- ½ medium pumpkin
- Salt and ground black pepper to taste
- 1 tbsp paprika
- 1 tsp turmeric
- 1 tbsp balsamic vinegar
- 1 lime juice only
- 1 cup paleo ranch dressing, optional

Directions:

1. With half of the pumpkin sliced into wedges of medium sizes, transfer them into the grill pan of your air fryer.
2. Set the timer to 20 minutes and allow cooking at 360 F.
3. After 20 minutes, open the air fryer.
4. Sprinkle the sliced pumpkins with the half of the seasonings, plus vinegar and lime.
5. Turn them over with thongs, and sprinkle the other half of the seasonings.
6. Then cook for an extra 5 minutes on either side at 390 F.
7. Serve with ranch dressing.

Spiced Pumpkin

Prep + Cook Time: 25 minutes | Servings: 2-3

Ingredients:

- 1½ lbs pumpkin (about 3 slices)
- 1 tbsp olive oil
- 3 cloves garlic, unpeeled
- Ground nutmeg
- Ground cinnamon
- Brown sugar
- Sea salt

Directions:

1. Using a brush, clean the pumpkin thoroughly, especially the skin, since we will be roasting with it.
2. Remove the seeds and discard them.
3. Ensure that your air fryer is preheated to 360 F.
4. Cut the pumpkin into cubes and slices, and transfer them into a clean bowl.
5. Spray some olive oil on the pumpkin, and rub on all surfaces.
6. Add the unpeeled garlic and season with ground nutmeg, ground cinnamon, sugar, and salt.
7. Transfer the pumpkin cubes/slices onto the baking sheet.
8. Move the baking sheet into the basket of the air fryer.
9. Allow air-roasting for 10-12 minutes, based on how thick the pumpkin slices or cubes are.

Butternut Squash Roasties

Prep + Cook Time: 15 minutes | Servings: 2

Ingredients:

- 1 small butternut squash
- 2 tbsp olive oil
- Mixed herbs chicken seasoning
- Salt and ground black pepper to taste

Directions:

1. Ensure that your air fryer is preheated to 360 F.
2. Peel the butternut squash and dice it.
3. With the butternut squash drizzled in olive oil, toss it in the unused mixed herb seasoning.
4. Then transfer it in the air fryer.
5. Set the timer to 10 minutes and allow cooking until you have a golden color appearance.
6. Serve alongside fresh herbs.

Pumpkin Tortilla Chips

Prep + Cook Time: 1 hour 10 minutes | Servings: 4

Ingredients:

- 2 tbsp olive oil
- 1 tbsp nutmeg
- Salt and ground black pepper to taste

Make the pumpkin tortillas:

- 10 oz plain flour
- 2 oz whole milk
- 1 oz butter
- 1 oz pumpkin pie puree
- 1 tbsp olive oil
- 1 tbsp mixed spice
- 1 tbsp nutmeg
- Salt and ground black pepper to taste

Directions:

1. Following the same way of making regular wraps, make the pumpkin tortillas as well. However, substitute less butter and less milk in the case of the pumpkin puree.
2. Cook the wraps in a frying pan, as usual.
3. To prepare the chips, brush one side of each of the six tortilla wraps with oil before stacking and cutting them into tortilla chip shapes.
4. Place them in the grill pan of the air fryer basket gently, and add sprinkles of salt, pepper, and nutmeg.
5. Set your air fryer to 400 F and allow cooking for 18 minutes or until they become golden brown.
6. Withdraw and serve alongside the pumpkin puree dipping sauce.

Air Fried Guacamole

Prep + Cook Time: 5 hours 25 minutes | Servings: 10

Ingredients:

- 1 egg
- 1 egg white
- 1/3 cup almond flour (coconut flour; tapioca or arrowroot powder)
- 3 oz gluten free panko (regular panko; wheat breadcrumbs)
- Cooking spray olive oil

Guacamole:

- 3 medium ripe avocados
- 1/3 cup chopped onion
- Juice from 1 lime
- 2 tsp cumin
- Fresh finely chopped cilantro to taste (about 1/3 cup)
- Sea salt and ground black pepper to taste
- 8 tbsp fine almond flour

Directions:

1. Get a clean bowl and in it, mix and mash all the guacamole ingredients, except the almond flour.
2. When the taste is what you desire, add the almond flour until the guacamole becomes as thick as the brownie batter. You may need to add extra tablespoons of almond flour to achieve the desired thickness. Add moderate lime juice, as excess will only make the guacamole loosen and wet. Place the bowl in the freezer and allow to harden for about 1-2 hours. Withdraw when the guacamole has hardened.
3. Use a non-stick foil or a parchment paper to line a baking sheet. Scoop out the hardened guacamole and shape it into a ball of a size of a ping pong ball. Transfer the ball-shaped guacamole on the baking tray. Do the same for the remaining guacamole.
4. Cover the tray with the non-stick foil and return to the freezer. Leave overnight or for 4 hours at least.
5. Ensure that your air fryer is preheated to 390 F.
6. Get a clean bowl and in it, beat the eggs together.
7. You may have to work in batches here, but at top speed. Spray a guacamole ball lightly with olive oil, and once sticky, dip it in the almond flour, then the egg mixture, and finally the panko crumbs. Do the same for the remaining guacamole balls, until the air fryer basket is filled. Make sure to leave a breathing space between the balls in the basket. All uncoated balls should be returned to the freezer.
8. Place the basket in the air fryer, and spray with a little olive oil.
9. Set the timer to 6-8 minutes and allow cooking until the outside appears golden brown. If the balls start cracking, remove them from the air fryer. Return them only when they are cold and firmer.
10. Now coat the uncoated balls and air-bake them.
11. Serve and enjoy.

Avocado Slices Recipe

Prep + Cook Time: 20 minutes | Servings: 2

Ingredients:

- 2 large avocados
- 3 limes juice and rind
- Salt and ground black pepper to taste
- 4 tbsp coriander
- 2 tbsp mexican seasoning
- 8 oz gluten free oats
- 3 tbsp Thousand Island
- 1 tbsp basil

Directions:

1. Remove the avocados' skin and chop them on the cutting board into shapes similar to the potato wedges.
2. Squeeze the juice in one of the limes over the chopped avocados.
3. Using pepper, salt, and a sprinkling of coriander, season the avocados to taste.
4. Blend the combination of the lime rind, seasoning, and the oats in a blender to produce a coarse mixture – just like the breadcrumbs.
5. Transfer the blended mixture into a shallow mixing bowl.
6. Immerse the avocados into the blended mixture.
7. Withdraw and place them on the grill pan of the air fryer.
8. Set the timer to 6 minutes and allow cooking at 360 F. Increase the heat to 400 F and allow to cook for another 3 minutes. Turn the avocados and let the other side to cook for another 3 minutes at the same heat.
9. Squeeze the remaining juice out of the lime and on to the air-fried avocado slices.
10. Serve alongside a preferred dipping sauce or a Thousand Island.

Avocado On Toast

Prep + Cook Time: 10 minutes | Servings: 4

Ingredients:

- 4 slices whole wheat bread
- 4 oz mashed avocado

Directions:

1. Allow a slice of toast to cook in the air fryer at 400 F for 4 minutes.
2. Turn it over and allow the other side to cook for an additional 4 minutes.
3. Spread the top of it with mashed avocado and serve.

Avocado Egg Boat

Prep + Cook Time: 10 minutes | Servings: 2

Ingredients:

- 2 medium avocados
- Salt and ground black pepper to taste
- Fresh chives
- Fresh parsley
- 4 small eggs

Directions:

1. Cut the avocados in half, thus giving you access to eject the stones and about 20% of the flesh. This makes the avocado wholes bigger.
2. Add salt, pepper, chives, and fresh parsley as seasonings.
3. Into each of the four halves, crack one egg and transfer them into the air fryer.
4. Allow cooking for 8 minutes at 360 F.
5. Add sprinkles of extra fresh parsley plus additional salt and pepper.
6. Serve.

Avocado Fries

Prep + Cook Time: 35 minutes | Servings: 4

Ingredients:

- 1½ tsp ground black pepper
- ½ cup (about 2 1/8 oz) all-purpose flour
- 2 large eggs
- 1 tbsp water
- ½ cup panko (Japanese-style breadcrumbs)
- 2 avocados, cut into 8 wedges each
- Cooking spray
- ¼ cup no-salt-added ketchup
- 2 tbsp canola mayonnaise
- 1 tbsp apple cider vinegar
- 1 tbsp Sriracha chili sauce
- ¼ tsp kosher salt

Directions:

1. In a clean shallow dish, combine the pepper and flour and stir thoroughly.
2. Get another shallow dish and beat eggs lightly while adding some water.
3. In the third shallow dish, put the panko and set aside.
4. Dip the avocado wedges into flour and shake off excess, then into the egg mixture, allowing any excess to drip off, and finally, dredge in the panko while pressing to adhere. Make a generous coating of the avocado wedges using the cooking spray.
5. In the air fryer basket, arrange the avocado wedges and allow to cook for 7-8 minutes at 400 F. Turn them halfway into cooking.
6. Meanwhile, combine the ketchup, mayonnaise, vinegar, and Sriracha in a separate small bowl to produce the sauce.
7. Withdraw the cooked wedges from the air fryer and sprinkle with salt.
8. Serve four avocado fries on each plate alongside two tablespoons of the sauce.

Zucchini Chips

Prep + Cook Time: 35 minutes | Servings:3- 4

Ingredients:

- 1 cup panko bread crumbs
- 3/4 cup grated Parmesan cheese
- 1 medium zucchini, thinly sliced
- 1 large egg, beaten
- Cooking spray

Directions:

1. Preheat an air fryer to 350 F before you begin preparing the zucchini.
2. Combine panko and Parmesan cheese on a plate. Dip 1 zucchini slice into beaten egg then into panko mixture, pressing to coat. Place zucchini slice on a wire baking rack and repeat with remaining slices. Lightly spray zucchini slices with cooking spray.
3. Place as many zucchini slices in the air fryer basket as you can without overlapping them.
4. Cook for 10 minutes. Flip with tongs. Cook for 2 minutes more. Remove from air fryer and repeat with remaining zucchini slices.

Flourless Mini Zucchini Fritter Bites

Prep + Cook Time: 25 minutes | Servings: 10

Ingredients:

- 4 oz zucchini
- 2 large eggs beaten
- 1 tsp mixed herbs
- 1 tsp oregano
- Salt and ground black pepper to taste
- 2 oz cheese
- 2 cups gluten free oats

Directions:

1. Preheat your air fryer to 360 F.
2. Start by grating your zucchini and removing any excess water from it by squeezing it out with your hands into a bowl.
3. Place your squeezed out zucchini and your beaten egg into a mixing bowl. Along with seasonings and cheese.
4. In a blender place your oats on the high setting and blend until they resemble fine bread crumbs.
5. Place the oats into the bowl a little at a time as it will go thick rather quickly.
6. Mix together and create bite sized balls.
7. Place in the air fryer for 12 minutes on 360 F.
8. Serve.

Guilt-Free Ranch Zucchini Chips

Prep + Cook Time: 25 minutes | Servings: 4

Ingredients:

- 1/8 tsp salt
- 1 pinch ground black pepper
- ¼ cup all-purpose flour
- ½ cup ranch dressing
- ¼ tsp garlic powder
- ½ cup whole wheat bread crumbs
- ¼ cup grated Parmesan cheese
- 2 zucchini, thinly sliced
- Cooking spray

Directions:

1. Ensure that your air fryer is preheated to 400 F.
2. Get a clean bowl and mix the salt, pepper, and flour.
3. Get another clean bowl and pour in the ranch dressing.
4. In a third bowl, mix the garlic powder, bread crumbs, and Parmesan cheese.
5. Dredge each piece of the zucchini in the flour mixture first, followed by the ranch dressing, and then coat either side while removing the excess dressing by shaking. Finally, dip into the breadcrumb mixture, while pressing the bread mixture lightly to adhere to the zucchini chip.
6. After adding some cooking spray, transfer the breaded zucchini chips in the air fryer basket. Maintain a single layer and leave breathing space.
7. Allow to cook for about 5-6 minutes or until the chips are browned.
8. Do the same for the other zucchini chips.
9. Serve.

Baked Zucchini Fries

Prep + Cook Time: 35 minutes | Servings: 1

Ingredients:

- Cooking spray
- 2 large egg whites
- Salt and ground black pepper to taste
- 2 tbsp grated Parmesan cheese
- ¼ tsp garlic powder
- ½ cup seasoned bread crumbs
- 3 medium zucchini sliced into sticks

Directions:

1. Ensure that your oven is preheated to 425 F.
2. Place a cooling rack inside a baking sheet.
3. Use some cooking spray to coat the rack and set aside.
4. Get a small bowl and in it, beat the egg whites, adding salt and pepper to taste.
5. Combine the cheese, garlic powder, and breadcrumbs in a separate bowl and mix well.
6. Dip the zucchini sticks into the egg mixture, the breadcrumb and cheese mixture.
7. Transfer the breaded zucchini onto the cooling rack, arranging them in a single layer.
8. Spray additional cooking spray on the top of the breaded zucchini.
9. Allow baking at 425 F for about 15-20 minutes.
10. Withdraw when the zucchini appears golden brown.
11. To serve, combine with Ranch or Marinara sauce for dipping.

Zucchini Rounds

Prep + Cook Time: 40 minutes | Servings: 4

Ingredients:

- 1 lb zucchini sliced into rounds
- 2 tbsp extra-virgin olive oil
- 1 tsp garlic powder
- 1 tsp kosher salt
- ½ tsp ground black pepper

Directions:

1. Ensure that your air fryer is preheated to 400 F.
2. With the ends of the zucchini cut off, cut them into rounds, each with a thickness of about ¼ inches.
3. Make a mixture of olive oil and seasonings in a clean small bowl.
4. Toss in the zucchini into the olive oil mixture and mix thoroughly.
5. Transfer the zucchini in the basket of the air fryer, and with the drawer closed, allow cooking for 30 minutes.
6. Endeavor to toss twice or thrice during the cooking to make sure that the zucchini browns evenly.

Zucchini Fritters

Prep + Cook Time: 30 minutes | Servings: 8

Ingredients:

- 4 oz plain flour
- 1 tbsp mixed herbs
- Salt and ground black pepper to taste
- 1 medium egg beaten
- 5 tbsp milk
- 5 oz zucchini, grated
- 3 oz onion, peeled and diced
- 1 oz cheddar cheese grated

Directions:

1. Combine your plain flour and the seasoning in a bowl.
2. Whisk the egg and milk separately and pour in the mixture into the bowl. Stir to make a smooth, creamy batter.
3. Grate the courgette and ensure that no excess moisture is retained before adding the onion.
4. Stir in the cheese.
5. You may add more cheese and flour to make the batter up to the required thickness.
6. Shape the batter into small burgers.
7. Arrange the shaped batter in the air fryer and allow cooking for 20 minutes at 390 F.
8. Withdraw and serve alongside a good dollop of mayonnaise.

Zucchini Gratin

Prep + Cook Time: 30 minutes | Servings: 4

Ingredients:

- 2 zucchini
- Salt and ground black pepper to taste
- 2 tbsp bread crumbs
- 4 tbsp grated Parmesan cheese
- 1 tbsp chopped fresh parsley
- 1 tbsp vegetable oil

Directions:

1. Ensure that your air fryer is preheated to 360 F.
2. After cutting the zucchini in half lengthways, slice each piece in half again through the middle.
3. Transfer the resulting eight pieces of zucchini into the air fryer basket.
4. Combine the freshly ground black pepper, salt, breadcrumbs, cheese, parsley, and oil in a separate bowl; mix thoroughly.
5. Divide the zucchini into two batches.
6. Transfer the first batch into the air fryer basket and top it with the breadcrumb and cheese mixture.
7. Allow frying for 15 minutes or until the gratin is golden brown.
8. Do the same for the other batch.

Ratatouille

Prep + Cook Time: 25 minutes | Servings: 4

Ingredients:

- 7 oz courgette and/or aubergine
- 2 tomatoes
- 1 onion, peeled
- 1 yellow bell pepper
- 2 tsp dried Provençal herbs
- 1 clove garlic, crushed
- ½ tsp salt
- Freshly ground black pepper
- 1 tbsp olive oil
- Small, round baking dish, 6-inch diameter

Directions:

1. Ensure that your air fryer is preheated to 390 F.
2. Make ½ -inch pieces of each of the courgette, aubergine, tomatoes, onion, and bell pepper by cutting.
3. Combine the Provencal herbs, vegetables, garlic, and ½ teaspoon salt and pepper to taste. Stir in a tablespoon of the olive oil.
4. Return the bowl into the air fryer basket and the basket back into the air fryer.
5. Allow the ratatouille to cook for 15 minutes. Stir once when cooking.
6. When cooked, serve the ratatouille alongside fried meat, including a cutlet or entrecote.

Roasted Cauliflower

Prep + Cook Time: 30 minutes | Servings: 2

Ingredients:

- 3 cloves garlic
- ½ tsp smoked paprika
- ½ tsp salt
- 1 tbsp peanut oil
- 4 cups cauliflower florets

Directions:

1. Ensure that your air fryer is preheated to 400 F.
2. Slice your garlic in half before smashing with your knife's blade. Combine the paprika, salt, and oil in a bowl. Finally, add the cauliflower while turning to coat.
3. Transfer the coated cauliflower into the air fryer and allow cooking until you have the desired crispiness. This may take up to 15 minutes, however, endeavor to shake at 5-minute intervals.
4. Serve.

Buffalo Cauliflower (ver. 1)

Prep + Cook Time: 25 minutes | Servings: 4

Ingredients:

For the Cauliflower:

- 4 cups cauliflower florets
- 1 cup panko breadcrumbs mixed with 1 tsp sea salt

For the Buffalo Coating:

- ¼ cup melted vegan butter (¼ cup after melting)
- ¼ cup vegan Buffalo sauce (Check the ingredients for butter. I used Frank's Red Hot)

For Dipping:

- Vegan mayo Cashew Ranch, or your favorite creamy salad dressing

Directions:

1. Start by melting your vegan butter in the microwave – pour it in a mug and place it in the microwave.
2. Whisk the melted butter in the buffalo sauce.
3. Grab each floret by the stem and dip in the buffalo-butter mixture, ensuring that the floret is well coated in the sauce. Do not worry if the part of the stem you are holding isn't saucy. Hold the floret over the mug until it doesn't drip anymore. Avoiding excessive dripping is necessary to ensure that your panko doesn't get clumpy or sticky.
4. Toss the dipped floret in the salt-panko mixture, while coating generously.
5. Transfer the coated florets into the air fryer basket – a single layer is not compulsory here.
6. Air fry at 350 F, without preheating, for about 14-17 minutes. Shake a few times while cooking and monitor the progress at the same time. Once you can see the florets getting almost browned, the cauliflower is ready to be served.
7. Serve alongside your preferred dipping sauce.

Buffalo Cauliflower Bites (ver. 2)

Prep + Cook Time: 55 minutes | Servings: 4

Ingredients:

- 1 large egg white
- 2 tbsp hot sauce (such as Franks Red Hot)
- 3 tbsp no-salt-added ketchup
- ½ head cauliflower, trimmed and cut into 1-inch florets (about 4 cups florets)
- ¾ cup panko (Japanese-style breadcrumbs)
- Cooking spray
- ¼ tsp black pepper
- 1 tsp red wine vinegar
- ¼ cup reduced-fat sour cream
- ¼ oz crumbled blue cheese (about 1 tbsp)
- 1 small garlic clove, grated

Directions:

1. Get a clean small bowl and in it, whisk together the egg white, hot sauce, and ketchup until you have a smooth mixture.
2. Toss the panko into a large bowl.
3. Combine the cauliflower florets and ketchup mixture in a separate large bowl and allow the florets coat generously. You may have to work in batches here.
4. Toss the cauliflower into the panko to coat, before coating it again generously with a cooking spray.
5. Move the first batch of the cauliflower into the air fryer basket.
6. Allow cooking at 320 F for about 20 minutes, or until you have crispy and golden brown florets.
7. Do the same for the other batches of the cauliflower.
8. Meanwhile, get a small bowl and in it, combine the pepper, vinegar, sour cream, blue cheese and garlic. Stir well till you have a uniform mixture.
9. Serve the cooked cauliflower alongside the blue cheese sauce.

Spicy Cauliflower Stir-Fry

Prep + Cook Time: 35 minutes | Servings: 4

Ingredients:

- 1 head cauliflower cut into florets
- 3/4 cup onion white, thinly sliced
- 5 cloves garlic finely sliced
- Salt and ground black pepper to taste
- 1 tbsp Sriracha or other favorite hot sauce
- 1½ tbsp tamari or gluten free tamari
- ½ tsp coconut sugar
- 1 tbsp rice vinegar
- Soy sauce to taste
- 2 scallions for garnish

Directions:

1. Place the cauliflower in the air fryer. Use an insert if your air fryer has holes in the base.
2. With the heat set to 350 F and time 10 minutes, allow cooking.
3. Once the timer goes off, open the air fryer and grab the pot by the handle. Withdraw and shake before sliding it back into the compartment.
4. Toss in the sliced onion, stir and cook for ten more minutes.
5. Toss in the garlic too, and stir. Allow cooking for an additional 5 minutes.
6. Get a clean small bowl and in it, combine the pepper, sriracha, salt, coconut sugar, rice vinegar, and soy sauce into a mixture,
7. Pour the mixture on the cauliflower and mix. Allow cooking for five more minutes. All the juice will be retained inside if you use an insert.
8. Sprinkle scallions over the top of the cauliflower as a form of garnish. Serve.

Orange Sesame Cauliflower

Prep + Cook Time: 1 hour 15 minutes | Servings: 4

Ingredients:

- 2/3 cup water
- 1/3 cup all-purpose flour
- 1/3 cup cornstarch
- ½ tsp salt
- ½ tsp ground black pepper
- 1 medium head cauliflower, cut into florets
- 4 tbsp vegetable oil
- 1 orange
- 2 tbsp soy sauce
- 2 tbsp rice vinegar
- 2 tbsp ketchup
- 2 tbsp brown sugar
- 1 tbsp toasted sesame oil
- 2 cloves garlic, minced
- 1 tsp cornstarch
- Sliced green onion
- Toasted sesame seeds

Directions:

1. Get a large, clean bowl and in it, whisk water, flour, cornstarch, salt, and pepper until you have a smooth mixture.
2. Toss in the cauliflower florets and stir until well coated.
3. Remove the cauliflower and place them onto a parchment paper-lined baking sheet. Allow chilling for 30 minutes.
4. Transfer the cauliflower into your air fryer. After drizzling with some vegetable oil, allow to cook for 22 minutes or until you have a tender browned cauliflower.
5. While cooking the cauliflower, measure one teaspoon of zest orange and set aside. Juice the orange to measure up to ¼ of the cup.
6. Get a clean saucepan and in it, make a mixture of the soy sauce, rice vinegar, orange juice, ketchup, brown sugar, sesame oil, and garlic. Place the saucepan containing the mixture on medium heat and allow to simmer.
7. Stir cornstarch with one teaspoon water until dissolved. Whisk into the sauce and allow cooking until you have glossy (takes about 2 minutes).
8. Withdraw the saucepan from the heat and pour in the orange zest.
9. Finally, toss in the cauliflower with the warm sauce. Add green onion and sesame seeds for garnishing.
10. Serve immediately.

Broccoli with Cheese Sauce

Prep + Cook Time: 25 minutes | Servings: 4

Ingredients:

- 6 cups broccoli florets (about 12 oz)
- Cooking spray
- 6 lower-sodium saltine crackers
- 4 tsp Aji Amarillo paste
- 1½ oz queso fresco (fresh Mexican cheese), crumbled (about 5 tbsp)
- 10 tbsp low-fat evaporated milk

Directions:

1. After coating your broccoli florets generously with cooking spray, divide into batches.
2. Transfer the first batch into the air fryer basket, and allow cooking at 375 F until they are tender-crisp (for about 6-8 minutes). Do the same for the other batch.
3. While the broccoli cooks, combine the saltines, Aji Amarillo paste, queso fresco, and the evaporated milk in a blender and process for about 45 seconds. Withdraw once you have a smooth blend into a microwave bowl.
4. Microwave the blend on 'high' for about 30 seconds.
5. Combine the broccoli with the cheese sauce and serve.

Cauliflower Rice Stuffed Peppers Budget Recipe
Prep + Cook Time: 30 minutes | Servings: 3

Ingredients:

- 1 yellow pepper
- 1 green pepper
- 1 red pepper
- 1 small onion peeled and diced
- 1 tsp garlic puree
- 1 tbsp olive oil
- 1 small courgette very thinly diced
- ¼ yellow pepper very thinly diced
- 1 large carrot very thinly diced
- 1 tsp fennel seeds
- 1 tsp mixed spice
- 1 tsp coriander
- 1 tsp chinese five spice
- Salt and ground black pepper to taste
- 1 small cauliflower shredded
- 3 tbsp soft cheese

Directions:

1. Pinch off the uppermost part of the peppers and pull out the stalk at the center.
2. Arrange pepper bottoms in the Airfryer and apply heat at 390 F for 5 minutes after which the peppers would appear firm and crispy.
3. In a separate pan, sauté the onion with garlic in olive oil at medium heat. Add vegetables and allow to fry for about 4 minutes before seasoning the mixture. After seasoning, put cauliflower in the same pan and mix with the previous contents to make cauliflower rice.
4. In the space from which the middle stalk and top of the peppers were removed, pour in cream cheese and cover with the cauliflower rice. Replace the cover, return the peppers to the air fryer and allow to simmer for about 10 minutes at a heat of 390 F.
5. The Cauliflower Rice Stuffed Peppers can now be served and enjoyed.

Honey Glazed Cauliflower Bites
Prep + Cook Time: 30 minutes | Servings: 4

Ingredients:

- 1 small cauliflower
- 1/3 cup gluten free oats
- 1/3 desiccated coconut
- 1/3 cup plain flour
- Salt and ground black pepper to taste
- 1 large egg beaten
- 1 tsp mixed herbs
- 2 tbsp honey
- 1 tsp mixed spice
- 1 tsp garlic puree
- ½ tsp mustard powder
- 2 tbsp soy sauce

Directions:

1. Ensure that your air fryer is preheated to 360 F.
2. Make small florets out of your cauliflower by chopping as required. This facilitates easy and fast cooking.
3. Get a clean bowl, and in it, combine the oats, coconut, flour, and add salt and pepper to taste. Set the mixture aside.
4. Get another clean bowl and in it, beat your egg and set aside.
5. Add mixed herbs alongside pepper and salt into the cauliflower to season it. Now roll the cauliflower in the eggs first, then in the oats mixture.
6. Transfer the rolled cauliflower into the air fryer and allow cooking for 15 minutes at 360 F.
7. While it is cooking in a large mixing bowl mix together the rest of your ingredients with a tablespoon.
8. Withdraw the cooked cauliflower and toss it entirely into the mixing bowl alongside the sticky substance.
9. With the aid of thongs (to avoid the cauliflower burning your hands), stir the cauliflower thoroughly to ensure even coating.
10. Return the coated cauliflower into the air fryer dish or a baking mat.
11. Allow cooking for an additional 5 minutes at 360 F. Serve on a bed of lettuce.

Cauliflower Cheese Tater Tots

Prep + Cook Time: 50 minutes | Servings: 12

Ingredients:

- 2 lbs fresh cauliflower
- 1 tbsp oats
- 4 oz bread crumbs
- 1 tbsp desiccated coconut
- 1 large egg
- 1 tsp garlic puree
- Salt and ground black pepper to taste
- 4 oz onion, peeled and thinly diced
- 1 tsp chives
- 1 tsp parsley
- 1 tsp oregano
- 5 oz cheddar cheese

Directions:

1. Transfer your chopped cauliflower (now florets) into the soup maker. Add some water and allow steaming for 20 minutes.
2. Meanwhile, prepare the breadcrumbs coating by combining the oats, breadcrumb, and coconut in a separate bowl. Beat your egg in another bowl.
3. Once the cauliflower is cooked, withdraw and drain the water.
4. Return into the soup maker, and add the garlic puree, salt, and pepper. Now blend until you have a mixture with the appearance of breadcrumbs. Transfer the blended mixture into a clean tea towel and squeeze it for few minutes. Stop when you are confident that all the water is drained.
5. Transfer the cauliflower into a mixing bowl alongside the onion and the rest of the herbs, plus the cheese. Mix thoroughly.
6. Shape the mixture into tater tots, and then roll the tots in the breadcrumbs.
7. Move the rolled tater tots into the air fryer and allow cooking at 360 F for 6 minutes.
8. Increase the heat to 390 F and allow cooking for an additional 10 minutes or until the cauliflower is hot in the middle and crispy on the outside.

Roasted Broccoli and Cauliflower

Prep + Cook Time: 30 minutes | Servings: 6

Ingredients:

- 3 cups broccoli florets
- ¼ tsp sea salt
- ½ tsp garlic powder
- 2 tbsp olive oil
- 3 cups cauliflower florets
- ¼ tsp paprika
- 1/8 tsp ground black pepper

Directions:

1. Ensure that your air fryer is preheated to 400 F.
2. Toss the broccoli florets into a large bowl suitable for microwaving. Set your microwave to 'high' and cook the florets for 3 minutes. Remove any accumulated liquid.
3. In the bowl containing the broccoli, combine the sea salt, garlic powder, olive oil, cauliflower, paprika, and black pepper. Transfer the mixture into the air fryer basket.
4. With the timer set at 12 minutes, allow the mixture to cook. After 6 minutes, toss in the vegetables, to ensure even browning.

Breaded Mushrooms

Prep + Cook Time: 15 minutes | Servings: 1

Ingredients:

- Breadcrumbs
- 3 oz grams finely grated Parmigiano Reggiano cheese
- 1 egg
- 0.5 oz button mushrooms
- Flour
- Salt and ground black pepper to taste

Directions:

1. Get a clean bowl and in it, make a mixture of the breadcrumbs, salt, pepper and the Parmigiano cheese. Set the mixture aside.
2. Get another bowl and beat an egg. Set aside also.
3. Using kitchen papers, pat-dry the mushrooms.
4. Roll the mushrooms in the flour, then dip in the egg, and finally in the breadcrumbs/cheese mixture, making sure that they are well coated.
5. Transfer the coated mushroom into the air fryer and allow cooking for 7 minutes at 360 F.
6. Shake once while cooking.
7. Serve the cooked mushroom while warm, alongside your preferred dipping sauce.

Stuffed Mushrooms with Sour Cream

Prep + Cook Time: 55 minutes | Servings: 24

Ingredients:

- 24 mushrooms, caps and stems diced
- ½ onion, diced
- 1 small carrot, diced
- ½ orange bell pepper, diced
- 2 slices bacon, diced
- 1 cup shredded Cheddar cheese
- ½ cup sour cream
- 1½ tbsp shredded Cheddar cheese, or to taste

Directions:

1. Combine the mushroom stems, onion, carrot, orange bell pepper, and bacon in a skillet. Cook and stir the mixture over medium heat until softened – this takes about 5 minutes. Pour in a cup of Cheddar cheese and sour cream. Continue cooking until the cheese has melted and the stuffing is mixed thoroughly – this takes about 2 minutes.
2. Ensure that your air fryer is preheated to 350 F.
3. Set the mushroom caps on the baking tray carefully. Add the stuffing to each mushroom following the heap style. Add sprinkles of about 1.5 tablespoons Cheddar cheese on top.
4. Transfer the tray of mushrooms into the air fryer basket and allow cooking for about 8 minutes, or until the cheese melts.

Mushroom Croquettes or Meat Croquettes

Prep + Cook Time: 25 minutes | Servings: 8

Ingredients:

- 4 oz mushrooms
- ¼ white onion
- 1 oz butter
- 1½ heaped tbsp flour
- ½ liter milk
- Ground nutmeg
- Salt to taste
- 2 oz breadcrumbs
- 2 tbsp vegetable oil

Directions:

1. Chop your mushrooms and onions into thin pieces. Get a saucepan and melt the butter in it, toss in the sliced onions and mushrooms and fry. Add the flour and stir well. Warm up the milk and stir it in bit by bit. Continue stirring while the mixture thickens. Add nutmeg and salt to taste. Leave the mixture in the refrigerator for 2 hours to cool.
2. Prepare the breadcrumb coating by combining the oil and the breadcrumbs. Continue stirring until you have a loose and crumbly mixture.
3. Roll 1 tablespoon of filling in the breadcrumbs until they are coated thoroughly. Now place it in the air fryer basket. Do the same for other breadcrumbs, until you have no more filing.
4. Ensure that your air fryer is preheated to 390 F.
5. Place the breadcrumbs into the basket and slide it into the air fryer. Set the timer for 8 minutes and fry the croquettes until they are brown and crispy.

Note:

You can make meat croquettes by replacing the mushrooms with 4 oz of finely-chopped beef or veal.

Shiitake Mushroom Chips

Prep + Cook Time: 20 minutes | Servings: 1-2

Ingredients:

- 8 oz Shiitake Mushroom
- Salt to tase

Directions:

1. Start by using cold water to rinse the Shiitake mushroom. Don't make the mistake of leaving it soaked in the water as the mushroom tends to absorb water
2. Bring up the Airfryer to heat of 360 F
3. Depending on your preference, you can either cut off the whole stem from the Shiitake mushroom or only remove the lower part of the stem
4. Cut the mushroom into slices. There are no hard and fast rules for the size of each slice. But note that if sliced too thin, it starts sticking to the bottom of the AirFryer pan and burns easily
5. Place the slices of mushroom in the pan and allow to fry for between 9 and 12 minutes or until your desired dryness for the mushroom has been achieved. Mid-way into the frying, you should either stir with a small ladle/spatula or gently shake the pan itself
6. After frying, sprinkle some salt on the now shrunken mushroom

Stuffed Garlic Mushrooms

Prep + Cook Time: 40 minutes | Servings: 4

Ingredients:

- 1 tsp garlic puree
- 1 oz onion, peeled and diced
- Salt and groundblack pepper to taste
- 1 tbsp olive oil
- 1 tbsp breadcrumbs
- 1 tsp parsley
- 6 small mushrooms

Directions:

1. Thoroughly mix the garlic, onion, salt, pepper, olive oil, breadcrumbs, and parsley
2. Rinse the mushrooms properly and pull out the middle stalks, then pour in the breadcrumb mixture to replace the central stalks in the center of the mushrooms.
3. Allow the mushrooms to boil for 10 minutes at a heat of 360 F, and you're done. You can now enjoy your air fryer stuffed Garlic Mushrooms

---

Stuffed Portobello Mushrooms

Prep + Cook Time: 45 minutes | Servings: 3

Ingredients:

- 3 portobello mushrooms
- 1 tbsp olive oil
- A dash of black pepper
- 1 medium red onion, diced
- 1 tsp minced garlic
- 1 green bell pepper, diced
- 1 tomato, diced
- Grated cheddar or mozzarella cheese
- 2 slices ham, chopped into small pieces
- Half tsp truffle salt

Directions:

1. Heat the AirFryer or an oven up to a heat of 320 F or 380 F respectively.
2. Get the mushrooms ready by washing them thoroughly and drying. Apply a thick film of olive oil to coat the mushrooms and rub it on your hands as well.
3. Get a big bowl, and mix the other ingredients: black pepper, onions, garlic, bell pepper, tomato, cheese, ham, and truffle salt inside it
4. Split open the mushroom caps and add portions of the mixture from the bowl into it. Depending on your preference, you could layer some more cheese atop the mushroom. Place the mushrooms either in the Airfry for 8 minutes at its initial heat of 320 F. If you're using an oven, allow the mushroom to get baked for between 12 and 15 minutes, but lower the heat by 10 degrees to 360 F
5. After the baking or frying is done, the meal is ready to be served with hard boiled eggs and salad.

Button Mushroom Melt

Prep + Cook Time: 40 minutes | Servings: 4

Ingredients:

- About 10 button mushrooms
- Salt and ground black pepper to taste
- Italian dried mixed herbs
- Olive oil
- Cheddar cheese, shredded
- Mozzarella cheese, grated
- Dried dill, optional as garnish

Directions:

1. Start by washing the mushrooms and cutting out their stems.
2. You might add a small sprinkle of salt here, black pepper, Italian dried mixed herbs but this is optional. Mushrooms are already tasty on their own, and adding more seasoning may make it turn out too spicy. Also, a little olive oil will aid in not allowing the mushrooms to dry out in the air fryer.
3. Heat the air fryer to a heat of 360 F for between 3 and 5 minutes
4. As the air fryer gets heated up, place the mushroom in the wire basket within the air fryer, ensure the hollow section is upwards. Sprinkle both cheddar and mozzarella cheese on top of each mushroom cap.
5. Allow the mushrooms to fry for between 7 and 8 minutes at 360 F.
6. The meal is ready to be served. If you so wish, you may add some green herbs like basil, dill, or parleys.

Brussels Sprouts

Prep + Cook Time: 20 minutes | Servings: 2

Ingredients:

- ½ tsp ground black pepper
- ½ tsp salt
- 1 tsp avocado oil
- 10 oz Brussels sprouts, trimmed and halved lengthwise
- 1 tsp balsamic vinegar
- 2 tsp crumbled cooked bacon, optional

Directions:

1. Ensure that your air fryer is preheated to 350 F.
2. Mix pepper, salt, and oil thoroughly in a clean bowl.
3. Add Brussels sprouts and turn to coat.
4. Allow air frying for 5 minutes. Stop and shake the sprouts, then cook for an extra 5 minutes.
5. Withdraw the sprouts and place in a serving dish.
6. Sprinkle with some balsamic vinegar and turn to coat.
7. Sprinkle with bacon. Serve.

Garlic-Rosemary Brussels Sprouts

Prep + Cook Time: 35 minutes | Servings: 4

Ingredients:

- ¼ tsp pepper
- ½ tsp salt
- 3 tbsp olive oil
- 2 garlic cloves, minced
- 1 lb Brussels sprouts, trimmed and halved
- ½ cup panko (Japanese) bread crumbs
- 1/2 tsp fresh rosemary, minced

Directions:

1. Ensure that your air fryer is preheated to 350 F.
2. Get a clean microwave-safe bowl, and in it, combine the first four ingredients.
3. Microwave the contents of the bowl for 30 seconds on 'high.'
4. Coat the Brussels sprouts with two tablespoons of the oil mixture, before transferring into the air fryer basket.
5. Set the timer for 4-5 minutes. Stop and stir the sprouts.
6. Resume air-frying while stirring every 4-5 minutes. Only stop when the sprouts are almost soft and are lightened browned (approximately after 8 minutes).
7. Toss the bread crumbs with rosemary and the leftover oil mixture, then sprinkle over sprouts.
8. Cook until you have browned and tender sprouts (for about 3-5 minutes).
9. Withdraw and serve immediately.

Brussels Sprouts with Bacon

Prep + Cook Time: 20 minutes | Servings: 2

Ingredients:

- 1 lb Brussels sprouts
- 4 slices back bacon
- Salt and ground black pepper to taste

Directions:

1. With the outside skin and the core of your Brussels sprouts removed, transfer them into the air fryer and allow cooking for 10 minutes at 360 F.
2. Meanwhile, dice your bacon and get rid of all the apparent fat. Place them in the bacon once the sprouts have cooked for 10 minutes.
3. With the bacon inside, set the timer for five minutes and 400 F.
4. Serve alongside pepper and salt.

Roasted Parsnips

Prep + Cook Time: 20 minutes | Servings: 4

Ingredients:

- 6 medium parsnips
- Salt and ground black pepper to taste

Directions:

1. Skin the Parsnips and cut them up in similarly sized diagonally shaped slices.
2. Arrange the sliced Parsnips inside the Instant Pot Steamer Basket and add a cup of warm water. Then place the basket in the Instant Pot and cover it by shutting the lid. The pot should now be put atop the steamer shelf (trivet)
3. The valve setting should be changed to "sealing" and the pressure set at "manual" while the pot is left to steam for 3 minutes
4. As soon as you here the pot beep, bleed off the pressure within it.
5. The parsnips should be drained to get rid of as much moisture as possible and placed on a chopping board.
6. The drained parsnips should be sprinkled with salt and pepper
7. After sprinkling, arrange the parsnips in the air fryer and allow to fry at a heat of 390 F for 8 minutes.

Curry Parsnip Fries

Prep + Cook Time: 1 hour | Servings: 1

Ingredients:

- Large parsnips
- Olive oil
- Curry powder to taste
- Sea salt to taste

Directions:

1. Heat the oven to 350 F
2. Skin the parsnips and slice them till they have the similitude of French fries
3. Spread a film of olive oil on a cookie sheet
4. Arrange the parsnips on the cookie sheet and add another film of olive oil on them too.
5. Season the parsnips with curry and some salt.
6. Allow it to bake for between 30 and 50 minutes or until it becomes soft and takes on a light brown color.

Everything Bagel" Kale Chips

Prep + Cook Time: 35 minutes | Servings: 2

Ingredients:

- 6 cups packed torn Lacinato kale leaves, stems and ribs removed
- 1 tbsp olive oil
- 1 tsp lower-sodium soy sauce
- ½ tsp dried minced garlic
- ¼ tsp poppy seeds
- 1 tsp white or black sesame seeds

Directions:

1. Rinse the Kale leaves thoroughly, then drain and dry them, totally removing all moisture. Pull the dried leaves apart and tear them into pieces that are between 1 and 0.5 inches long.
2. Toss together kale, olive oil, and soy sauce in a medium bowl, rubbing the leaves gently to be sure they are well coated with mixture.
3. Arrange a third of the Kale leaves in the air fryer basket, and allow to fry at a heat of 375 F for about three minutes. Shake the basket, then fry for another 3 minutes.
4. Place the now fried kale chips on a baking sheet, then season with garlic, poppy seeds, and sesame seeds before it loses the heat of cooking.
5. Repeat with remaining kale leaves.

Onion Rings

Prep + Cook Time: 25 minutes | Servings: 4

Ingredients:

- 2 tsp baking powder
- ¾ cup all-purpose flour
- ½ cup cornstarch
- 1 tsp salt
- 1 large onion, cut into rings
- 1 egg
- 1 cup milk
- 1 cup bread crumbs
- Cooking spray
- 2 pinches garlic powder, optional
- 2 pinches paprika, optional

Directions:

1. Get a small bowl and mix the baking powder, flour, cornstarch, and salt inside it. Roll the sliced onion in the flour mixture until it is covered within it.
2. Break the egg into the flour mixture, add milk, and whisk all together. Pick the coated onion slices and dip them in the batter until they get coated again. Drain them by arranging the rings on a wire rack until the batter stops drooping
3. Put the bread crumbs in a dish and add the onion slices to the crumbs successively, place the crumbs on the ring so the onion rings will be well covered with the crumbs. While pulling the onion rings out of the bread crumbs, tap them to make the batter and breadcrumb mixture stick properly.
4. Heat your air fryer, and get it up to 390 F. Keep in mind that instructions from the manufacturer should be followed to prevent damage to the equipment.
5. Arrange the onion rings in the frying basket and add a slight puff of cooking spray. Turn the onion rings over to the other side and lower the frying basket into the air fryer. Allow it to fry for between one and one and half minutes, then turn the onion rings over again. Allow frying for another one to one and a half minutes. You can then take out the rings and drain them using paper towels.
6. Alternatively, you can choose to sprinkle with paprika or garlic powder.

Onion Rings With Comeback Sauce

Prep + Cook Time: 60 minutes | Servings: 4

Ingredients:

- ½ tsp kosher salt, divided
- ½ cup (about 2 1/8 oz.) all-purpose flour
- 1 tsp smoked paprika
- 1 large egg
- 1 tbsp water
- 1 cup whole-wheat panko (Japanese-style breadcrumbs)
- 1 (10-oz.) sweet onion, cut into 1/2-in.-thick rounds and separated into rings
- Cooking spray
- 2 tbsp canola mayonnaise
- 1 tsp Dijon mustard
- ¼ tsp garlic powder
- ¼ tsp paprika
- ¼ cup plain 1% low-fat Greek yogurt
- 1 tbsp ketchup

Directions:

1. In a shallow dish, thoroughly mix a quarter teaspoon of salt with flour and smoked paprika.
2. Break the egg in another dish and beat it with water.
3. In yet another dish, add a quarter teaspoon of salt to panko and stir them together.
4. Dip the rings of onion slices in the flour mixture, totally submerging them and shaking off extraneous flour. Then drench the onion rings in the egg mixture as well, again, be sure to shake off any extra egg mixture. Finally, dip the onion rings in the panko mixture, apply some pressure on it and generously apply cooking spray to both sides of the rings.
5. Arrange the onion rings by stacking them on each other and placing them inside the air fryer basket in batches. Then allow them to cook for 5 minutes at 375 F. Turn them over and allow to cook for another five minutes. By this time they would have a golden brown color as well as a crispy texture on both sides. While frying other batches, ensure to keep the already fried onion rings covered so as not to let them grow cold.
6. While the onion rings are being fried, make a sauce by mixing mayonnaise, mustard, garlic powder, paprika, yogurt, and ketchup together.
7. Each serving may contain two tablespoons of the well-mixed sauce and between 5 and eight onion rings.

Roasted Peppers (Bell Peppers)

Prep + Cook Time: 15 minutes | Servings: 3

Ingredients:

- 1 lb mixed bell peppers

Directions:

1. Remove the pepper tops by slicing them off.
2. Using a firm grip, pull out the stalk and get rid of all the seeds at once.
3. Now dice the peppers into large and medium pieces.
4. Transfer the pepper pieces in the air fryer and allow cooking for 8 minutes at 360 F.
5. Withdraw after 8 minutes and serve while still warm.

Vegan Stuffed Bell Peppers

Prep + Cook Time: 50 minutes | Servings: 6

Ingredients:

- 2 tsp dried mixed herbs
- 2 cloves garlic, minced
- 1 carrot, diced
- 1 small onion, diced
- ½ cup peas
- 1 potato, diced
- 1 vegan bread roll, diced
- 6 green bell peppers - tops, seeds, and membranes removed (tops reserved)
- 1/3 cup shredded vegan cheese

Directions:

1. In a clean bowl, combine the mixed herbs, garlic, carrot, onion, peas, potato, and bread.
2. After dicing the tops of the green bell pepper, toss them into the bowl. Mix thoroughly.
3. Ensure that your air fryer is preheated to 350 F.
4. Stuff the peppers equally with the filling.
5. Transfer the stuffed peppers into the air fryer basket.
6. Allow cooking until tender and hot throughout – this takes about 20 minutes.
7. Stir in the shredded vegan cheese and cook until melted – this takes an additional 5 minutes.

Green Salad with Roasted Pepper

Prep + Cook Time: 30 minutes | Servings: 4

Ingredients:

- 1 red bell pepper
- 3 tbsp yoghurt
- 2 tbsp olive oil
- 1 tbsp lemon juice
- Salt to taste
- Freshly ground black pepper to taste
- 2 oz rocket leaves
- 1 romaine lettuce, in broad strips

Directions:

1. Ensure that your air fryer is preheated to 390 F.
2. Place the basket containing the bell pepper into the air fryer and allow cooking for 10 minutes. This will roast the bell pepper until you have their skin mildly charred.
3. Withdraw the roasted bell pepper into a bowl and cover it using a plastic wrap or a lid.
4. Allow the covered pepper to rest for 10-15 minutes.
5. After resting, cut the bell pepper into four sections, while removing the skin and the seeds.
6. In a clean bowl, mix a dressing of 2 tablespoons of the moisture from the bell pepper, yogurt, olive oil, and the lemon juice. Add salt and pepper to taste.
7. Add the rocket leaves and the lettuce into the dressing. Finally, garnish your salad with the bell pepper strips.

Celery Root Fries

Prep + Cook Time: 50 minutes | Servings: 4

Ingredients:

- 3 cups water
- 1 tbsp lime juice
- ½ celeriac (celery root), peeled and cut into 1/2-inch sticks

Mayo Sauce:

- 1 tsp powdered horseradish
- 1/3 cup vegan mayonnaise
- 1 tbsp brown mustard
- 1 tbsp olive oil
- 1 pinch salt
- Ground black pepper to taste

Directions:

1. In a bowl, add water and lime juice to celery roots. Stir the mixture together and leave it for a third of an hour
2. Heat the air fryer to a heat of 390 F
3. Prepare vegan mayo sauce by adding together horseradish powder, vegan mayonnaise, and mustard in a bowl. Cover the mixture and keep it in the refrigerator.
4. Remove water from the celery root sticks and allow to dry before putting in a separate bowl. Add some oil to the fries and sprinkle salt and pepper over it. Turn the fries over to allow a uniform coating to form.
5. Place the drained and dried celery root sticks in the air fryer basket and cook for about 10 minutes after which you can check to see how cooked it is. Shake the basket and cook for eight more minutes till the fries take on a crisp texture and brown color.
6. Now bring out the vegan mayo sauce from the refrigerator and serve alongside the fries.

Grilled Tomatoes

Prep + Cook Time: 17 minutes | Servings: 3

Ingredients:

- 3 medium beefcake tomatoes
- Salt and ground black pepper to taste
- 1 tsp oregano

Directions:

1. With the tomatoes chopped into two halves, transfer them into the air fryer grill pan.
2. Add sprinkles of salt, oregano, and pepper.
3. Allow cooking for 8 minutes at 360 F.
4. Reduce the heat to 320 F and allow to cook for an extra 5 minutes. This is to let the tomatoes to cook in the middle.
5. Serve.
6. The essence of chopping the tomatoes in half is to get equal sizes and ensure that each tomato has a bottom.

Stuffed Tomatoes and Broccoli

Prep + Cook Time: 25 minutes | Servings: 2

Ingredients:

- ¼ cup cheddar cheese, grated
- ¼ cup broccoli, chopped
- 1 organic tomato (preferably big size)
- 4-5 florets broccoli
- Butter (unsalted)
- Pinch of natural country herbs

Directions:

1. Ensure that your air fryer is preheated to 360 F.
2. Get a clean small bowl and in it, mix the grated Cheddar cheese and the chopped broccoli.
3. Remove the pulps and seeds from the tomato.
4. Stuff the empty tomato with the cheddar and broccoli mixture.
5. Transfer the stuffed tomato into the air fryer basket, add the florets of the broccoli, and finally some butter on top.
6. Allow the tomato to air bake for 12 or 15 minutes.
7. Sprinkle some herbs on the melted cheese.
8. Serve.

Air Fryer Pickles

Prep + Cook Time: 45 minutes | Servings: 2

Ingredients:

- 32 dill pickle slices
- ½ cup all-purpose flour
- ½ tsp salt
- 3 large eggs, lightly beaten
- ½ tsp garlic powder
- 2 tbsp dill pickle juice
- ½ tsp cayenne pepper
- 2 tbsp snipped fresh dill
- 2 cups panko (Japanese) bread crumbs
- Cooking spray
- Ranch salad dressing, optional

Directions:

1. Ensure that your air fryer is preheated to 425 F.
2. Allow the pickles to stand on a paper towel until the liquid is almost absorbed – this takes about 15 minutes.
3. Get a shallow bowl, and in it, make a mixture of flour and salt.
4. Get another shallow bowl and combine whisked eggs, garlic powder, pickle juice, and cayenne.
5. In a third shallow bowl, mix the dill and panko.
6. Dip the pickles in the flour mixture, ensuring the even coating of both sides and shake to get rid of excess. Dip again in the egg mixture, and finally in the crumb mixture, and pat to ensure that the coating stays.
7. Spray the air fryer basket and the pickles with the cooking spray. You may work in batches if your air fryer is small.
8. Arrange the pickles in a single layer inside the air fryer basket.
9. Allow cooking for 7-10 minutes or until you have crispy and golden brown pickles.
10. Turn the pickles and spray with extra cooking spray.
11. Resume cooking until you have golden brown and crispy pickles – it takes about 7-10 minutes.
12. Serve immediately, with ranch dressing (optional).

Spicy Dill Pickle Fries

Prep + Cook Time: 35 minutes | Servings: 10

Ingredients:

- 1½ (16 oz) jars spicy dill pickle spears
- 1 cup all-purpose flour
- ½ tsp paprika
- 1 egg, beaten
- ¼ cup milk
- 1 cup panko bread crumbs
- Cooking spray

Directions:

1. Pat the drained pickles dry.
2. Mix the flour and paprika in a bowl.
3. Get another bowl and in it, mix the beaten egg and milk.
4. Place your panko in a third bowl.
5. Ensure that your air fryer is preheated to 400 F.
6. Dip each pickle in the flour mixture, followed by the egg mixture, and finally in the breadcrumbs. Ensure that the pickles are well coated.
7. Transfer the coated pickles on a plate and do the same for the remaining pickles.
8. Spritz some cooking spray on the coated prickles before placing it in the air fryer basket. You may cook in batches to ensure that the fryer is not overcrowded.
9. Allow cooking for 14 minutes; after 7 minutes, turn the pickles to allow the other side cook.

Roasted Okra

Prep + Cook Time: 25 minutes | Servings: 1

Ingredients:

- ½ lb okra, ends trimmed and pods sliced
- ¼ tsp salt
- 1 tsp olive oil
- 1/8 tsp ground black pepper

Directions:

1. Ensure that your air fryer is preheated to 350 F.
2. Get a clean bowl and in it, combine okra, salt, olive oil, and pepper. Stir the mixture gently.
3. Place in a single layer in the air fryer basket.
4. Allow cooking in the air fryer for 5 minutes.
5. Toss and cook for an additional 5 minutes.
6. Toss again and allow cooking for an extra 2 minutes.
7. Withdraw and serve instantly.

Ratatouille, Italian-Style

Prep + Cook Time: 50 minutes | Servings: 4

Ingredients:

- ½ large yellow bell pepper, cut into cubes
- ½ large red bell pepper, cut into cubes
- ½ onion, cut into cubes
- 1 medium tomato, cut into cubes
- 1 zucchini, cut into cubes
- ½ small eggplant, cut into cubes
- 1 fresh cayenne pepper, diced
- 2 sprigs fresh oregano, stemmed and chopped
- 1 clove garlic, crushed
- 5 sprigs fresh basil, stemmed and chopped
- Salt and ground black pepper to taste
- 1 tsp vinegar
- 1 tbsp white wine
- 1 tbsp olive oil

Directions:

1. Ensure that your air fryer is preheated to 400 F.
2. Get a clean bowl and in it, toss in the bell peppers, onion, tomato, zucchini, and the eggplant. Include the cayenne pepper, oregano, garlic, basil, salt, and pepper also. Mix thoroughly to combine properly. Drizzle in vinegar, wine, and oil. Mix the entire mixture to coat all the vegetables.
3. Transfer the vegetable mixture into a baking dish and transfer it into the air fryer basket.
4. Allow cooking for 8 minutes.
5. Stir, and cook for an additional 8 minutes.
6. Stir again and resume cooking until the vegetables are soft. Ensure to stir every 5 minutes, 10 to 15 minutes more.
7. With the dish still inside the air fryer, turn it off for 5 minutes.
8. Remove the dish and allow to rest for 5 minutes. Serve.

Air-Fried Asparagus

Prep + Cook Time: 20 minutes | Servings: 2-4

Ingredients:

- ½ bunch of asparagus, with bottom 2 inches trimmed off
- Avocado or olive oil in an oil mister or sprayer
- Himalayan salt to taste
- Ground black pepper to taste

Directions:

1. After placing your trimmed asparagus spears in the air-fryer basket, spritz it lightly with cooking oil.
2. Add sprinkles of salt and a tiny bit of black pepper.
3. With the basket inside the air-fryer, allow baking for 10 minutes at 400 F.
4. Serve once baked.

Asparagus Fries

Prep + Cook Time: 25 minutes | Servings: 6

Ingredients:

- 1 large egg, beaten
- 1 tsp honey
- ½ cup Parmesan cheese, grated
- 1 cup panko bread crumbs
- 12 asparagus spears, trimmed
- 1 pinch cayenne pepper, optional
- ¼ cup Greek yogurt
- ¼ cup stone-ground mustard

Directions:

1. Ensure that your air fryer is preheated to 400 F.
2. Get a long, narrow dish, and in it combing egg and honey. Beat together and set aside.
3. In a separate plate, combine the Parmesan cheese and panko.
4. After coating each asparagus stalk in the egg mixture, roll it also in the panko mix and allow thorough coating.
5. Arrange six spears in the air fryer and allow cooking to the desired brownness – this takes 4 to 6 minutes. Do the same for the other spears.
6. Get a small bowl, and in it, mix the cayenne pepper, yogurt, and mustard.
7. Serve the asparagus spears with the dipping sauce.

Artichoke Hearts

Prep + Cook Time: 30 minutes | Servings: 1-2

Ingredients:

- 1 cup arrowroot flour (gluten free & easily digestible)
- 1 tbsp organic herb de provence
- 1-2 eggs
- 1 bag of frozen artichoke hearts
- Cooking spray

Directions:

1. Get a clean bowl, and in it, combine a cup of Arrowroot Flour alongside Herb de Provence. Mix well.
2. Get another bowl and make an egg wash by whisking 1-2 eggs.
3. Pick each artichoke and dip in the egg mixture before the flour mixture. Ensure generous coating in both instances, while avoiding the contamination of the egg wash by the excess flour mix from your hands.
4. Ensure that our air fryer basket remains non-sticky by coating oil.
5. Allow the chips to cook for 15 minutes under the chips feature.
6. Flip the artichokes after about 7 minutes using your thongs.

Jalapeno Poppers

Prep + Cook Time: 50 minutes | Servings: 2-3

Ingredients:

- 8 oz of cream cheese I used a dairy-free cream cheese
- ¾ cup gluten-free tortilla or bread crumbs
- ¼ cup fresh parsley
- 10 jalapeno peppers halved and deseeded

Directions:

1. Combine the cream cheese and half of the crumbs first before adding the parsley.
2. Fill each piece of pepper with this mixture.
3. Press the top of each pepper into the other ¼ cup of crumbs, thus creating the top coating.
4. Allow the peppers to cook in the air fryer at 370 F for 6-8 minutes. If you are using a conventional oven, just set the temperature to 375 F and the time, 20 minutes.
5. Allow the peppers to cool before serving.

Crispy Jalapeno Coins

Prep + Cook Time: 15 minutes | Servings: 1-2

Ingredients:

- 2-3 tbsp coconut flour
- Pinch of garlic powder
- Pinch of onion powder
- Cajun seasoning for extra kick, optional
- Salt and ground black pepper to taste
- 1 jalapeno, sliced and seeded if desired
- 1 egg, raw, mixed well
- Cooking spray or oil mister

Directions:

1. Ensure that your air fryer is preheated to 400 F.
2. Mix your ingredients thoroughly, except egg and jalapeno.
3. Using a paper towel, remove the excess water in the jalapeno slices by patting them dry.
4. Then dip each slice in the egg and wash dry in the mixture. Toss to coat. You may reapply until it is sticking well.
5. Transfer the coated jalapeno slices in the air fryer, while arranging them in a single layer.
6. Spray lightly with some cooking oil.
7. Allow cooking until coins are crispy and nice. Turn once during the cooking time, depending on the size of the slices.
8. Serve while hot.

Roasted Rainbow Vegetables

Prep + Cook Time: 35 minutes | Servings: 4

Ingredients:

- ½ sweet onion, cut into 1-inch wedges
- 4 oz fresh mushrooms, cleaned and halved
- 1 zucchini, cut into 1-inch pieces
- 1 yellow summer squash, cut into 1-inch pieces
- 1 red bell pepper, seeded and cut into 1-inch pieces
- Salt and ground black pepper to taste
- 1 tbsp extra-virgin olive oil

Directions:

1. Ensure that the air fryer is preheated as presented in the manufacturer's guidelines.
2. In a large, clean bowl, combine the onion, mushrooms, zucchini, summer squash, and red bell pepper.
3. Add the black pepper, salt, and olive oil, then toss to mix.
4. Arrange the vegetables in the air fryer basket so that they maintain an even layer.
5. Air-fry until you have roasted vegetables – this takes about 20 minutes, but you must stir after about 10 minutes of cooking time.

Roasted Winter Vegetables

Prep + Cook Time: 30 minutes | Servings: 6

Ingredients:

- 10 oz parsnips
- 10 oz celeriac
- 2 red onions
- 10 oz 'butternut squash'
- 1 tbsp fresh thyme needles
- 1 tbsp olive oil
- Salt and ground black pepper to taste

Directions:

1. Ensure that your air fryer is preheated to 390 F.
2. Cut the peeled parsnips and celeriac into 2 cm cubes.
3. Cut the peeled onions into wedges.
4. Divide the 'butternut squash' into two, get rid of the seeds, and cut them all into cubes.
5. Combine the cut vegetables with the olive oil and thyme.
6. Add seasoning to taste.
7. Transfer the cut vegetables into the air fryer basket and allow roasting for 20 minutes. Remove the vegetable once they are nicely brown and done.
8. It is advisable to stir the vegetables while roasting, but only once.

Healthy Mediterranean Vegetables

Prep + Cook Time: 30 minutes | Servings: 4

Ingredients:

- 1 large courgette
- 1 green bell pepper
- 1 large parsnip
- 1 medium carrot
- 2 oz cherry tomatoes
- 6 tbsp olive oil
- 2 tsp garlic puree
- 1 tsp mixed herbs
- 1 tsp mustard
- 2 tbsp honey
- Salt and ground black pepper to taste

Directions:

1. At the base of your air fryer, cut up the courgette and the green pepper. Peel and dice the parsnip and carrot, and toss in the cherry tomatoes in whole while still on the vine. This gives the mixture some extra flavor.
2. After drizzling three tablespoons of olive oil, cook the mixture for 15 minutes at 360 F.
3. While cooking, combine the remaining ingredient into a baking dish suitable for your air fryer.
4. Remove the cooked vegetables from the base of your air fryer and transfer them into the baking dish.
5. Shake well to ensure that the marinade covers all parts of the vegetables.
6. After sprinkling little extra pepper and salt, allow cooking for 5 minutes at 390 F.
7. Serve.

Veggie Bake Cakes

Prep + Cook Time: 20 minutes | Servings: 2

Ingredients:

- 1 tbsp plain flour
- Leftover vegetable bake

Directions:

1. Ensure that your air fryer is preheated to 360 F.
2. Combine the flour and the leftover vegetable bake to form a thick dough.
3. Insert your baking mat into the air fryer.
4. Place the vegetable bake mixture on the baking mat inside the air fryer.
5. Allow cooking for 12 minutes at 360 F.
6. Serve.

Vegan Veggie Balls

Prep + Cook Time: 45 minutes | Servings: 6

Ingredients:

- 3 oz parsnips
- 3 oz carrot
- 4 oz sweet potato
- 8 oz cauliflower
- 2 tsp oregano
- 2 tsp garlic puree

- 1 tsp mixed spice
- 1 tsp chives
- 1 tsp paprika
- 1 cup gluten free oats
- ½ cup desiccated coconut
- Salt and ground black pepper to taste

Directions:

1. Combine the vegetables in your food processor and blend until the raw vegetables appear like breadcrumbs.
2. Transfer them into a tea towel and get rid of the excess water by ringing out the towel, with the resulting mixture firm.
3. Place the dry vegetables in a mixing bowl, and combine it with the remaining ingredients.
4. Mix thoroughly and mold into medium-sized balls.
5. Transfer the balls into the fridge and allow them to stay for up to 2 hours. This will make them firmer.
6. From the fridge, move them into the air fryer and allow cooking for 10 minutes at 320 F.
7. After the first 10 minutes, roll over the balls to the other side and cook for 10 minutes more at 390 F.
8. Serve the cooked vegetable balls.

Easy Sage and Onion Stuffing Balls

Prep + Cook Time: 20 minutes | Servings: 8

Ingredients:

- 4 oz sausage meat
- ½ tsp garlic puree
- ½ small onion peeled and diced
- 3 tbsp breadcrumbs
- 1 tsp sage
- Salt and ground black pepper to taste

Directions:

1. Get a clean mixing bowl and in it, combine all the ingredients and mix well.
2. Mold the ingredient mixture into balls of medium sizes.
3. Transfer the molded balls into the air fryer and allow cooking for 15 minutes at 360 F.
4. Serve.

Purple Yam Fries with Sour Cream Sriracha Sauce

Prep + Cook Time: 40 minutes | Servings: 4

Ingredients:

- 1 1/3 lbs ube (purple yam), peeled and cut into 1/4-inch-thick fries
- 1 tsp sriracha-flavored salt
- 2 tsp olive oil
- 2 tsp sriracha sauce, or more to taste
- 1/3 cup sour cream

Directions:

1. Ensure that your air fryer is preheated to 320 F.
2. Assemble the yam fries in a bowl.
3. Add the sriracha-flavored salt and the olive oil.
4. Toss to allow the fries coat evenly and transfer into the air fryer basket.
5. Allow cooking for 16 minutes. Increase the heat to 400 F.
6. Shake the basket and continue cooking for an extra 5 minutes.
7. Combine the sriracha sauce and the sour cream in a bowl.
8. Serve the yam fries alongside the sauce.

Air Fryer Tofu

Prep + Cook Time: 20 minutes | Servings: 4

Ingredients:

- 1 block of extra firm tofu, pressed
- 1 tbsp smoked paprika
- ¼ cup cornstarch
- Salt and ground black pepper to taste

Directions:

1. Press the tofu and cut into small-sized or squared pieces.
2. Combine the smoked paprika and cornstarch. Sprinkle the mixture over the tofu pieces. Add salt and pepper to taste.
3. Transfer the seasoned tofu into the air fryer.
4. With the temperature set at 370 F, allow cooking for 12 minutes, or more – if you want crispier tofu.
5. Shake the tofu to stir them up at 4 minutes intervals. Pay close attention to the cooking to avoid burning the tofu.
6. Serve the cooked tofu and enjoy.

Tofu Scramble

Prep + Cook Time: 40 minutes | Servings: 3

Ingredients:

- 1 block tofu chopped into 1-inch pieces
- 1 tsp turmeric
- ½ tsp onion powder
- ½ cup chopped onion
- 2 tbsp olive oil
- 2 tbsp soy sauce
- ½ tsp garlic powder
- 2½ cups chopped red potato 1-inch cubes, 2-3 potatoes
- 4 cups broccoli florets

Directions:

1. Get a medium sized bowl and in it, combine the tofu, turmeric, onion powder, onion, 1 tablespoon olive oil, soy sauce, and garlic powder. Keep somewhere and allow mixture to marinate.
2. In another small bowl, place the potatoes and 1 tablespoon olive oil. Air fry both for 15 minutes at 400 F and shake midway into cooking, once.
3. Shake the potatoes again before adding the tofu. Keep the remaining marinade.
4. Allow the potatoes and tofu to cook for 15 extra minutes at 370 F.
5. Meanwhile, place the broccoli in the remaining marinade. You may add a bit extra soy sauce to ensure that the broccoli is well coated. Do not allow the broccoli to get too dry.
6. Only toss it into the air fryer from 5 minutes to the end of the cooking time.

Air Fryer Rutabaga

Prep + Cook Time: 25 minutes | Servings: 4

Ingredients:

- 1 large swede
- 1 tbsp parsley
- Salt and ground black pepper to taste
- 1 tsp garlic puree

Directions:

1. Dice the peeled swede and transfer them into the instant pot steamer basket.
2. Lower the steamer shelf and place the steamer basket on top.
3. Add a cup of warm water and place the lid on the Instant Pot.
4. With the valve set to sealing, allow cooking on manual pressure for about 4 minutes.
5. Release the pressure on the Instant Pot immediately after 4 minutes.
6. After draining the swede, mix it in the combined seasoning and garlic puree.
7. Transfer the mixed swede into the air fryer basket and allow cooking for 14 minutes at 360 F.
8. Serve.

Crispy Toasted Sesame Tofu

Prep + Cook Time: 1 hour 20 minutes | Servings: 4

Ingredients:

- 2 (14-oz) pkg. extra-firm tofu, drained and cut into 1-inch cubes
- Cooking spray
- 2 tbsp lower-sodium soy sauce
- 1 tbsp plus 1 tsp honey
- ¼ cup fresh orange juice (from 1 orange)
- 1 tbsp plus 1 tsp toasted sesame oil
- 1 tsp rice vinegar
- ½ tsp cornstarch
- 2 pkg. boil-in-bag brown rice (such as Uncle Bens)
- ½ tsp kosher salt
- 1 tbsp toasted sesame seeds
- 2 tbsp chopped scallions

Directions:

1. Ensure that your air fryer is preheated to 200 F.
2. With the tofu arranged on a plate pre-lined with multiple paper towel layers, cover the paper with extra paper towels, and finally a second plate.
3. Put a weight on top and set aside for 30 minutes.
4. After that, coat the tofu with cooking spray and divide into two batches.
5. Arrange the first batch in the air fryer basket following a single layer. Allow cooking at 375 F for about 15 minutes or until you have golden brown and crispy pieces.
6. Turn the tofu halfway during cooking. Retain the cooked tofu in the air fryer so that they remain warm.
7. Cook the second batch of the tofu.
8. While at it, combine the soy sauce, honey, orange juice, sesame oil, rice vinegar, and cornstarch in a small saucepan. Whisk constantly over high heat and bring to boil. Stop when the sauce thickens – this takes about 2-3 minutes. Withdraw and set aside.
9. Prepare your rice by following the directions on the package. Add salt to taste.
10. Place the tofu in the soy sauce mixture.
11. With the rice divided equally into four bowls, top each bowl with the tofu.
12. Finally, add sprinkles of sesame seeds and scallions. Serve.

Crispy, Sweet Beet Chips

Prep + Cook Time: 1 hour 10 minutes | Servings: 4

Ingredients:

- 3 medium-size red beets (about 1½ lbs), peeled and cut into 1/8-inch thick slices (about 3 cups slices)
- 2 tsp canola oil
- 3/4 tsp kosher salt
- ¼ tsp black pepper

Directions:

1. Get a large bowl and in it, combine pepper, salt, oil, and the sliced beets.
2. Divide the beets into two, place one half into the air fryer basket.
3. Set the timer to 25-30 minutes and the heat to 320 F.
4. Cook while shaking the basket every 5 minutes. Withdraw when dry and crisp.
5. Do the same for the other half of the beets.

German Pancakes

Prep + Cook Time: 20 minutes | Servings: 6

Ingredients:

- 3 whole eggs
- 1 cup whole wheat flour (Substitutes: oat flour)
- 1 cup almond milk (Substitutes: coconut milk; reduced fat milk; 2% whole milk)
- 2 heaping tablespoons unsweetened applesauce
- Pinch of salt

Directions:

1. While your air fryer is heating at 390 F, place in the cast iron tray or ramekin.
2. Blend all the ingredients for the batter until you have a smooth mixture. You may add tablespoons of milk and/or applesauce to reduce the thickness of the batter.
3. Add some non-stick baking spray to the cast iron tray, before pouring in a serving of the batter.
4. Allow air frying for 6-8 minutes. It is normal if the top comes out a bit firmer – it is the effect of the air fryer. Plus it ensures that the pancake gets a considerably firm outer coating/edges that soften after cooling.
5. Keep the remaining batter in an air-tight container and place it in the fridge. This ensures that it stays fresh for use every morning.
6. Garnish to taste and serve.

Garnish ideas:

Fresh berries

Swerve confectioners sugar

Raw unsweetened cacao nibs (for crunch and antioxidants)

Greek yogurt

Maple syrup (optional)

Lemon Slice Sugar Cookies

Prep + Cook Time: 30 minutes | Servings: 2

Ingredients:

- 1 package (3.4 ounces) instant lemon pudding mix
- ½ cup unsalted butter, softened
- ½ cup sugar
- 1 large egg
- 2 tbsp 2% milk
- 1 tsp baking powder
- 1-1/2 cups all-purpose flour
- ¼ tsp salt
- 2/3 cup confectioners' sugar
- 2 to 4 tsp lemon juice

Directions:

1. Get a large, clean bowl, and in it, combine the pudding mix, cream butter, and sugar. Mix until you have a light and soft mixture. Now, beat in the egg and milk.
2. Get another bowl, and in it, combine the baking powder, flour and salt, whisk and beat slowly into a creamed mixture.
3. Halve the dough, and shape each half into a 6 inches long roll, on a lightly floured rolling surface. Wrap each roll and place in the fridge for 3 hours or until they are firm enough.
4. Ensure that your air fryer is preheated to 325 F. Cut the unwrapped dough crosswise into ½ inches slices, and transfer them into the air fryer basked that is already lined with a foil. Maintain a single layer of arrangement.
5. Set the timer to 8-12 minutes and cook until you have light brown edges. Withdraw the basket and allow to cool for 2 minutes. Remove to wire racks and leave until they cool completely. Do the same for the remaining dough.
6. Get a clean small bowl, and in it, combine the confectioners' sugar alongside lemon juice. Mix until you have a drizzling consistency, and drizzle the mixture over the cookies. Leave until the mixture sets over the cookies.
7. It is possible that you make your dough two days before the cooking date. If this is the case, simply wrap and place the dough in a resealable container, and refrigerate.
8. You may also use the freezing option, which involves keeping the wrapped logs in a resealable container and freezing it. Simply unwrap the frozen logs and cut them into slices whenever you are ready to use them.
9. In the case of frozen logs, cook by following the same steps as above, but increase the cooking time by about 2 minutes.

Churros with Chocolate Sauce

Prep + Cook Time: 1 hour 30 minutes | Servings: 10

Ingredients:

- ½ cup water
- ¼ cup, plus 2 tbsp unsalted butter, divided
- ¼ tsp kosher salt
- ½ cup (about 2 1/8 oz.) all-purpose flour
- 2 large eggs
- 1/3 cup granulated sugar
- 2 tsp ground cinnamon
- 3 tbsp heavy cream
- 4 oz bittersweet baking chocolate, finely chopped
- 2 tbsp vanilla kefir

Directions:

1. In a small saucepan, placed over medium-high heat, combine water, ¼ cup of the butter and salt. Allow boiling before reducing the heat to medium-low. Now add flour and stir very well using a wooden spoon. Stop stirring when the dough is smooth – this takes about 30 seconds. Then continue cooking, while stirring consistently, until the dough starts pulling away from the sides of the pan and a film starts forming at the base of the pan – this takes about 2-3 minutes.
2. Remove the dough from the saucepan and transfer into a medium bowl. Continue stirring until it is slightly cooled –for about 1 minute. Now, add the eggs one after the other, while stirring. Only stop stirring when the egg-dough mixture is completely smooth after all the eggs have been added.
3. Transfer the mixture into a piping bag fitted with a medium star tip. Allow it to chill for 30 minutes.
4. Pipe 6 pieces, each 3-inch long, of the dough mixture into the air fryer basket, arranging them in a single layer. Allow cooking at 380 F for 10 minutes or until they are golden. Do the same for the unused dough.
5. In a clean medium bowl, combine the sugar and cinnamon. Brush the cooked churros with the remaining melted butter, before rolling them in the sugar mixture to ensure even coating.
6. Get a microwavable bowl and combine the cream and chocolate. Transfer the bowl into the microwave and microwave on HIGH until you have a smoothly-melted mixture – this takes about 30 seconds. After cooking for 15 seconds, stir the mixture.
7. At the end of the 30 seconds, stir in the kefir.
8. Combine the churros with the chocolate sauce when serving.

Half Dipped Chocolate Biscuits

Prep + Cook Time: 30 minutes | Servings: 6

Ingredients:

- 4 oz butter
- 4 oz white sugar
- 8 oz self raising flour
- 1 tsp vanilla essence
- 1 small egg beaten
- 2 oz milk chocolate

Directions:

1. Get a clean mixing bowl, and in it, combine the butter, sugar, and flour. Rub the butter into the flour until you have the mixture appearing like breadcrumbs.
2. Now pour in the vanilla essence and the egg, gradually, until the mixture turns into a dough.
3. Shape the dough into walnut-sized balls. Transfer the balls into the air fryer.
4. Allow cooking at 360 F for 15 minutes.
5. With the biscuits cooling, melt the milk chocolate in the air fryer – at 360 F for 4 minutes. While melting, stir constantly, the mixture is clearly in the liquid form.
6. Dip one side of the cool biscuits in the chocolate. Transfer them into the fridge and allow them to refrigerate for an hour.
7. Serve the set biscuits.

Chocolate Cake

Prep + Cook Time: 30 minutes | Servings: 4

Ingredients:

- Cooking spray
- 3 ½ tbsp butter, softened
- ¼ cup white sugar
- 1 tbsp apricot jam
- 1 egg
- 6 tbsp all-purpose flour
- Salt to taste
- 1 tbsp unsweetened cocoa powder

Directions:

1. Ensure that your air fryer is preheated to 320 F.
2. Get a small fluted pan and spray with some cooking spray.
3. Combine butter and sugar into a clean bowl. Beat the mixture with an electric mixer until you have a creamy and light mixture. Now toss in the jam and egg, and mix thoroughly. Sift in the flour, salt, cocoa powder and mix well again.
4. Transfer the batter into the sprayed pan, and return it into the air fryer basket.
5. Cook in the air fryer until a toothpick inserted into the center of the cake comes out unstained – this takes about 15 minutes.

Chocolate Cupcakes with Cream Cheese Frosting Recipe

Prep + Cook Time: 25 minutes | Servings: 8

Ingredients:

- ¼ of the mixture chocolate cake batter
- 3 oz butter
- 9 oz brown sugar
- 14 oz soft cheese
- 1 tbsp vanilla essence
- 3 tbsp organic cocoa powder

Directions:

1. The first step is to make the cake batter – simply mix it like you were making a chocolate cake. Set aside when ready.
2. Get eight small cupcake cases. Flour the base of each, as well as the sides. This prevents them from getting sticky.
3. Pour in the cake batter into each of the cases until they are ¾-filled.
4. Transfer them into the air fryer and allow cooking at 400 F for 7 minutes.
5. To make the cream frosting, combine the butter, brown sugar, soft cheese, and vanilla in a clean mixing bowl. Use a hand mixer to mix until the mixture is creamy and smooth.
6. Transfer the frosting into the freezer and leave for an hour. This makes it firm up a bit.
7. With the aid of the cake decorating kit, add ¼ of the set frosting cake into the cake decorator.
8. Using a fork, mix in the cocoa powder in the bowl until the mixture appears nice and chocolate in color.
9. Add the rest of the mixture into the cake decorating kit, and swirl the cupcake layer right on the top of the buns.
10. Keep the buns in the fridge for 20 minutes before serving.

Strawberry "Pop Tarts"

Prep + Cook Time: 1 hour 55 minutes | Servings: 6

Ingredients:

8 oz quartered strawberries (about 1 ¾ cups)

¼ cup granulated sugar

½ pkg (14-oz) refrigerated pie crusts

Cooking spray

1 ½ tsp fresh lemon juice (from 1 lemon)

½ cup (about 2 oz) powdered sugar

½ oz rainbow candy sprinkles (about 1 tbsp)

Directions:

1. In a medium microwavable bowl, combine the strawberries and granulated sugar. Stir until uniform, and leave for 15 minutes while stirring occasionally. Then microwave the mixture on HIGH until reduced and shiny – this takes about 10 minutes. Stir halfway through cooking, i.e., after 5 minutes. Leave the microwaved mixture to cool completely – this takes about 30 minutes.
2. On a lightly floured surface, roll the pie crust into a 12-inch circle. Cut the dough into 12 pieces of 2.5 x 3-inch rectangles, and reroll the scraps (if any). Using a spoon, add about two teaspoons of the strawberry mixture into the center of the six dough rectangles, leaving a border of about 0.5 inches. Brush the edges of the filled dough rectangles with water, and top with the remaining dough rectangles. Seal by pressing the edges with your fork. Use some cooking spray to coat the tarts generously.
3. Transfer 3 tarts into the air fryer basket, maintaining a single layer. Allow cooking at 350 F for 10 minutes or until golden brown. Do the same for the other tarts. Withdraw the cooked tarts onto a wire rack and allow them to cook thoroughly, for about 30 minutes.
4. In a small bowl, combine lemon juice and powdered sugar and whisk until smooth. Spoon-glaze the mixture over the cooled tarts, with some sprinkles of candy.

Doughnuts

Prep + Cook Time: 2 hours 15 minutes | Servings: 6

Ingredients:

- ¼ cup warm water, warmed (100F to 110F)
- 1 tsp active dry yeast
- ¼ cup, plus ½ tsp granulated sugar, divided
- 2 cups (about 8 ½ oz) all-purpose flour
- ¼ tsp kosher salt
- 1 large egg, beaten
- 2 tbsp unsalted butter, melted
- ¼ cup whole milk, at room temperature
- 1 cup (about 4 oz) powdered sugar
- 4 tsp tap water

Directions:

1. Get a clean small bowl, and in it, combine water, yeast and ½ teaspoon of the granulated sugar. Leave until the mixture is foamy – for about 5 minutes.
2. Get a clean medium bowl, and in it, combine flour, salt, and remaining 1/4 cup granulated sugar. Add the yeast mixture, egg, butter, and milk. Using a wooden spoon, stir the mixture until you have a soft dough forming.
3. On a lightly floured surface, turn the dough out and knead until it is smooth – this takes about 1-2 minutes. Transfer the smooth dough into a lightly greased bowl and cover. Keep it in a warm place until it has risen into the 2x volume – this takes about 1 hour.
4. Return the risen dough onto a lightly floured surface and gently roll to ¼-inch thickness. Using a 3-inch round cutter, cut out eight doughnuts from the dough. Remove the center using the 1-inch cutter. Transfer the doughnuts and the doughnut holes to a lightly-floured surface and cover loosely with plastic wrap. Leave for about 30 minutes to allow the doughnut double in volume.
5. Now, arrange two doughnut holes and two doughnuts in the air fryer basket following a single layer. Allow cooking at 350 F for 4-5 minutes or until golden brown. Do the same for the remaining doughnut holes and doughnuts.
6. Get a clean medium bowl and combine the powdered sugar and tap water. Whisk until the mixture is smooth. Now dip the doughnuts and holes in the glaze, placing each on a wire rack set over a rimmed baking sheet. This ensures that the excess glaze drips off.
7. Leave until the glaze hardens – for about 10 minutes.

Almost Guilt-Free Cinnamon Doughnut

Prep + Cook Time: 15 minutes | Servings: 2-3

Ingredients:

- 14 oz plan flour/all-purpose flour
- 1 cup milk
- 1½ tsp instant yeast
- 1.5 oz butter
- 4 oz brown sugar
- ½ tsp ground cinnamon

Directions:

1. Combine all your ingredients in the bread maker pan in the order provided by your manufacturer.
2. With the bread maker set to DOUGH setting, allow it to run till it stops.
3. Roll dough out until you have a thickness of ¾ - inch. Cut the doughnuts using your doughnuts cutter.
4. Ensure that your air fryer is preheated to 305 F. Bake 3-4 doughnuts at once, for 5 minutes or until they are golden brown.

Donuts Recipe

Prep + Cook Time: 20 minutes | Servings: 8

Ingredients:

- 1/3 cup granulated sugar
- ½ to 1 tsp cinnamon (adjust to your taste)
- 4 tbsp dark brown sugar (try to remove or break up any clumps)
- Pinch of allspice
- 1 can Pillsbury Grands Flaky Layers biscuits (8 biscuits; can use generic brands as well — I used Hy-Vee biscuits!)
- 3 tbsp butter, melted

Directions:

1. Combine the sugar, cinnamon, brown sugar and allspice in a cereal- or soup-sized bowl. Mix and keep.
2. Without flattening the biscuits, remove them from the can. Cut holes out of the center of each of the biscuits using a 1-inch circle biscuit cutter.
3. Move the donuts into the air fryer basket, and air fry for 5 minutes at 350 F. For the holes, fry for 3 minutes at the same temperature. You may divide the donuts and holes into batches, depending on the size of your air fryer.
4. Withdraw each hole or donut and immediately paint butter over their entire surface using a pastry brush.
5. Drop the painted holes and donuts into the sugar mixture, submerging them to ensure an even and generous coating. Shake off the excess gently.
6. Serve the holes and donuts while warm.

Honey Glazed Pineapple Fries

Prep + Cook Time: 15 minutes| Servings: 2

Ingredients:

- 4 oz fresh pineapple
- 2 tsp cinnamon
- 2 tbsp honey

Directions:

1. Chip the peeled pineapple into chunky chip sizes.
2. Arrange the fries in the grill pan placed in your air fryer. Maintain a long neat row, without gaps.
3. Allow cooking in the air fryer for 390 F for 3 minutes.
4. Turn the fries over using thongs and allow cooking for another 3 minutes at 390 F.
5. Withdraw the grill pan and sprinkle the pineapple fries with cinnamon, before glazing them with honey using a pastry brush.
6. Serve immediately while warm.

Peach Hand Pies

Prep + Cook Time: 55 minutes | Servings: 8

Ingredients:

- 2 (5-oz) fresh peaches, peeled and chopped
- ¼ tsp table salt
- 1 tsp vanilla extract
- 3 tbsp granulated sugar
- 1 tbsp fresh lemon juice (from 1 lemon)
- 1 tsp cornstarch
- 1 pkg (14-oz) refrigerated piecrusts
- Cooking spray

Directions:

1. Get a clean medium bowl, and in it, combine peaches, salt, vanilla, sugar, and lemon juice. Stir well. Leave for 15 minutes but stir occasionally. Drain the peaches, keeping one tablespoon liquid. Now stir cornstarch into the reserved liquid, and add the mixture into the drained peaches.
2. Make eight 4-inch circles out of the piecrusts. Add the filling in the center of each circle – about one tablespoon per circle. Brush the edges with water before folding the dough over the filling. This forms half-moons. Seal by crimping the edges with a fork. On the top of the pies, cut three small slits. Now spray the pies generously with cooking spray.
3. Transfer the pies into the air fryer basket – 3 at once in a single layer. Allow cooking for 12-14 minutes at 350 F, until the pies are golden brown.
4. Do the same for the other pies.

Baked Apple

Prep + Cook Time: 40 minutes| Servings: 2

Ingredients:

- 1 medium apple or pear
- ¼ tsp cinnamon
- 2 tbsp raisins
- 2 tbsp chopped walnuts
- ¼ tsp nutmeg
- 1½ tsp light margarine, melted
- ¼ cup water

Directions:

1. Ensure that your air fryer is preheated to 350 F.
2. Cut the pear or apple in half, around the middle, to gain access to scrape out some of the flesh.
3. Place the pear or apple at the base of the air fryer, or in the frying pan of the air fryer (if available).
4. Get a clean small bowl, and in it, combine the cinnamon, raisins, walnuts, nutmeg, and margarine.
5. Add the mixture to the center of the pear or apple halves.
6. Add some water into the pan, and bake the halves for 20 minutes.

Apple Pie

Prep + Cook Time: 55 minutes | Servings: 8

Ingredients:

For the dough:

- ½ lemon
- 4 oz superfine sugar
- 4 oz butter or margarine
- Salt to taste
- 9 oz self-rising flour

For the filling:

- 3 lbs tart apples
- ½ oz currants
- 5 tbsp apricot jam
- 2 tbsp vanilla custard
- Pinch of cinnamon
- 2 oz golden raisins
- 8 oz sugar

For decoration:

- Powdered sugar

Directions:

1. Grate and peel off the clean lemon, and squeeze the fruit.
2. Combine the sugar, butter, lemon juice, lemon peel, and a pinch of salt. Finally, rub the self-rising flour into the butter mixture.
3. Slice the peeled apples and combine with currants, apricot jam, custard, cinnamon, raisins, and sugar.
4. Roll the dough out to 10 -inch or divide into three and roll out to 8 -inch each, depending on the size of your air fryer tin. Either way, grease the tin(s) with some melted butter while placing a sheet of parchment paper on them.
5. Put the dough into the tin and press down until level. Make holes into the base of the tin(s) with a fork, to prevent the buildup of air bubbles. Now spread the filling on the top, and bake the cake. If you use an Avance XL, bake for 50 minutes at 320 F, and for 30 minutes at 320 F for Viva.
6. After baking, leave the cake in the tin until it is cool, then sprinkle with powdered sugar.

Mini Apple Pie

Prep + Cook Time: 30 minutes | Servings: 8

Ingredients:

- 1 oz butter
- 3 oz plain flour
- ½ oz caster sugar
- Water
- 2 medium red apples
- Pinch cinnamon
- Pinch caster sugar

Directions:

1. The first step is to make your pastry. Do this by combining the butter and plain flour in a mixing bowl, while rubbing the fat into the flour. Add the sugar and stir thoroughly. Add water to moisten the ingredients, so that they can form into a nice dough.
2. Once the dough is formed, knead it well until you have a nice smooth texture.
3. Cover your pastry tins with butter, to prevent sticking.
4. Roll out the pastry, and fill the tins with the pastry.
5. Place your peeled and diced apples into the tins too.
6. Add sprinkles of cinnamon and sugar.
7. Add an extra pastry layer to the top. Include a few fork markings to leave some breathing spaces.
8. Allow cooking for 18 minutes in the air fryer.

Apple Chips

Prep + Cook Time: 15 minutes | Servings: 2

Ingredients:

- 6 large red apples
- 1 tsp olive oil
- 1 pinch cinnamon

Directions:

1. Place your sliced apples in the air fryer.
2. Drizzle with some olive oil and allow cooking at 360 F for 10 minutes or until you have crisp apples.
3. With your cinnamon present in a large bowl, toss in the cooked apple chunks.
4. Serve.

Airfryer Soft Chocolate Brownies with Homemade Caramel Sauce

Prep + Cook Time: 40 minutes | Servings: 6

Ingredients:

- 4 and ½ oz butter
- 2 oz chocolate
- 6 oz brown sugar
- 2 medium eggs beaten
- 2 tsp vanilla essence

- 4 oz self raising flour
- 2 tbsp water
- 4 oz caster sugar
- 5 oz milk

Directions:

1. Ensure that your air fryer is preheated to 360 F.
2. The first step is to make your chocolate brownies. This is done by melting 4 oz of the butter and chocolate over medium heat in a suitable pan. Then stir in the brown sugar, medium eggs, and vanilla essence respectively. Finally, add the self-rising flour. Mix well and transfer the mixture into a greased dish, sizeable enough to fit into your air fryer.
3. With the dish in the air-fryer, allow cooking for 15 minutes at 360 F.
4. With the brownies cooking, prepare your caramel sauce. Start by combining water and caster sugar in a pan on medium heat. Leave until the sugar is melted. Increase the heat and continue cooking for an additional 3 minutes or until the mixture is light brown. Remove from the heat and allow to cool for 2 minutes, before stirring in ½ oz butter. Continue stirring until all the butter is melted. Finally, add the milk, gradually.
5. Leave the caramel sauce to cool.
6. Withdraw the cooked brownies and chop them into squares. Transfer the squares into a plate, alongside some sliced banana.
7. Cover them with the cool caramel sauce. Serve.

---

5 Ingredient Chocolate Mug Cake

Prep + Cook Time: 15 minutes | Servings: 1

Ingredients:

- 5 tbsp caster sugar
- ¼ cup self raising flour
- 1 tbsp cocoa powder
- 3 tsp coconut oil
- 3 tbsp whole milk

Directions:

1. Combine all ingredients in a clean mug and mix thoroughly to ensure that the cocoa is uniformly present in the cake.
2. Transfer the mug into the air fryer. Set the heat to 390 F and allow cooking for 10 minutes.
3. Rinse and do the same for other mugs until all the chocolate has been made.
4. Serve.

5 Ingredient Flourless Chocolate Cake

Prep + Cook Time: 2 hours 15 minutes | Servings: 1 large cake

Ingredients:

- 10 bananas
- 4 tbsp honey
- 10 tsp organic cocoa powder

- 8 large eggs
- 1 large avocado

Directions:

1. Ensure that your air fryer is preheated to 360 F.
2. Combine all ingredients into the blender (except the avocado) and blend until a smooth chocolate cake mixture is formed.
3. Divide the mixture into two – set aside one half, and divide the other half into two cake baking tins. Transfer the tins into the air fryer and leave for 35 minutes at 360 F.
4. After 35 minutes, withdraw the cake tins and let them rest on the wire rack and cool.
5. To the other half of the cake mixture, add the avocado until the paste is of your preferred thickness.
6. Sandwich a small layer in between two cakes. You may use the rest as a lovely chocolate icing around the cake.
7. Keep the cake in the fridge for about an hour to set the icing.
8. Serve.

Butter Cake

Prep + Cook Time: 35 minutes | Servings: 4

Ingredients:

- Cooking spray
- 7 tbsp butter, at room temperature
- ¼ cup and 2 tbsp white sugar
- 1 egg
- 1 pinch salt, or to taste
- 1 and 2/3 cups all-purpose flour
- 6 tbsp milk

Directions:

1. Ensure that your air fryer is preheated to 350 F.
2. Get a small fluted tube pan and spray with some cooking spray.
3. In a clean bowl, use your electric mixer to mix butter and ¼ cup white sugar plus two tablespoons of white sugar until you have a light and creamy mixture. Add the egg and mix lightly until the batter is soft and smooth. Stir in salt and flour. Add the milk and mix batter thoroughly.
4. Move the batter into the sprayed pan, and level the surface with the back of a spoon.
5. Transfer the pan into the air fryer basket and allow baking for 15 minutes, or until an inserted toothpick comes out clean of the cake.
6. Remove the cake from the pan and set aside to cool for about 5 minutes.

Banana Cake

Prep + Cook Time: 45 minutes | Servings: 4

Ingredients:

- Cooking spray
- 3½ tbsp butter, at room temperature
- 1/3 cup brown sugar
- 1 egg
- 1 banana, mashed

- 2 tbsp honey
- 1 cup self-rising flour
- 1 pinch salt
- ½ tsp ground cinnamon

Directions:

1. Ensure that your air fryer is preheated to 320 F.
2. Get a small fluted tube pan and spray with some cooking spray.
3. In a clean bowl, use your electric mixer to mix butter and sugar until you have a light and creamy mixture.
4. Mix the egg, banana, and honey in a different bowl. Combine the banana mixture and butter mixture and whisk until the new mixture is smooth.
5. Sift in flour, salt, and cinnamon and mix again until smooth.
6. Move the batter into the sprayed pan, and level the surface with the back of a spoon.
7. Transfer the pan into the air fryer basket and allow baking for 30 minutes, or until an inserted toothpick comes out clean of the cake.
8. Remove the cake from the pan and set aside to cool for about 5 minutes.

Peppermint Lava Cakes

Prep + Cook Time: 35 minutes | Servings: 4

Ingredients:

- 2/3 cup semisweet chocolate chips
- ½ cup butter, cubed
- 1 cup confectioners' sugar
- 2 large eggs
- 2 large egg yolks

- 1 tsp peppermint extract
- 6 tbsp all-purpose flour
- 2 tbsp finely crushed peppermint candies, optional

Directions:

1. Ensure that your air fryer is preheated to 375 F.
2. Get a microwavable bowl and in it, melt the chocolate chips and butter for 30 seconds.
3. Stir the mixture until smooth, and whisk in the confectioners' sugar, eggs, egg yolks, and peppermint extract. Mix until well combined and fold in flour.
4. Grease and flour four 4-oz.-ramekins generously.
5. Pour in the batter into the greased ramekins, without overfilling them.
6. Transfer the ramekins into the air fryer basket and allow cooking until a thermometer reads 320 F, and the cake edges set. This will take about 10-12 minutes, however, ensure that you do not overcook.
7. Withdraw the cake from the oven and leave for 5 minutes. Run a knife gently around the sides of the ramekins severally until the cake is loosened. Invert onto dessert plates.
8. Finally, add sprinkles of crushed candies and serve immediately.

Frugal Pineapple Cake

Prep + Cook Time: 55 minutes | Servings: 4

Ingredients:

- 9 oz self raising flour
- 4 oz butter
- 4 oz caster sugar
- 4 oz pineapple chopped into chunks
- 4 oz pineapple juice
- 2 oz dark chocolate grated
- 1 medium eggs
- 2 tbsp whole milk

Directions:

1. Ensure that your air fryer is preheated to 390 F.
2. Grease the cake tin generously.
3. Get a clean bowl, and in it, combine the flour and butter, rubbing the butter into the flour until the mixture appears like breadcrumbs.
4. Now stir in the sugar, followed by the pineapple pieces and juice, and finally the dark chocolate. Set aside the mixture.
5. Get a jug, and in it, combine the beaten egg and milk.
6. Mix the liquid to the breadcrumbs mixture until there is a soft cake mixture.
7. Allow the mixture to cook in the air fryer at 390 F for 40 minutes.
8. Withdraw and leave for 10 minutes to cool before serving.

Carrot Cake

Prep + Cook Time: 55 minutes | Servings: 2-3

Ingredients:

- 1 tsp ground cinnamon
- 5 oz self-raising flour
- 2 large eggs
- 4 oz sugar
- 4 oz canola oil
- 1 oz milk
- Pinch of salt
- 4 oz carrot, shredded
- 1½ oz mixed fruits

Directions:

1. Combine the ground cinnamon and self-rising flour in a clean bowl. Keep away.
2. Get another bowl and in it, combine the eggs and sugar and mix slightly. Add oil, milk, and a pinch of salt. Mix well and evenly.
3. Transfer the egg mixture into the sifted flour bowl. Mix the egg mixture into the flour mixture using the "cut and fold" method.
4. Fold in the shredded carrots and mixed fruits gradually using the same "cut and fold."
5. Ensure that your air fryer is preheated to 360 F for 5 minutes.
6. Transfer the mixture into the baking pan and cover with aluminum foil with random holes in it.
7. Move the baking pan into the air fryer, and set the heat to 320 F and timer to 35 minutes.
8. Once the timer goes off, remove the foil and continue baking for about 3-5 minutes, or until you have a golden brown cake surface.

Fruit Crumble Mug Cakes

Prep + Cook Time: 35 minutes | Servings: 4

Ingredients:

- 4 plums
- 1 small peach
- 1 small apple
- 1 small pear
- Handful blueberries
- 1 oz brown sugar
- 1 tbsp honey
- 4 oz plain flour
- 2 oz butter
- 1 oz caster sugar
- 1 oz gluten free oats

Directions:

1. Ensure that your air fryer is preheated to 320 F.
2. With the aid of the core equipment, get rid of the cores and stones from the fruit before dicing it into tiny square pieces.
3. Transfer the diced fruits into the base of the mugs, distributing them among the four mugs. Add sprinkles of brown sugar and honey generously, covering all the fruit. Set aside.
4. In a clean mixing bowl, combine the flour, butter, and caster sugar. Rub the fat into the flour and continue until you have an appearance of fine breadcrumbs. Now add the oats and mix well.
5. Cover the tops of the mugs with a layer of the crumble.
6. Transfer the mugs into the air fryer and allow cooking for 10 minutes. Raise the heat to 390 F and allow cooking for an additional 5 minutes. This ensures that there is a lovely crunch on the top of your crumble.

Flourless Key Lime Cupcakes

Prep + Cook Time: 35 minutes | Servings: 6

Ingredients:

- 8 oz soft cheese
- 10 oz Greek yoghurt
- 2 large eggs
- 1 large egg yolk only
- 2 limes juice and rind
- ¼ cup caster sugar
- 1 tsp vanilla essence

Directions:

1. With the aid of a wooden spoon or a hand mixer, combine the soft cheese and the Greek yogurt, until you have a creamy and nice mixture with the appearance of a mayonnaise.
2. Beat in the eggs and mix again before adding the limes, sugar and vanilla essence. Mix again.
3. By now, you should have a lovely creamy mixture, enough to fill up 6 cupcake cases. If you have excess, set it aside.
4. Transfer the cupcakes into the air fryer and allow baking for 10 minutes at 320 F. Raise the heat to 360 F and allow cooking for another 10 minutes.
5. With the cupcakes in the air fryer, remove the contents of your bowl into a cupcake nozzle. Transfer it into the fridge and leave for about 10 minutes.
6. Once the cupcakes are done, set aside on a baking tray for 10 minutes to allow cooling.
7. Create the top layer of your cool cupcakes with the aid of the nozzle. Move them into the fridge and leave for 4 hours, to ensure that the topping sets properly.
8. Decorate the cake with the spare limes.

Ricotta and Lemon Cheesecake

Prep + Cook Time: 40 minutes | Servings: 8

Ingredients:

- 1 lemon
- 18 oz ricotta
- 2 tsp vanilla essence
- 5 oz sugar
- 3 eggs, beaten
- 3 tbsp corn starch
- 8-inch round oven dish

Directions:

1. Ensure that your air fryer is preheated at 320 F.
2. Zest and juice the lemon.
3. Get a clean bowl and in it, add the ricotta with the vanilla essence, sugar, 1 tbsp lemon juice and the lemon zest. Combine by mixing until you have the desired consistency.
4. Add the eggs to the mixture one after the other, while stirring. Stir in the corn starch, and mix thoroughly.
5. Transfer the mixture into the oven dish and the dish into the air fryer basket. Allow cooking for 25 minutes, or until the center of the cheesecake is set.
6. Withdraw and set the dish up on a wire rack to allow cooling.
7. You may serve with a digestive biscuit crumbled over the top for an upside-down cheesecake.

New York Cheesecake

Prep + Cook Time: 55 minutes | Servings: 8

Ingredients:

- 4 oz brown sugar
- 8 oz plain flour
- 4 oz butter
- 2 oz butter, melted
- 1 ½ lbs soft cheese
- 2 cups caster sugar
- 3 large eggs
- 1 tbsp vanilla essence
- 2 oz quark

Directions:

1. The first step is making the biscuit base. Start by combining the sugar and the plain flour in a clean bowl. Mix the fat into the sugar and flour until you have a breadcrumb-like mixture. Make the mixture into biscuit shapes and place them on the baking mat of your air fryer. Allow cooking for 15 minutes at 360 F.
2. Apply little flour to the sides and bottom of the springform pan.
3. Break the cooked biscuits into small pieces, and mix them with the melted mixture. Transfer the mixture to the base of the springform pan.
4. Combine the soft cheese and the sugar in a different mixing bowl, and mix thoroughly using a hand mixer. Ensure that the sugar is mixed into the cheese to give a thick creamy mixture.
5. In a clean bowl, crack in the eggs and add the vanilla. Mix well with a fork.
6. Stir in the quark into the springform pan, and finally, pour in the cheesecake batter. Using the spatula, press down the cheesecake's tops and sides. This ensures flat, smooth edges, which will come out as expected after cooking.
7. Allow cooking for 30 minutes at 360 F. Leave in the air fryer for an additional 30 minutes after cooking to keep it warm.
8. Withdraw and place the cake in the fridge. Leave for six hours to ensure the proper setting of the cake. Serve once set.

Caramel Cheesecake

Prep + Cook Time: 55 minutes | Servings: 8

Ingredients:

- 1 can condensed milk
- 6 digestives
- 2 oz butter, melted
- ½ lb caster sugar
- 1 lb soft cheese
- 1 tbsp vanilla essence
- 4 large eggs
- 1 tbsp chocolate, melted

Directions:

1. Place the can of condensed milk in your Instant Pot without the can wrappings getting under the water. Set your Instant Pot to MANUAL, seal, and allow cooking for 40 minutes.
2. Ensure that your airfryer is preheated to 360 F
3. Using your hands, apply some flour on the base and sides of the springform plan to ensure that it does not get sticky.
4. Hammer the digestive biscuits with a rolling pin inside a sandwich bag or its wrappers to form crumbles.
5. Combine the biscuit crumbles and the melted butter inside the springform pan. Mix well with your hands to ensure it pushes down on the base.
6. Get a clean mixing bowl, and in it, combine the sugar and the soft cheese until you have a nice and soft mixture. For best results, use a hand mixer. Add the vanilla essence and the eggs, and mix well with the mixer. Set aside.
7. Cool the condensed milk when it is done. Then open it up and empty the caramel into the bowl. With the aid of a fork, mix it in before placing the mixture over the biscuit base, in the springform pan.
8. Use your spatula to make it smooth and level.
9. Allow cooking at 360 F for 15 minutes, reduce the heat to 320 F and cook for another 10 minutes, and finally cook at 300 F for 15 minutes.
10. After cooking, remove from the air fryer and place in the fridge for like 6 hours.
11. This allows the cake to set before drizzling small amounts of leftover caramel and melted chocolate.
12. Serve.

Freshly Baked Banana Bread

Prep + Cook Time: 40 minutes | Servings: 1

Ingredients:

- ½ lb self raising flour
- ¼ tsp bicarbonate of soda
- 3 oz butter
- 5 oz caster sugar
- 2 medium eggs
- 4 oz chopped walnuts
- 1 lb bananas weight with peeling

Directions:

1. Ensure that your air fryer is preheated to 360 F.
2. Slot in the greased tin into the air fryer.
3. Combine the flour and the bicarbonate of soda.
4. Get another bowl and in it, cream the butter and sugar to produce a pale and soft mixture. Then add the eggs one after the other, while adding a little flour in the process.
5. Stir in the unused flour and walnuts.
6. Mash the peeled bananas, and place them in the mixture.
7. Fill the tin with the banana-bread mix and allow cooking in the air fryer for 10 minutes at 360 F. Reduce the heat to 340 F and cook for an additional 15 minutes.
8. Withdraw and serve.

Chocolate Banana Bread Recipe

Prep + Cook Time: 30 minutes | Servings: 8

Ingredients:

- 3 bananas
- 3 small eggs
- 3 oz coconut oil
- 1 tbsp vanilla essence
- 2 tbsp honey
- 4 tbsp gluten free oats
- 4 tbsp banana flour
- 3 tbsp kakosi cacao powder

Directions:

1. Get a mixing bowl, and in it, mash up the bananas.
2. In another bowl, crack the eggs and combine it with the coconut oil, vanilla essence, and the honey. Use your hand mixer to mix thoroughly until you have a smooth mixture.
3. Blend the gluten-free oats in the blender until you have a mixture that looks like coarse breadcrumbs.
4. Pour in the blended oats into the mixing bowl containing the banana flour, and add the cacao. Mix thoroughly.
5. Apply a little extra banana flour to the sides and base of the air fryer baking pan. This ensures that the pan doesn't get sticky.
6. Place the baking pan inside the air fryer, and pour in the banana bread mixture.
7. Allow cooking for 18 minutes at 360 F or until you have a cocktail stick coming out clear from the center of the cake.
8. Serve alongside chocolate sauce.

Chocolate Chip Zucchini Bread Recipe

Prep + Cook Time: 35 minutes | Servings: 4

Ingredients:

- 13 oz self raising flour
- 11 oz zucchini/courgette
- 2 tbsp vanilla essence
- 10 oz brown sugar
- 9 oz olive oil
- 1 tsp nutmeg
- 2 tsp cinnamon
- 3 large eggs, beaten
- Dieter's green tea
- 1 oz cocoa powder
- 7 oz dark chocolate chips

Directions:

1. Ensure that your air fryer is preheated to 360 F.
2. Apply a little flour to the sides and base of your air fryer baking pan. Set it aside.
3. Grate the zucchini and set aside.
4. Get a large mixing bowl and in it, combine the vanilla extract, brown sugar, olive oil, nutmeg, cinnamon and eggs. Mix thoroughly using a hand mixer until you have a soft and light mixture.
5. Fold in the flour, green tea, and cocoa powder. Do the same for the grated zucchini, alongside the dark chocolate chips.
6. Add the batter into the baking pan, return it into the air fryer, and allow cooking at 360 F for 20 minutes.

Don't Go Heatin' the House Gluten-Free Fresh Cherry Crumble

Prep + Cook Time: 1 hour 20 minutes | Servings: 4

Ingredients:

- 1/3 cup butter
- 3 cups pitted cherries
- 10 tbsp white sugar, divided
- 2 tsp lemon juice
- 1 cup gluten-free all purpose baking flour
- 1 tsp vanilla powder
- 1 tsp ground nutmeg
- 1 tsp ground cinnamon

Directions:

1. Cube butter and place in freezer until firm, about 15 minutes.
2. Preheat air fryer to 325 F.
3. Combine pitted cherries, 2 tablespoons sugar, and lemon juice in a bowl; mix well. Pour cherry mixture into baking dish.
4. Mix flour and 6 tablespoons of sugar in a bowl. Cut in butter using fingers until particles are pea-size. Distribute over cherries and press down lightly.
5. Stir 2 tablespoons sugar, vanilla powder, nutmeg, and cinnamon together in a bowl. Dust sugar topping over the cherries and flour.
6. Bake in the preheated air fryer. Check at 25 minutes; if not yet browned, continue cooking and checking at 5-minute intervals until slightly browned. Close drawer and turn off air fryer. Leave crumble inside for 10 minutes. Remove and allow to cool slightly, about 5 minutes.

Cranberry Muffins

Prep + Cook Time: 30 minutes | Servings: 4

Ingredients:

- 3 oz flour
- 1 tsp cinnamon
- 1½ tsp baking powder
- Pinch of salt
- 3 tbsp sugar
- 1 small egg, beaten
- 2 oz melted butter
- 3 oz milk
- 3 oz dried cranberries
- 8 paper muffin cups

Directions:

1. Ensure that the air fryer is preheated to 390 F.
2. Double up the muffin cups so that you have a total of four cups.
3. Get a clean bowl, and in it, sift in the flour and add cinnamon, baking powder, a pinch of salt, and sugar. Mix thoroughly.
4. Get another bowl, and in it, beat the egg lightly, adding the melted butter, and the milk. Mix well.
5. Stir the egg mixture into the flour, and add the cranberries. Mix well.
6. Place the batter into the doubled muffin cups, and move them into the air fryer basket carefully.
7. Return the basket into the air fryer, and allow baking for 15 minutes, or until you have golden brown, cooked muffins. Leave the muffins to cool in the cups.

Easy Chocolate Muffins

Prep + Cook Time: 30 minutes | Servings: 12

Ingredients:

- 7 oz self raising
- 8 oz caster sugar
- 1 oz cocoa powder
- 3 oz milk chocolate
- 4 oz butter
- 2 medium eggs
- 5 tbsp milk
- Water as needed
- ½ tsp vanilla essence

Directions:

1. Ensure that your air fryer is preheated to 360 F.
2. Get a large mixing bowl, and in it, combine the sugar, cocoa, and the flour.
3. Rub in the butter to arrive at a consistency similar to that of breadcrumbs.
4. Get a small mixing bowl and crack the eggs into it. Add the milk and mix thoroughly.
5. Pour in the egg/milk mixture into the large mixing bowl containing the flour/cocoa mixture and stir thoroughly.
6. Pour in the vanilla essence and mix well – you may add some water if the mixture is too thick. Stop when you have a bun mix or something close.
7. With the aid of your rolling pin, bash the milk chocolate in a sandwich bag until there are different sizes. Transfer it into the bowl and mix again thoroughly.
8. Fill the bun cases with the mixture and move the filled cases into the air fryer.
9. Allow cooking at 360 F for 9 minutes, and another 6 minutes at 320 F. Serve.

Apricot and Blackberry Crumble

Prep + Cook Time: 35 minutes | Servings: 4

Ingredients:

- 8 oz fresh apricots
- 1 tbsp lemon juice
- 4 oz fresh blackberries
- 3 oz sugar
- 4 oz flour
- 2 oz cold butter, in cubes
- 1 tbsp cold water
- Pinch of salt
- Shallow, round cake tin, 6 -inch diameter

Directions:

1. Ensure that your air fryer is preheated to 390 F.
2. Slice the apricots into two and get rid of the stones. Now cut the halves into cubes.
3. Transfer the cubes and blackberries into a bowl containing the lemon juice and 1 oz of sugar. Mix well.
4. Spread the fruit mix over the already-greased cake tin.
5. Get another bowl, and in it, combine the flour with the remaining sugar, butter, one tablespoon cold water, and a pinch of salt. Mix until you have a reasonable consistency. Now use your fingertips to form the mixture into a crumbly mixture.
6. Distribute the crumbly mixture over the fruit equally, and press the top layer lightly.
7. Move the bowl into the air fryer basket, and allow baking for 20 minutes or until there is a golden brown color.
8. Serve while hot, cold, or lukewarm, alongside ice cream, vanilla sauce, or whipped cream.
9. You may replace the apricots with mangos, pears, and apples – you will get the same amazing results. Likewise, you can combine raspberries, fresh cranberries, or blueberries.

Pumpkin Muffins

Prep + Cook Time: 25 minutes | Servings: 12

Ingredients:

- 2 cups gluten free oats
- 1 cup pumpkin puree
- ½ cup honey
- 1 tsp coconut butter
- 2 medium eggs beaten
- 1 tbsp cocoa nibs
- 1 tsp nutmeg
- 1 tbsp vanilla essence

Directions:

1. Combine all ingredients into the blender and blend until the mixture is smooth.
2. Add the mixture into little muffin cases, filling up 12 different cases.
3. Transfer the filled cases into the air fryer.
4. Allow cooking for 15 minutes at 360 F.
5. Serve when cool.

Raspberry Crumble

Prep + Cook Time: 40 minutes | Servings: 2-3

Ingredients:

- 1 (6 oz) tub fresh raspberries
- 1 tsp cornstarch
- 1 tbsp white granulated sugar
- 4 tbsp (½ stick) of cold butter, chopped into small cubes
- ¼ cup light brown sugar
- 1/3 cup old fashioned oats
- ¼ cup all-purpose flour
- Whipped cream or ice cream to serve

Directions:

1. Pat dry the washed raspberries, before moving them into the bowl containing the cornstarch and white sugar. Leave for about 10 minutes for the mixture to macerate.
2. Meanwhile, place the cubes of cold butter, brown sugar, oats and the all-purpose flour in the food processor and pulse until the mixture appears like crumbs.
3. Make two mini pie pans out of the macerating raspberries and the juices released (4-inches each).
4. Top each pie with the oat-butter crumble and transfer them into the air fryer basket.
5. Allow air frying at 350 F for 15 minutes.
6. Serve while warm, alongside ice cream or whipped cream and some more berries.

Cinnamon Apple Chips with Almond Yogurt Dip

Prep + Cook Time: 30 minutes | Servings: 4

Ingredients:

- 1 (8-oz) apple (such as Fuji or Honeycrisp)
- 2 tsp canola oil
- 1 tsp ground cinnamon
- Cooking spray
- ¼ cup plain 1% low-fat Greek yogurt
- 1 tsp honey
- 1 tbsp almond butter

Directions:

1. Slice your apple into thin slices on a mandolin.
2. Transfer them into a bowl containing the oil and cinnamon – toss to ensure even coating.
3. Into the sprayed air fryer basket, arrange 7-8 slices in a single layer. Allow cooking for 12 minutes at 375 F. Ensure that you turn the slices at 4-minute intervals while rearranging the slices to flatten them. This is necessary because the slices will move while cooking. The slices will only appear completely crisp after cooling, not after withdrawing from the air fryer.
4. Do the same for the other apple slices.
5. Meanwhile, get a small bowl, and in it, combine the yogurt, honey, and the almond butter until you have a smooth mixture.
6. Serve by placing 6-8 apple slices on each plate, alongside a small dollop of dipping sauce.

Double-Glazed Cinnamon Biscuit Bites

Prep + Cook Time: 50 minutes | Servings: 8

Ingredients:

- ¼ tsp ground cinnamon
- 1 tsp baking powder
- 2 tbsp granulated sugar
- 2/3 cup whole-wheat flour
- 2/3 cup all-purpose flour
- ¼ tsp kosher salt
- 4 tbsp cold salted butter, cut into small pieces
- 1/3 cup whole milk
- Cooking spray
- 3 tbsp water
- 2 cups (about 8 oz.) powdered sugar

Directions:

1. In a medium bowl, combine the cinnamon, baking powder, granulated sugar, flours, and salt. Whisk into a consistent mixture.
2. Add the butter; cut the butter into mixture with the aid of two knives or a pastry cutter. Ensure that the butter is well-combined with the flour to form a dough that appears like coarse cornmeal.
3. Pour in the milk, stir together until the dough forms into a ball.
4. Transfer the dough onto a floured surface. Knead until you have a smooth dough forming a cohesive ball – this takes about 30 seconds.
5. Now cut the dough into 16 equal pieces. Form each piece into a smooth ball by rolling lightly.
6. Place eight balls into an already-sprayed air fryer basket without the balls overlapping one another.
7. Respray the donut balls with cooking spray.
8. Allow cooking at 350°F for 10-12 minutes or until you have browned and puffed donuts.
9. Withdraw the cooked donuts carefully and place them on a wire rack over foil.
10. Allow cooling for about 5 minutes. Do the same for the other donut balls.
11. In another medium bowl, combine water and powdered sugar. Whisk until you have a smooth mixture. Apply half of the glaze over the donut balls.
12. Leave again for 5 minutes to allow cooling, before glazing again.
13. Allow the excess glaze to drip off. Serve.

Delicious British Lemon Tarts

Prep + Cook Time: 35 minutes | Servings: 8

Ingredients:

- 4 oz butter
- 1 oz caster sugar
- 8 oz plain flour
- 1 large lemon zest and juice
- Pinch nutmeg
- 4 tsp Mrs Darlington's lemon curd

Directions:

1. Get a clean large mixing bowl, and in it, prepare your shortcrust pastry by combining the butter, sugar, and flour following the rubbing-in method. Once you have a mixture that appears like fine breadcrumbs, add the lemon rind and juice as well as the nutmeg. Mix again thoroughly, and if required, add little water to ensure that the ingredients combine well into a soft dough.
2. Roll out the pastry with some flour.
3. Use little pastry cases or small ramekins to rub some flour around them, to prevent them from getting sticky. Then add your nice and thin pastry. A thin pastry is necessary to ensure that the cooked pastry doesn't end up too thick.
4. Into each of the mini tart containers, add ½ teaspoon lemon curd before cooking for 15 minutes at 360 F.
5. Once cooked, leave for a couple of minutes to cool. Serve.

Stuffed Baked Apples

Prep + Cook Time: 35 minutes | Servings: 2

Ingredients:

- 2 small apples
- 1 tbsp raisins
- 2 sheets of ready-to-use puff pastry, 10 x 10 cm
- 2 tbsp milk
- Pizza pan, 15 cm diameter

Directions:

1. Ensure that your air fryer is preheated to 360 F.
2. Core the peeled apples, and create some extra space in the hollowed-out core by scrapping some extra apple off.
3. Combine the jam and the raisins.
4. Place each apple on a slice of dough, while filling the core with the raising mixture. Fold the dough around the apple and enclose it completely.
5. Transfer the stuffed apples onto the pizza pan. Allow the dough seams to face down while brushing the dough with milk.
6. Move the pizza pan into the air fryer basket, and allow baking for 20 minutes or until the stuffed apples appear golden brown and done.
7. Remove and leave the baked apples to cool. Serve while lukewarm, alongside a scoop of ice cream or vanilla quark (curd cheese).
8. Instead of raisins and jam, you may decide to fill the apples with:
   a. Chopped dried apricots Cinnamon and ½ tablespoon of soft brown sugar
   b. Raisins, ½ tablespoon of grated orange peel, plus ½ tablespoon brown sugar
   c. Dried cranberries, one teaspoon scrapings of vanilla pod, and ½ tablespoon sugar.

Apple Dumplings

Prep + Cook Time: 40 minutes | Servings: 8

Ingredients:

- 2 tbsp sultana raisins
- 1 tbsp brown sugar
- 2 sheets puff pastry
- 2 small apples, peeled and cored
- 2 tbsp butter, melted

Directions:

1. Ensure that your air fryer is preheated to 320 F.
2. Apply some aluminum foil as lining for the air fryer basket.
3. Get a clean bowl, and in it, combine the sultanas and brown sugar.
4. On a clean work surface, place a soft pastry sheet and with the apple placed on the sheet, fill the core with the sultana mixture. Fold the pastry around the apple such that it is entirely covered. Do the same for the remaining filling, apple, and pastry.
5. Transfer the dumplings into the already-prepared air fryer basket.
6. Brush the dumplings with melted butter before cooking for 25 minutes or until you have soft, golden brown apples.

Apple Cinnamon Dessert Empanadas

Prep + Cook Time: 35 minutes | Servings: 12

Ingredients:

- 2 tbsp raw honey
- 1/8 tsp nutmeg
- 1 tsp cinnamon
- 1 tsp vanilla extract
- 2 apples, diced
- 1 tsp water
- 2 tsp cornstarch
- 12 empanada wrappers
- 1 tsp olive oil spray

Directions:

1. In a saucepan on medium-high heat, combine honey, nutmeg, cinnamon, vanilla, and apples. Cook for 2-3 minutes while stirring until you have soft apples.
2. In a different bowl, combine water and the cornstarch. Transfer the mixture into the pan and cook for an extra 30 seconds while stirring.
3. On a clean flat surface, lay out the empanada wrappers, adding the apple mixture to each wrapper.
4. Close and roll each empanada into a half, pinching the crust along the edges. Now roll each side inward and continue twisting until you have a closed crust.
5. Brush empanadas with olive oil.
6. Transfer the wrapped empanadas into the air fryer basket. Feel free to stack them.
7. Allow cooking for 8 minutes at 400 F.
8. Turn and flip the empanadas after 8 minutes, then allow cooking for an extra 10 minutes.
9. Allow to cool and serve.

Tarte Tatin

Prep + Cook Time: 45 minutes | Servings: 2

Ingredients:

- 2 oz cold butter, in thin slices
- 4 oz flour
- 1 egg yolk
- 1 large, firm apple (Elstar, Jonagold)
- 1 oz sugar
- Small, round fixed-base cake pan, 6 -inch diameter

Directions:

1. With the 1 oz butter slices cut into sizable bits, mix them into the combination of the flour and egg yolk. If required, add some drops of water, and knead the mixture into a smooth ball of dough.
2. Roll out the dough to a 6 -inch circle on a floured work surface.
3. Ensure that your air fryer is preheated to 390 F.
4. Core the peeled apple, and slice it into 12 separate wedges.
5. Return the unused butter slices into the pan, add sprinkles of sugar, and the apple wedges, following a circular pattern.
6. Cover the apple wedges with the rolled-out dough, while pressing the dough down along the inside edge of the cake pan.
7. Transfer the cake pan into the air fryer basket, and allow baking for 25 minutes or until the Tarte Tatin is done.
8. Once the baking is completed, place a plate on the cake pan, and flip while holding both the cake pan and the plate. This way, you have moved the tart into the plate.
9. Serve while hot or lukewarm alongside vanilla sauce or ice cream.

Pineapple with Honey and Coconut

Prep + Cook Time: 25 minutes | Servings: 4

Ingredients:

- ½ small fresh pineapple
- ½ tbsp lime juice
- 1 tbsp honey
- ¼ liter ice cream or mango sorbet
- Parchment paper

Directions:

1. Ensure that your air fryer is preheated to 390 F.
2. Leaving ½ inch of the edge unlined, line the base of the basket with baking parchment.
3. Cut the pineapple into eight sections by cutting lengthways. Remove the skin, alongside the deep crowns, as well as the tough core.
4. Combine, in a bowl, the lime juice, and the honey. Now brush the pineapple sections with the mixture before transferring them into the air fryer basket. Add sprinkles of coconut on top.
5. With the basket in the air fryer, set the cooking time to 12 minutes or until the pineapple and the coconut appear golden brown.
6. Place the pineapple sections on plates, alongside a sufficient amount of ice cream.

Cherry Clafoutis

Prep + Cook Time: 45 minutes | Servings: 4

Ingredients:

- 8 oz fresh cherries or 1 jar of cherries, well-drained
- 2-3 tbsp crème de cassis or vodka
- 1 egg
- 5 oz sour cream
- 2 oz flour
- Pinch of salt
- 2 tbsp sugar
- 2/3 tbsp butter
- Powdered sugar
- Small, low cake pan, 6 -inch diameter

Directions:

1. After pitting the cherries, combine them with the kirsch or crème de cassis in a clean bowl.
2. Ensure that your air fryer is preheated to 360 F.
3. Get another bowl, and in it, combine the egg, sour cream, flour, a pinch of salt, and sugar until you have thick but smooth dough. If required, add one or two drops of water.
4. Transfer the batter into the buttered cake pan, and place the cherries over the top of the batter evenly. Lastly, make the remaining butter into small bits and place them evenly on the top.
5. Transfer the cake pan into the air fryer basket and allow baking until the clafoutis is golden brown and done – this takes about 25 minutes.
6. Once done, withdraw and dust the clafoutis with plenty of powdered sugar.
7. Serve in slices while lukewarm.

Chocolate Chip Oatmeal Cookies

Prep + Cook Time: 35 minutes | Servings: 6

Ingredients:

- 1 cup butter, softened
- 3/4 cup sugar
- 3/4 cup packed brown sugar
- 2 large eggs
- 1 tsp vanilla extract
- 3 cups quick-cooking oats
- 1-1/2 cups all-purpose flour
- 1 package (3.4 oz) instant vanilla pudding mix
- 1 tsp baking soda
- 1 tsp salt
- 2 cups (12 oz) semisweet chocolate chips
- 1 cup chopped nuts

Directions:

1. Preheat air fryer to 350 F. Line the air fryer basket with foil.
2. In a large bowl, combine butter and sugars until light and fluffy. Beat in eggs and vanilla. Combine the oats, flour, dry pudding mix, baking soda and salt; gradually add to creamed mixture and mix well. Stir in chocolate chips and nuts.
3. Form into balls using one tablespoon of dough; flatten slightly. Place shaped dough 2 in. apart onto foil-lined air fryer basket. Air fry for 8-10 minutes or until lightly browned. Remove to wire racks. Repeat with remaining dough.

Shortbread Heart Cookies

Prep + Cook Time: 30 minutes | Servings: 2

Ingredients:

- 9 oz plain flour
- 6 oz butter
- 3 oz caster sugar
- 1 tsp vanilla essence
- Chocolate buttons

Directions:

1. Ensure that your air fryer is preheated to 360 F.
2. Get a sizable mixing bowl and in it, combine all the ingredients, except the chocolate, and rub the fat into the other ingredients.
3. After a while, the fat will rub into the other ingredients to produce a nice soft dough.
4. Once the dough is big enough, roll it out and use your cutter to cut into heart shapes.
5. Transfer the shapes into the air fryer lined with a baking sheet, while leaving some space between the shapes. Allow cooking for 10 minutes at 360 F.
6. After 10 minutes, open the air fryer, and add the chocolate buttons on the top of the half-done dough.
7. Resume cooking for an additional 10 minutes at 320 F.
8. Serve the cookies alongside marshmallows and hot chocolate.

Dark Chocolate Chunk Cookies

Prep + Cook Time: 25 minutes | Servings: 8

Ingredients:

- 4 oz brown sugar
- 5 oz butter
- 2 medium eggs, beaten
- Pinch of salt
- 1 tbsp honey

- 2 oz caster sugar
- 2 tsp vanilla essence
- 11 oz self raising flour
- 4 oz dark chocolate (70-75% cocoa)

Directions:

1. Form a nicely creamed mixture by beating the brown sugar into the butter. The mixture should not have the gritty brown sugar texture.
2. Stir in the egg, salt, honey, sugar, and vanilla. Mix slightly at first before using the hand mixer to mix thoroughly for some minutes until you have a consistent mixture.
3. Pour in the flour and mix well again.
4. Make the mixture into cookie shapes using your hands, and layer them onto a chopping board or a clean worktop.
5. With your hands, break the dark chocolate into quarter chunks. Push each chunk into the top of the cookies such that they stay at the top without appearing when cooked.
6. Transfer them onto the grill pan of the air fryer.
7. Allow cooking for 10 minutes at 350 F.
8. Serve alongside milk.

Soft Chocolate Chip Cookies

Prep + Cook Time: 25 minutes | Servings: 12

Ingredients:

- 6 oz butter
- 1½ oz coconut sugar
- 3 oz brown sugar
- 3 tbsp whole milk
- 1 tbsp cocoa powder

- 1 tsp vanilla essence
- 4 tbsp honey
- 10 oz self raising flour
- 3 handfuls chocolate chips

Directions:

1. Ensure that your air fryer is preheated to 360 F.
2. In a clean mixing bowl, combine the butter and sugar. Mix the fat into the sugar with the aid of your hand mixer, until the mixture is soft and light.
3. Combine the milk, cocoa powder, flour, vanilla, and honey in a separate bowl. Mix thoroughly with a fork.
4. Coat your hands with flour to ensure that the cookie mixture does not stick to them.
5. Now roll in the chop chips or crushed chocolate using your hands.
6. Using your hands still, mix for some time to ensure that the chips are coated evenly and generously.
7. Roll out the coated mixture into 12 small cookie balls.
8. Transfer the balls into a silver foil sheet or a baking sheet placed in the air fryer.
9. Allow cooking for 15 minutes at 360 F.
10. Serve alongside milk.

Soft White Chocolate Chip Cookies

Prep + Cook Time: 30 minutes | Servings: 4

Ingredients:

- 4 oz butter
- 3 oz brown sugar
- 1 oz whole milk
- 1 oz honey
- 6 oz self raising flour
- 2 oz white chocolate

Directions:

1. Soften the butter to taste by beating slightly, before adding the sugar. Beat the sugar into the butter until the mixture is soft and light.
2. Stir in the milk, honey, flour, and white chocolate. Mix thoroughly.
3. Shape the mixture into cookies, and transfer them into the air fryer.
4. Allow cooking at 360 F until the mixture is chips are cooked in the middle – this takes about 18 minutes.
5. Serve.

Peanut Cookies

Prep + Cook Time: 30 minutes | Servings: 12

Ingredients:

- 1 lb all-purpose flour
- 9 oz peanut butter
- 3 oz icing sugar
- 5 oz vegetable oil
- Pinch of salt

Glaze:

- 1 egg yolk

Directions:

1. In a clean mixing bowl, combine all the ingredients and mix thoroughly and evenly with your hand. Stop when you have a soft dough.
2. Withdraw the frying basket and close the air fryer. Now preheat to 340 F.
3. Line the basket with baking sheet.
4. On a clean working surface, roll the dough into balls of 1 -inchin diameter.
5. Arrange the balls in the lined frying basket and glaze the surface of the balls with egg yolk.
6. Allow baking until the top is golden brown – this takes about 10-12 minutes.
7. If your preference is a crunchy crust cookie, extend the baking time by a few minutes.

10 Minute Smartie Cookies

Prep + Cook Time: 14 minutes | Servings: 8

Ingredients:

- 3 tbsp cocoa
- 7 oz self raising flour
- 4 oz caster sugar
- 4 oz butter
- 1 tsp vanilla essence
- 2 oz white chocolate
- 5 tbsp milk
- 1/3 tube of Smarties

Directions:

1. Ensure that your air fryer is preheated to 360 F.
2. Get a large mixing bowl, and in it, combine the cocoa, flour, and sugar.
3. Rub in the butter, and then stir in the vanilla essence. Mix thoroughly.
4. With the aid of a rolling pin, smash the white chocolate to produce small- and medium-sized chocolate chips. Combine the chocolate chips with the milk and add the mixture into the cookie mix. Mix the new mixture thoroughly.
5. Knead the mixture until you have a soft and nice mixture. If required, feel free to add a little extra milk.
6. Roll out the mixture again, and cut into biscuit shapes with the aid of your cookie cutter.
7. Place the Smarties into the top of the cookies, such that they are midway into the cookie.
8. Transfer the cookies onto a baking sheet in the air fryer and allow cooking at 360 F for 10 minutes.
9. Serve alongside milk.

Butterless Strawberry Sugar Cookies

Prep + Cook Time: 30 minutes | Servings: 10

Ingredients:

- 1 cup caster sugar
- 1 cup brown sugar
- ¾ cup olive oil
- ¼ cup coconut oil
- 2 medium eggs
- 1 tbsp vanilla essence
- 1 tbsp honey
- 3 cups self raising flour
- 4 tbsp gluten free oats
- 1 cup diced strawberries

Directions:

1. Ensure that your air fryer is preheated to 360 F.
2. In a clean mixing bowl, combine the sugars and oils. Mix with a hand mixer to form a smooth and creamy mixture.
3. Combine the mixture with eggs, the vanilla essence, and the honey. Mix again with the hand mixer until the eggs are well beaten into the cookie batter.
4. With the aid of a fork, mix in the flour and oats gradually. Continue until you have a uniformly-combined cookie batter.
5. Clean the strawberries and add them into the batter. Mix with your hands.
6. Transfer the cookie dough onto the baking pan of the air fryer – 6 cookie dough balls per batch.
7. Allow cooking at 360 F for 12 minutes.
8. Once the timer goes off, withdraw the cookies onto a cooling rack.
9. Repeat the process for the rest of the dough, until there are 12 strawberry sugar cookies.
10. Serve.

Soft and Creamy Chocolate Cookie Dough

Prep + Cook Time: 30 minutes | Servings: 6

Ingredients:

- 4 oz butter
- 3 oz brown sugar
- 6 oz self raising flour
- 4 tbsp honey
- 4 oz chocolate
- 1 tbsp milk

Directions:

1. Ensure that your air fryer is preheated to 320 F for 10 minutes.
2. Get a large bowl, and in it, beat the butter until soft, then add the sugar.
3. Cream the mixture until it is soft and light.
4. Stir in the flour and honey, and mix thoroughly.
5. With the aid of a rolling pin, smash the white chocolate to produce small- and medium-sized chocolate chips. Combine the chocolate with the chips and milk. Stir thoroughly.
6. Add the cookie dough into a tin.
7. Move the tin into the baking sheet layered in the air fryer.
8. Allow cooking at 320 F for 20 minutes.
9. Serve.

Super Simple Shortbread Chocolate Balls

Prep + Cook Time: 20 minutes | Servings: 9

Ingredients:

- 2 tbsp cocoa
- 3 oz caster sugar
- 1 tsp vanilla essence
- 9 oz plain flour
- 6 oz butter
- 9 chocolate chunks

Directions:

1. Ensure that your air fryer is preheated to 360 F.
2. Combine the cocoa, sugar, vanilla and flour into a small bowl. Mix well.
3. After rubbing in the butter, knead the mixture well into a smooth dough.
4. Make balls out of the dough, and place a chunk of chocolate at the center of each ball, while ensuring that the chocolate chunk is not visible at all.
5. Transfer the chocolate shortbread balls into the air fryer basket lined with a baking sheet. Allow cooking at 360 F for 8 minutes. Reduce the heat to 320 F and cook further for 5 minutes – this ensures that the balls are well and evenly cooked.
6. Withdraw and serve.

4 Ingredient Airfryer Strawberry Jam Tarts

Prep + Cook Time: 20 minutes | Servings: 9

Ingredients:

- 1 oz caster sugar
- 4 oz butter
- 9 oz plain flour
- Water as needed
- Strawberry jam

Directions:

1. Ensure that your air fryer is preheated to 360 F.
2. In a large mixing bowl, combine the sugar, butter, and flour, while rubbing the fat into the sugar and flour. Stop when the mixture appears like breadcrumbs. You may add little water to form a firm pastry dough.
3. Get nine little pastry cases, and grease each. Place the pastry into the base and the sides of the cases.
4. Add two teaspoon of strawberry jam or raspberry into the base, before transferring them into the air fryer.
5. Allow cooking at 360 F until the pastry is well cooked – it takes about 10 minutes.
6. Withdraw and serve.

Half Cooked Lemon Biscuits

Prep + Cook Time: 15 minutes | Servings: 9

Ingredients:

- 8 oz self raising flour
- 4 oz caster sugar
- 4 oz butter
- 1 small lemon rind and juice
- 1 small egg
- 1 tsp vanilla essence

Directions:

1. Ensure that your air fryer is preheated to 360 F.
2. In a clean bowl, combine the flour and sugar and mix thoroughly. Rub in the butter until you have a mixture that appears like breadcrumbs. Shaking the bowl regularly is recommended – it makes the fat bits move to the top, such that you see what is left to rub in.
3. Stir in the lemon juice and vanilla essence and rind as well as the egg.
4. Mix well and knead to produce a soft and nice dough.
5. Roll out the dough and cut into biscuits of medium sizes.
6. Transfer the biscuits into the baking sheet laid in the air fryer.
7. Allow cooking at 360 F for 5 minutes.
8. Transfer the cooked biscuits onto a cooling tray, and add sprinkles of icing sugar.

Banana Puff Pastry

Prep + Cook Time: 20 minutes | Servings: 3

Ingredients:

- 2 puff pastry sheet, thawed
- 3 bananas, peeled

Directions:

1. Form thin slices from the puff pastry sheet by slicing it.
2. Wrap the rolled pastry around the banana. You may have to make more strips if required.
3. Roll the strips together – two at a time.
4. Transfer the wrapped banana into the air fryer basket.
5. Set the timer to 8-10 minutes and the heat to 360 F.
6. Allow cooking until golden brown.
7. To minimize the need for cleaning, you may use aluminum foil to line the frying basket.

Banana Boat S'mores

Prep + Cook Time: 15 minutes | Servings: 2

Ingredients:

- 2 ripe but firm bananas
- 2 tbsp of semi-sweet chocolate chunks
- 2 tbsp of mini marshmallow
- 2 tbsp of golden graham cereal
- Ice-cream and chocolate sauce, optional garnish

Directions:

1. With the aid of a sharp paring knife, cut each banana lengthwise, along the inside curve. Then cut out a strip of the banana peel – about 1/2 inch in size.
2. Mush the banana gently using a fork to ensure that the chocolate chunk, the marshmallow, and the golden graham cereal can be stuffed in the banana easily.
3. Add a tablespoon of the mini marshmallow, golden graham, and chocolate chunks inside each banana boat.
4. Transfer the studded bananas into the air fryer basket.
5. Allow air frying for 8 minutes at 370 F.
6. Withdraw from the fryer and leave to cool for 5 minutes.
7. Serve alongside a drizzle of chocolate sauce (if you like) and some ice-cream.

Printed in Great Britain
by Amazon